HOW TO USE
V**O**ICE *for* LIFE

A comprehensive guide to the Voice for Life
scheme for choir trainers and teachers

CONTENTS

RS✦M

HOW TO USE

VOICE for LIFE

Project editor: Tim Ruffer

Written by Anthony Marks with additional material by Colin Davey

Voice for Life was developed by Leah Perona-Wright in consultation with experienced practitioners from across the UK and beyond. These include: Gordon Appleton, Colin Baldy, Roger Brice, Chris Broughton, Lesley Cooper, June Cox, Colin Davey, Paul Ellis, Rosemary Field, Peter Futcher, Susan Gardner, Ameral Gunson, John Harper, Esther Jones, Sally Leeming, Hilary Llystyn Jones, Sue Moore, David Ogden, Keith Roberts, Sheila Robertson, Ben Saunders, John Wardle, Alistair Warwick, Geoff Weaver and Jenevora Williams. We are grateful for their contributions.

Design and layout: Anthony Marks
Illustrations: Hilary Perona-Wright
Editorial assistance: Julian Elloway

Printed in the United Kingdom.

ISBN 978-0-85402-217-5

THE ROYAL SCHOOL OF CHURCH MUSIC
19 The Close, Salisbury, Wiltshire, SP1 2EB
Tel: +44 (0)1722 424848   Fax: +44 (0)1722 424849
E-mail: education@rscm.com Website: www.rscm.com
Registered charity no. 312828

Distributed exclusively in North America by GIA Publications, Inc.
7404 S. Mason Ave., Chicago, IL 60638
Toll free: 800 442 1358 Website: www.giamusic.com

Singing is a very special human attribute, and singing with others is a wonderful human experience. Singing has been cherished for thousands of years, and nurtured by Christians since the earliest days of the Church. Choral singing is a social activity: it links individuals to the group and builds community. It is an important part of the way in which many Christian communities express their worship of God. It is a metaphor for heaven itself.

The RSCM encourages, equips and resources singers in many different ways. It gathers them together for training and inspiration, and provides sung music to fit with the spoken parts of worship. From the 1960s it has promoted dedicated schemes for training singers. *Voice for Life*, the third of these, is an all-age scheme: it recognizes that singing is an activity for the whole span of life. It can be used in church, in schools and colleges, or in the wider community – in small singing groups or larger choirs. While most musical instruction separates individual tuition from collective music-making, *Voice for Life* develops individuals within the choral group. It enables each individual to develop within the context of the choir, and of the wider worshipping community.

Every choir needs a leader to inspire, train and direct it. That person must make use of all kinds of musical and social skills. To enable singers to use their voices well, he or she needs an understanding of basic vocal technique as well as of choral training. It is important too for the choir's director to help singers improve their sight-reading and aural skills, appreciate musical repertoire, and understand the context of the choir's singing. The five modules of the *Voice for Life* scheme articulate these features.

This book, *How to Use Voice for Life*, is the essential resource for choir trainers as they deliver the scheme. It supports all the modules and provides invaluable help and advice for training, assessing and developing singers as they progress through their *Voice for Life* workbooks. In addition, there are many other *Voice for Life* publications and resources to supplement the scheme: see pages 10–11 for a complete list.

Voice for Life is challenging and demands commitment. But it is rewarding and through it both individuals and the whole singing group or choir can greatly develop their talents. They will grow in confidence and skill, give pleasure and enrichment to those who hear them, and help to inspire the worship of the gathered community.

Andrew Reid,
Director, RSCM

Icons The icons in this book mean:

 Important information

 Something to think about

 See the singer's workbook

 Caution!

 Teaching aim

 Teaching tip

 Refers to a specific *Voice for Life* level

 A singing exercise or activity

About Voice for Life

Voice for Life is the RSCM's acclaimed choral education scheme. It is for choirs and singers of all ages, and for the people who train them. A vast resource, it provides a clear framework to encourage and develop singing within communities, whatever they may be – schools, churches or wider organisations. It is delivered by means of a range of teaching and learning materials (print and online), specially created graded repertoire, recordings, accessories and motivational items, and training courses.

This book is the key source of information and advice for choir trainers about using *Voice for Life* with a choir or group of singers. There are many other resources available to help you train, assess and motivate singers. These include further publications for choir trainers, workbooks for singers, graded repertoire collections, and medals, badges, and wallcharts. For more information see pages 10–11, or visit **www.rscmshop.com/voice-for-life.html** for full details.

Training a choir is both a challenge and a joy. The *Voice for Life* scheme contains a wealth of teaching materials and plenty of useful advice on the practicalities of running a choir. *Voice for Life* is systematic but not rigid – used well, it will enable you to train your choir or group more effectively, and to help singers grow as people as well as musicians. Most of the training and assessment arises naturally within the flow of the scheme, as part of music-making.

Voice for Life involves you as choir trainer or teacher, and every member of your choir or group. Each singer is involved both as part of a team and as an individual. The balance between training the group and training the individual is an essential feature of *Voice for Life* because it enables you to give individuals confidence and training even while you are working with the whole group. Importantly, this simultaneously strengthens individuals' commitment and contribution to the group.

Establishing and running a *Voice for Life* scheme requires musical and organizational skills, and a level of work and engagement. If you are reading this introduction, clearly you are prepared to consider investing the necessary time and effort. This book aims to help you to navigate the scheme smoothly and effectively so that you and your singers get the maximum results and enjoyment from *Voice for Life*.

On the following pages, you will find answers to some of the questions that choir trainers ask most frequently about *Voice for Life*. Read these first – they provide a useful introduction to all aspects of the scheme.

Use the workbooks!
Just as this book is the choir trainer's essential guide to *Voice for Life*, so singers have vital publications of their own: the five workbooks, one for each level (see opposite). You are strongly advised to ensure that singers use them, as they form the main focus of their engagement with the scheme. You should also become very familiar with the workbooks yourself as they are the backbone of the resource.

The workbooks address each topic of *Voice for Life* systematically, in terms that users will easily understand. They include a range of advice, support and activities for singers to use outside rehearsals in their own time. Some of the material from them is reproduced in this volume, but it is advisable to own your own copies too and know your way around them. This book is full of references to the workbooks, shown by the icon on the left; be sure to follow these.

How is *Voice for Life* structured?

There are five levels in *Voice for Life,* providing training for singers of all levels from beginner to advanced. The levels are designed for use by singers of any age; all singers will work through exactly the same levels (although in some cases it may not be necessary for experienced singers to start the scheme at the very beginning).

The *Voice for Life* levels are as follows:

White

Light Blue

Dark Blue

Red

Yellow

Voice for Life is also divided into five modules, each of which explores a particular aspect of choral singing. There is material for each module at each level, so that throughout the scheme singers work on all modules, developing a range of skills simultaneously. The modules are as follows:

- *Module A: Using the voice well* addresses good vocal technique. At lower levels, singers learn the physical sensations of good posture and breathing; at higher levels, singers study the physiology of voice production. Throughout, practical exercises are used to develop tone, range, diction, and choral and performing skills. Module A materials begin on page 13 of this book.

- *Module B: Musical skills and understanding* develops knowledge of music notation and theory, and encourages singers to demonstrate this through sight-reading and aural skills. Practical exercises help singers to understand the music they see, hear and sing. Module B materials begin on page 91 of this book.

- *Module C: Repertoire* helps singers to understand the musical and historical contexts of the music they sing. A range of music analysis tasks draw on the theoretical understanding gained in Module B, while research activities and projects encourage singers to gather, understand and present information about what they are singing. Module C materials begin on page 161 of this book.

- *Module D: Belonging to the choir* explores what it means to be part of a choir, addressing issues such as commitment, punctuality and responsibility. Module D materials begin on page 187 of this book.

- *Module E: Choir in context* explores how the choir interacts with its surroundings. A choir does not exist in isolation. Although it is a community in its own right, it is also part of a wider community. In this module, projects and discussions help singers to explore the wider context of their choir's existence: Why do they sing in that particular choir? Why does the choir exist? For whom does it sing? How does the choir benefit its members and those outside the choir? Module E materials begin on page 195 of this book.

How do I use *Voice for Life* with my choir?

Voice for Life is flexible; it fits around your choir's schedule. Much of the training will become part of your normal rehearsal time; for example, the vocal exercises can be incorporated as warm-ups at the beginning of choir practice, or to break up the rehearsal. As a choir trainer, you probably already undertake specific training on posture, breathing, diction, and so on – but *Voice for Life* provides a robust structure and measurable targets which make this training much more effective.

Voice for Life doesn't demand to be used in a particular way – it allows you (and your singers) to work with the materials in a fashion that is suitable to you. Because the targets cover the full range of activities in all the modules, at any given time it is easy to steer individual singers to parts of the scheme that they need to focus on – while still using choral rehearsals to develop your choir as a group. In practice you will find that singers start to drive this process as they explore the workbook activities.

You may find it helpful to take some training sessions with small groups (or you could ask senior members of the choir to do this). While this may eat into the choir's general schedule, it will be repaid by the progress your singers make. Some choir trainers find that if they set aside 20 minutes or so at the start of rehearsals for workbook activities, this gives singers – especially young ones – the opportunity to calm down and focus before singing practice starts.

It can also be useful to allow a little time before or after each rehearsal for assessments or evaluation, or just talking to singers about their progress and which activities they should undertake next. This could be as little as 10 to 15 minutes a week, depending on the assessment tasks involved. Even a relatively short amount of time will allow you to check the progress of your singers and try some practical tests with them.

As you become familiar with the structure of *Voice for Life* and its resources, you will find that the scheme adapts itself to your schedule and practice rather than the other way around.

Do all my singers have to participate in *Voice for Life*?

In theory, no. If some choir members choose not to follow the scheme formally, it will not matter. But in practice, if you are using *Voice for Life* as your choir-training resource, all choir members will be taking part in most of the activities anyway. Singers gain a sense of inclusion and motivation from participating – as well as a sound musical education with measurable outcomes.

Some choir trainers make participation in the scheme a condition of choir membership; others are more flexible. This is your choice. It may be unwise to exclude keen singers simply because they don't want to follow the workbooks; but the sense of cohesion the scheme creates is a valuable asset to the choir.

Can I have different singers at different *Voice for Life* levels?

Yes. In fact it is unlikely that all your singers will be at the same level at any one time. You should attend to each individual at each level but this need not be too time-consuming if you are well organized. Use the workbooks and, perhaps, delegate senior choir members to help you. Some choir trainers organize occasional brief sessions to monitor and motivate groups of singers who are all at a similar level.

How do singers progress through the levels?
At each level of *Voice for Life*, there are targets for each module. These are listed at the back of each workbook with boxes for you to sign and date, and are also listed in this book at the start of each module. Familiarizing yourself with the targets will help you train singers effectively, as you will know what is required at any given time.

The targets require singers to do a range of things as appropriate for their level and the module:

- fill in sections of the workbook (self-assessment, commentary, puzzles, research)

- demonstrate in rehearsals and performances that they have understood the contents of a particular module or section

- show practical performance and musicianship skills

- display theoretical and historical understanding (assessed by means of puzzles, activities and projects in the workbooks, or through discussion with other singers or the choir trainer)

- be reliable, helpful members of the choir

Some targets need to be tested by you (or by senior choir members) on occasions you specify when you think an individual singer is ready. Others need to be undertaken over a period of time. Still others assess evolving skills that will become evident from a singer's performance or behaviour within the choir. You, the choir trainer, should check that singers successfully complete each target. Make sure you sign and date each one, as this provides both a progress record and a source of motivation.

When all the targets in all the modules are completed and signed, the singer has finished the level. You should sign the declaration at the very back of the workbook. Additionally, depending on your choir's custom, you can award a certificate, badge, ribbon and medal. (See pages 10–11 for a list of these items.) The singer then moves on to the next level, to a new set of challenges, targets and achievements.

How do I pace my singers as they work through *Voice for Life*?
Choral musicianship is a durable asset that takes years to acquire, so let singers take their time. Different competences will develop at different stages, and no two singers are alike. The workbooks are constructed so that singers will make steady progress: if you work methodically through the targets, the ideas will really sink in. Encourage singers to approach *Voice for Life* in a spirit of discovery, not competition.

While it is normal to want to see rapid progress, try to resist pressure (from parents, or from singers themselves) to finish the 'tests' and get to the next badge or medal as quickly as possible. If you push singers too fast, or award the next level simply because they have been in the choir for a certain length of time, their development will not be durable. They may flounder at the higher level and drop out as a result. To avoid this, be sure that your singers are really ready to move up.

Make it clear from the outset that *Voice for Life* is about developing as a musician – not about passing tests, or even length of membership of the choir.

What special skills do I need to deliver *Voice for Life*?
These can be divided roughly into five groups:

- **Musicianship skills:** you will need to understand how music works and be comfortable teaching this to others. If your knowledge of music theory is limited, you can learn it along with your singers from the *Voice for Life* resources; or delegate theory training to someone in your choir with the necessary skills.

- **Organizational skills:** you will need to manage your time and your choir's time carefully. Keeping abreast of your singers' needs as they progress through the scheme requires an ability to see both the overview and the detail. Delegation skills are useful too as you will need other senior choir members to help you.

- **Pastoral and interpersonal skills:** you will need to be diplomatic and persuasive to motivate and coax the best from your singers.

- **Singing and performing skills:** you will need at least some basic singing ability (see page 15 for more about this). Bear in mind that you can ask skilled singers in your choir to help train others.

- **Choir-training skills:** techniques specific to training a choir are covered in *The Voice for Life Guide to Choir Training*. Skills directly related to the *Voice for Life* modules are included in this book.

If you are not a trained singer yourself, consider having a few lessons in basic singing technique – specifically posture, breathing and tone production. While you can learn from books, you need to know how good singing feels, not just what to say. You could also arrange for a singing teacher to observe you training your choir and give feedback and guidance. You can also gain a lot by observing experienced choir trainers at work and attending relevant courses. *Church Music Skills*, a distance-learning course run by the RSCM, helps choir trainers of all standards to develop their skills.

How do I find my way around *How to Use Voice for Life*?
This book is divided into five main sections, one for each of the modules outlined on page 5. Each section has an introduction which gives advice on how to train singers for the module targets. Because the material in each module is different, each section is organized slightly differently. (For example, some of the material is organized level by level; some is more general.) This is explained in the introduction to each section.

Each section contains references to the workbooks so that you can see at a glance where singers have questions to consider, exercises to complete or support materials to read. Where relevant, the answers to the questions are included; in some cases you are advised to check an answer or discuss a topic with your singer. This will help you to assess each target.

At the end of the book you will find master copies of all the photocopiable pages from the workbooks, so that you will always have a source from which to make worksheets and write-in resources for singers. (In some cases, you might like to put the photocopied page on the choir-room wall for everyone to use.) Permission to photocopy is clearly indicated in the margin of each page.

The RSCM Bronze, Silver and Gold awards
Each level of *Voice for Life* is assessed informally by you, the choir trainer: you award singers their badge and/or ribbon and medal. In order to support you and affirm the *Voice for Life* levels achieved within the choir, the RSCM provides a parallel external system of awards assessed through formal examinations: the Bronze, Silver and Gold awards. Each of these has its own syllabus and regulations. These come with guidelines to prepare the candidate and the choir trainer fully for the examinations.

In recognition of their achievement, successful candidates are entitled to wear a prestigious medal cast in the appropriately coloured metal (bronze, silver or gold), worn on distinctive ribbons. Bronze awards are worn with a green ribbon, Silver awards with a purple ribbon and Gold awards with a dark red ribbon.

 How do these awards relate to the *Voice for Life* levels?
The *Voice for Life* scheme and the Bronze, Silver and Gold awards fit together as shown below:

White

Light Blue

Dark Blue

Bronze

Red

Silver

Yellow

Gold

Voice for Life provides excellent training and preparation for the Bronze, Silver and Gold awards: a singer who has completed the targets in the Dark Blue workbook is well prepared for the Bronze award; the Red and Yellow levels provide the same support for Silver and Gold awards respectively. Similarly, the Bronze, Silver and Gold awards provide an externally validated affirmation of the *Voice for Life* 'colour' levels that have been awarded informally by the choir trainer.

You can find further details of the awards at

www.rscm.com/education/vfl/singingAwards.php

 What if I have a singer who does not want to take the external awards?
This is not a problem. *Voice for Life* can be used on its own to provide training and motivation. There is no need to take the Bronze, Silver and Gold awards if your singer is unhappy about undertaking a formal assessment. You may find however that their opinion changes as they make progress and their skills develop.

Voice for Life *resources*

 Here is a summary of *Voice for Life* resources that will help you to train and motivate singers through the scheme. A more detailed list is available at:

www.rscmshop.com/voice-for-life.html

 Books for choir trainers
This book, *How to Use Voice for Life*, is your essential guide to delivering the scheme as it is presented to singers in the workbooks.

The Voice for Life Guide to Musicianship is a complete resource for choir trainers and the singers they work with. It contains detailed advice, exercises and activities to help prepare singers for the Module B musicianship targets – aural tests and sight-reading – at White, Light Blue, Dark Blue, Red and Yellow levels and for the tests in the RSCM Bronze, Silver and Gold awards.

The forthcoming *Voice for Life Guide to Choir Training* addresses other important topics for choir trainers relating to the practicalities of running and training a choir.

 Books for singers
The *Voice for Life* Singer's Workbooks are the core of the scheme. They contain practical advice, training exercises, games, puzzles and activities and are also the main place for you to record and monitor the progress of each individual singer (via the target check-list and declaration at the back of each one). Encourage every member of your choir to own – and use! – the appropriate book for their level.

- White level workbook
- Light Blue level workbook
- Dark Blue level workbook
- Red level workbook
- Yellow level workbook

The Voice for Life Chorister's Companion is a handy pocket-sized book that provides everything a chorister needs to know about the routines and practices of church choirs. It exists in two versions – paperback and cloth-bound hardback (the latter is often used by choirs for presentation purposes). Candidates for the RSCM awards will also find much to help them prepare for their exams.

 Rewards: certificates, badges, medals and ribbons
The principal record of a singer's progress is the declaration you sign at the back of each workbook. But many choirs also mark singers' achievements in other ways. The RSCM offers a range of badges, medals, ribbons and certificates for all the 'colour' levels of the scheme and the Bronze, Silver and Gold awards too. For details of all available items see:

www.rscmshop.com/voice-for-life/vfl-certificates.html   and

www.rscmshop.com/voice-for-life/vfl-medals-ribbons.html

Registers and record-books
There are a number of items to help you monitor attendance, progress and standards across your choir. You can use these as a private record, though some choir trainers find that a chart on general display in the rehearsal room is a powerful motivator. Details of these, and of other useful ways to record and reward singers' service in the choir, are available at:

www.rscmshop.com/voice-for-life/voice-for-life-resources.html

Repertoire
The RSCM publishes numerous collections which were specifically created as choral resources within *Voice for Life*. Other publications are suitable for use within the scheme and contain training notes to help you use them to maximum effect. This means that you always have access to carefully selected and graded choral (and solo) materials – repertoire and service books alike – for each 'colour' level and for the Bronze, Silver and Gold awards too. Details can be found at:

www.rscmshop.com/voice-for-life/voice-for-life-songbooks.html

www.rscmshop.com/voice-for-life/repertoire-for-vfl-awards.html

www.rscmshop.com/voice-for-life/vfl-festival-service-books.html

The catalogue of publications is always growing, so you are advised to return to the site often to remain up-to-date with the latest materials.

The *Voice for Life* pages of the RSCM website
For more information about the *Voice for Life* scheme, visit:

www.rscm.com/voiceforlife or www.rscm.com/vfl

Here you will find all manner of help, support and resources for the scheme.

What singers say

Over the years various *Voice for Life* practitioners have collected comments from members of the scheme. You will find these reproduced throughout this book.

'In some ways, when I started using Voice for Life *with the choir, things didn't change much at first. I certainly didn't have to revolutionize the way I worked. Then I realized that everything was just starting to 'click' somehow. The singers liked the workbooks; I was able to be more organized; everyone seemed to be moving in the same direction. And best of all – the singing got better.'*

Margaret, organist and choir trainer

'I had to change choirs when we moved house. I'd done Voice for Life *in the old choir, and the new choir had it too. That made changing much easier as I knew what to expect.'*

Kyle, 11

MODULE A

Using the voice well

CONTENTS

Module A: Using the voice well

This module is concerned with all aspects of vocal technique. It shows singers the physical sensations and sounds of healthy singing, and at the higher levels develops understanding of the physiology of the voice. The general aims of Module A are:

- to help singers understand and apply the principles of good vocal technique

- to develop their understanding of the physiology of singing, and to encourage use of this knowledge to improve their skills

- to point out the differences between choral and solo singing

- to make singers aware of the need to exercise the voice regularly

Each of these aims is assessed by means of the targets for each level, which are listed on pages 16–18 and at the back of each workbook.

How Module A is organized

The module is divided into five principal topic sections:

- Posture (page 19)

- Breathing (page 29)

- Tone and range (page 46)

- Diction (page 77)

- Performance (page 85)

These topics are of course interlinked, and in practice you will often address them simultaneously rather than sequentially. Not all of them are covered in the same depth at all levels but they are developed systematically throughout *Voice for Life*.

How to use this part of the book

This part of the book contains advice and practical exercises to help you train singers in the module with confidence. Starting on page 20, the material for each topic listed above is presented level by level, so you can easily see what needs to be covered at each stage. Within each topic, for each level, you will find in the following order:

- aims for you as a choir trainer – an overview of what you should achieve with your singers for the level

- key training points for the level, together with a summary of the relevant exercises and activities from the workbooks

- training hints and tips, and, where appropriate, more detailed information about a particular topic at a particular stage

- a key to the activities and puzzles in the workbooks (verbatim quotations from the workbooks are shown on a grey background)

Thinking about Module A

The necessity of regular training for athletes is widely understood. Sprinters, for example, do not spend all their time running 100 metres: if they were to do this at top speed without preparation, they would not perform well, and may risk serious injury. Instead they engage in various exercises, as part of an often gruelling regime, to improve general fitness and strengthen muscles.

Like athletes, singers need regular training and exercise to develop muscles and vocal functions. In singing, nothing works in isolation; each muscle group depends on the rest. If a set of muscles or vocal function is weak or working poorly, the others will compensate. This can spoil the sound and cause fatigue. Regular practice ensures that singers are strong enough to meet the demands of rehearsals and performances.

It is vital to establish healthy technical foundations from the start. *Voice for Life* reflects this: before singers are even asked to produce a single note, the first activity in the White level workbook (page 4) addresses posture, breathing and relaxation. These basics pertain throughout the scheme, however advanced singers may become.

Your voice is with you for life, and needs exercise. Use the exercises on the following pages to give your singers a vocal work-out at each rehearsal. You can incorporate them as warm-ups, or perhaps halfway through a practice to work on one particular aspect of technique. Remember too that all choir members will benefit from individual practice. Encourage them to use the exercises in their workbooks at home.

Keeping the body fit and healthy involves more than just exercise. Other factors affect the voice, such as diet. Just as athletes have to consider what they eat, so singers need to be aware of how food and drink affects the voice. There are voice-care tips below, and in the singer's workbooks. A good understanding of the physiology of the voice is important so that singers know how to take care of their own 'instrument'.

Finally, always encourage your singers to take part in other singing activities and to take advantage of any opportunity for individual singing lessons. Singing lessons enable an individual to master vocal techniques and grow in confidence and musical understanding – these skills are all beneficial to the life of the choir. Singing as part of a choir can help to improve a singer's sight-reading ability and general musical understanding: this helps with the progress and development of each individual.

Thinking about your own singing

Don't worry if you are a bit unsure about your own singing ability. Try the exercises yourself before working on them with singers, and you will see that the basics of vocal technique are simpler than you might imagine. Practise on your own, or try the exercises with a group of singers. In the latter case, you will be able to work through any problems together: this can enhance your sense of connection to the choir.

Tip: If you decide to work alone, try recording yourself to assess your progress. Do not worry too much about the quality of your voice – it is unlikely that anyone will judge it. (A number of excellent professional choir directors would never consider singing in public.) But a basic understanding of how your own voice works is invaluable when working with others. Consider taking some singing lessons yourself. This way you can learn new techniques, which you can then pass on more successfully to your choir. There is nothing more valuable than another pair of ears.

Module A: Targets

White level

To complete Module A, singers must:

- understand the need for regular practice
- stand and sit with good posture while singing, holding music appropriately
- demonstrate good breath control using the exercises on pages 8 and 9 of the singer's workbook
- sing with focus and concentration in rehearsals, performances and services
- follow the conductor at key moments in a piece (such as the start and end)

Light Blue level

To complete Module A, singers must:

- understand the need for regular practice
- understand how to stand and sit while singing, and demonstrate good posture in rehearsals and performances
- demonstrate good breath management by singing with an even tone
- have found a comfortable register in which to sing, and demonstrate this by singing with even tone an ascending and descending scale of an octave
- sing with clear diction, producing good pure vowels and clear consonants
- be able to sing a verse of a hymn or song with clear diction and projection, good even tone, and continuity between the notes of a phrase

Dark Blue level

To complete Module A, singers must:

- understand the need for regular practice
- understand how to stand and sit well while singing, and demonstrate this during rehearsals and performances without being reminded
- have developed the good breath management learnt at Light Blue and demonstrate this by singing with a good even tone to the end of each line or phrase, with control of dynamics
- understand appropriate places to breathe in a piece of music

- have developed the range of the comfortable register found at Light Blue level and sing with resonance. Singers will demonstrate this by singing an ascending and descending scale of an octave with resonance throughout.

- sing with clear diction, producing good, pure vowels and clear consonants

- be able to sing a hymn, song or psalm, in a comfortable register with a range of up to an octave, and sing a small portion (such as one verse) unaccompanied, maintaining good intonation throughout

 **Red level**

To complete Module A, singers must:

- understand the need for regular practice

- understand the need for good posture, consistently and as second nature standing and sitting well in rehearsals and performances

- understand the basic mechanics of breathing

- have developed good breath management and demonstrate this with a good even tone and control of dynamics

- understand where it is appropriate to breathe in the music, and why, and understand how to achieve the effect of no breathing in a piece or phrase, using staggered breathing as part of the choir

- understand the basic mechanics of vocal sound production

- understand the different registers of the voice and how to access them

- have developed the range and resonance of the voice, and demonstrate this by singing an ascending and descending scale of at least an octave on any vowel, with resonance throughout, placing the sounds correctly and avoiding a break in the resonance

- understand the need for clear diction and how to use diction appropriately (according to the style of the music, demonstrating this in rehearsal and performance)

- understand the difference between solo and choral singing, contributing to the overall sound while blending the voice with the ensemble as a whole

- sing accurately and musically a carefully prepared short solo or solo line in a service, concert or similar public event

Module A: Targets

To complete Module A, singers must:

- understand the need for regular practice
- understand what makes good posture and be aware of the effects of bad posture on vocal production
- understand that posture can help prepare the mind for singing and is an important part of communication, and of presenting an image of confidence and professionalism
- understand the mechanics of breathing, using this understanding to prepare the voice for singing
- sing with good breath support and be able to sing long notes and phrases with an even tone and without a decline of energy or support towards the end
- use the back muscles to strengthen the sound
- sing with resonance throughout the vocal range
- sing without tightening the jaw, or pushing or crushing the larynx downwards
- blend the different registers of the voice and move between them with agility
- sing with a variety of vocal tones
- understand the difference between solo and choral singing
- contribute to the choral sound while blending the voice with the ensemble as a whole, without compromising good vocal technique
- sing with clear diction to create appropriate style and expression
- use vowels to produce resonance, and ensure that consonants are clear without interrupting the flow of the tone
- have performed three contrasting pieces with a range of over an octave. These must be sung (optionally from memory) demonstrating agility, good articulation and diction, good breath control and intonation, and a variety of vocal tone.
- have sung confidently, accurately and musically a solo or solo line in a concert or service

What singers say

'A year's systematic approach to vocal training has revolutionized my approach to singing. Learning to support the sound properly has developed and extended the top end of my vocal range. High notes are no longer a strain or worry, and the sound is less driven and more resonant throughout the vocal compass. Newly-learned techniques I can now pass on to my church choir with very noticeable and beneficial results. I would heartily recommend every would-be choir trainer to take at least a few singing lessons: I just wish I had taken such a step thirty years ago!'

Peter, organist and choirmaster

To establish the importance of posture, it is helpful to tell singers that the body is a musical instrument and that it needs to be correctly held, played and maintained. You have to stand or sit as well as possible when singing, to maximize the potential of the voice. The best way to achieve this is through good posture and exercise. Singers are never too advanced to work on their posture and to study the effect it has on the way they sing. Even the facial muscles need to be exercised.

Point out too that much of our communication with others occurs through body language rather than verbally. As well as affecting the voice itself, posture affects the audience or congregation because it gives an impression of confidence even when singers are under the pressure of performance. Singers who sit or stand well create an impact even before they begin to sing. If they look focused and professional, the audience or congregation will relax and enjoy the music.

The warm-up exercises below will help singers of all ages and levels with their posture. They make singers aware of the body, aid relaxation and emphasize that singing is not just an activity of the mouth. Use these when warming up the choir before a rehearsal. They can also be used to break up the middle of a session, when posture may have lapsed. (This may mean moving to a part of the rehearsal room where there is space for everyone to move about, unrestricted by pews or chairs.)

 Exercises: warming up the body and face muscles

- Tense all your muscles, clenching your fists and hunching your shoulders up. Hold for a few seconds, then relax. Repeat several times.

- Roll your shoulders, one at a time, then both together, in either direction. Roll your head slowly on your neck, opening your mouth as you reach the top so as not to strain your neck.

- Tense your facial muscles tightly, then open your mouth and eyes as wide as possible, before slowly letting them relax completely.

- Reach up slowly with your hands and arms and then stretch upwards until you are on tiptoe. Then curl the spine slowly downwards, hanging the head and neck, with hands and arms towards the floor. Hang there for a few moments, swaying gently from side to side. Then straighten up to a good upright standing posture.

- Move your jaw round and round or pretend you are chewing a toffee.

- Shake your hands by your side, as though shaking off water.

 Tension in the body can be heard in the singing voice, so it is vital to avoid this by developing and maintaining good posture. The key areas where tension can develop are the jaw, neck and shoulders. Encourage your singers to use these exercises to help them relax when they are aware of tension building up.

To help singers understand how to stand and sit while singing, and how to hold their music

White level introduces the basics of posture (standing and sitting); and how to hold music while singing. Simple practical experiments are used to demonstrate the effects of good posture on the sound and feel of the voice. In the workbook, puzzles and self-assessment help singers to identify good posture.

Key points for White level posture
When standing to sing, singers should have:

- tall posture with an upright head
- relaxed shoulders
- a straight back, but not rigid
- relaxed knees (not locked)
- weight balanced evenly on both feet
- feet slightly apart and firmly on the ground

If a singer's posture is poor, tension starts to creep into various muscles in the body. This gradually affects the singing voice, making it feel and sound tired.

Tip: In your warm-up, when working with beginners or young singers, try asking what *they* think makes good posture when standing to sing. It is good to encourage them to put what they know into words rather than always being told by their choir trainer or teacher.

Sitting or standing?
Generally, it is better to stand than sit while singing, but with good posture it is still possible to sing well while sitting. If your singers sit to sing, encourage the following:

- upright posture in head and neck
- relaxed shoulders
- a straight back, but not rigid
- both feet firmly on the ground (with young children whose feet do not reach the ground, simply encourage them to sit as well as they can, without slouching)

Discourage singers from crossing their legs when they sit to sing, as this twists the body and restricts airflow.

Tip: In order to introduce good posture, you need to help your singers get rid of any tension that has crept into the body during the day. It is good to begin a rehearsal with some relaxation exercises like the ones on the previous page. Gentle stretches, rolling the shoulders and massaging the face can all help to relax your singers so they are ready to assume a good posture for singing.

Holding music

Singers often need to hold books or scores. The way they do this affects their posture and the sound they make. It also affects whether or not they can see the conductor.

If music is held too high (see left), it covers the mouth, blocking the sound.

If the music is held too low (see right), the sound goes straight down to the floor.

Either way, the singer cannot see the conductor properly. In addition the singer will not be seen or heard well by the congregation or audience.

Encourage singers to hold their music so they can see you conducting over the top of it by moving only their eyes, not their heads (see right).

 Tip: For part of your practice or rehearsal, stop giving spoken directions altogether. This will encourage singers to watch you for instructions and to find suitable positions for themselves and their music.

 In the workbook

- *Page 4*   Check singers' answers and discuss if necessary.
- *Page 5*   Check singers' answers and discuss if necessary.
- *Page 6*   The singers with good posture are shown below.

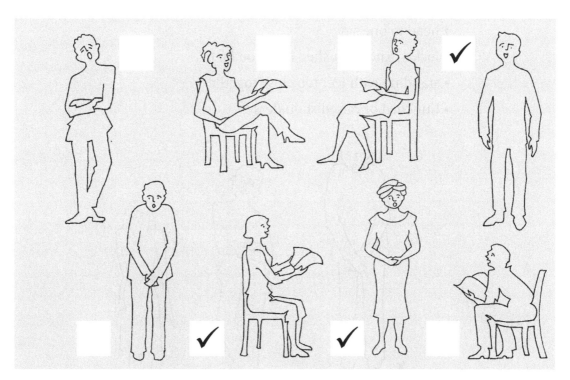

- *Page 7*   Check singers' answers and discuss if necessary.

To help singers understand how to stand and sit while singing; to encourage good posture in rehearsals and performances; to help singers recognize and understand the effects of good and bad posture on the voice

Light Blue level develops the basic concepts introduced at White level, addressing aspects of both good and bad posture, standing and sitting. In the workbook, puzzles and self-assessment help singers to identify good and bad posture.

Key points for Light Blue level posture

When singing, the whole body is involved. Good posture is essential to sing well; bad posture has a bad effect on the voice.

When standing to sing, singers should have:

- tall posture with an upright head
- relaxed shoulders
- a straight back, but not rigid
- relaxed knees (not locked)
- weight balanced evenly on both feet
- feet slightly apart and firmly on the ground

Tip: Be constantly vigilant about your own posture. As a choir trainer, you must set a good example for singers.

Some ways of standing cause tension and may affect the sound of the voice:

- a slumped back
- head to one side
- locked knees (pushed back too far)
- standing with feet too close together
- hunched or raised shoulders

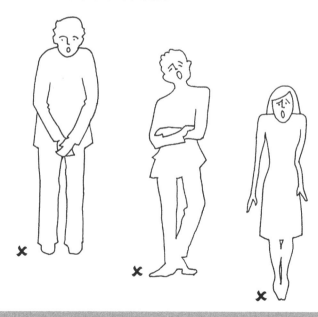

When sitting to sing, singers should have:

- upright posture in head and neck
- relaxed shoulders
- a straight back, but not rigid
- both feet firmly on the ground

 Some ways of sitting cause tension and may affect the sound of the voice:

- hunched or slumped in the seat
- hunched shoulders, neck or upper body
- crossed legs

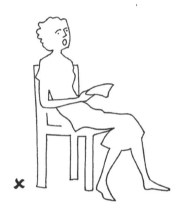 

 Tip: Praise singers who demonstrate good posture. They will feel good and others will want to feel the same by adopting a similar approach.

Some choir trainers use a code word or gesture to prompt singers to check their posture from time to time. This shorthand can be useful because it avoids too frequent repetition of verbal instructions (which singers can start to ignore).

 In the workbook

- *Page 4*
  1. Head on one side, arms folded, weight on one leg, feet together
  2. Hunched or raised shoulders, feet together
  3. Hunched or raised shoulders, slumped back

- *Page 5*   Check singers' answers and discuss if necessary.

- *Page 6*   Puzzle
  1. Hunched back/leaning forward
  2. Crossed legs
  3. Slumped in seat

- *Page 6*   Self-assessment: Check singers' answers and discuss if necessary.

Posture: Dark Blue level

 To ensure singers stand and sit well in rehearsals and performances without any reminder
At Dark Blue level, the principles of good posture learned at Light Blue should start to become second nature.

 Key points for Dark Blue level posture
Having taught singers how to stand and sit for Light Blue, you now need to check and correct their posture during rehearsals and performances. As they progress, singers should start to monitor their own posture automatically, but it takes time to acquire this habit: you can help with gentle reminders and tips. Building on the basics of good posture that your singers have already learned, check on the following:

- the whole body should be well balanced, with legs, hips and knees flexible rather than locked in one position
- the shoulders should be loose
- breathing should be steady and natural

 As singers move through *Voice for Life*, other skills and challenges need concentration, such as reading music or singing longer, more complex pieces. If singers get distracted or lazy during practice or performance, posture may suffer. To prevent this, it is a good idea to make frequent changes between standing and sitting.

Explain regularly to your singers that good posture will make them feel, look and sound better. Encourage them to listen to the ensemble and recognize their value as a singer within that group. But while you (and they) should be vigilant about posture, remember that constant reminders about it may cause your singers to 'tune you out'. So try to find a variety of ways – explicit and otherwise – of keeping singers aware of how they stand or sit.

Praise those who set a good standard and those who show improvement, however small. Remind singers that, no matter how large the choir, it will be obvious to an audience or congregation if even one member looks bad or does not participate fully. It affects the impression that the whole choir is trying to create.

 Don't forget that the way singers hold their music affects their posture. Music should be well in front, at a good height; not so low that the sound falls to the floor, and not so high that the sound is obstructed by the copy. Your singers need a clear line of sight from the music to the conductor so that they can follow the conductor while keeping a good posture. (The workbook contains details.)

 In the workbook

- *Page 4*   Standing to sing: 1. Bad   2. Good   3. Bad
- *Page 4*   Sitting to sing: 1. Good   2. Bad
- *Page 5*   Holding your music: 1. Bad   2. Good   3. Bad
- *Page 5*   Self-assessment: Check singers' answers and discuss; write comments in the last box on the page (if possible, make these constructive points for improvement rather than criticisms)

Module A: Using the voice well

To help singers understand the need for good posture; to encourage consistent posture in rehearsals and performances; to help singers recognize the effects of posture on the voice and begin to diagnose and remedy postural problems

By Red level, good posture should be second nature. Singers should now begin to understand and explain how and why posture affects the voice.

Key points for Red level posture

When discussing posture, point out how particular ways of holding the body influence the voice. This will help singers to understand the physiology of singing. For example:

- Is the weight evenly distributed on both feet? If not, the body will be off balance causing tension in leg, back and neck muscles.

- Are knees, shoulders, hips and legs relaxed? If any of these are locked while singing, muscle tension will restrict breathing and cause constriction in the throat.

- Is the music held correctly? Too high or too low causes tension in the neck and back, and restricts singers' view of the conductor.

- Do singers' feet point towards the conductor? If not, the torso or neck may be twisted.

- Are singers sharing music? If so, allow them to experiment to find a way to hold the copy so that they can both see it, while both maintaining a good posture.

- Are singers making full use of good posture, using their music only as a tool and remembering to sing into the building, communicating with the audience?

Explain to singers that any tension present in the body will be heard in the voice. The key areas where tension can develop are the jaw, neck and shoulders. Refer to the warm-up and relaxation exercises on page 19 (these also appear on page 5 of the Red workbook). These help to make singers aware of the body and aid relaxation. They emphasize that singing is not just an activity of the mouth.

Tip: If singers are cold, they may instinctively raise their shoulders to keep warm. This creates tension. As far as possible, ensure that your rehearsal space is warm (though not too warm – this can make singers drowsy and sluggish). If only a cold hall is available, then advise your singers to wrap up warmly – and make sure you allow them to keep their coats or jackets on while rehearsing.

In the workbook

- *Page 4*   Puzzle: Answers 3, 7, 8 and 10 are good; the rest are bad

- *Page 4*   Posture comments: check and discuss singers' answers. Only the third and fourth singers from left have good posture.

- *Page 5*   Puzzle: Left-hand column, descending: 6, 4, 10, 8
  Right-hand column, descending: 1, 3, 5, 2, 9, 7

To help singers understand what makes good posture; to encourage awareness of the effects of bad posture on vocal production; to help singers understand that posture is an important part of performance and presentation

At Yellow level, singers will gain a more detailed understanding how posture affects singing and know something of the physiological aspects of vocal production.

 Key points for Yellow level posture

Good posture allows the muscles to function to their optimum level. Bad posture impairs the working of the muscles and, therefore, the voice. If the body is not correctly aligned – if the bones are not in the right place – the workings of the muscles will be impaired. Balanced posture depends on the correct alignment of the head, neck, back, pelvis and legs.

 Tip: Before you discuss this topic with your singers, study the diagram here and see how it relates to your own posture.

- Notice how, when the posture is balanced, the mouth, larynx and spinal column all relate to each other.

- Keep your spine straight (aligned as shown). This allows the diaphragm to work properly, and helps your back muscles to function to their optimum level in supporting the sound.

- Do not let your shoulders sag or your head move too far forward, as this impairs the working of the neck muscles.

- Your head weighs about 15lb (more than 6kg). If it is in the wrong position, your muscles have to work harder to keep your body balanced. (If you ever have to sing while kneeling, balance your head properly without pushing your chin forward.)

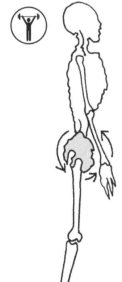 **Stretching the spine**

If the area around the lower spine aches after standing for a while (and singing may involve long periods of standing), it has probably curved too far inwards. Try stretching the base of the spine by turning your pelvis as shown on the left:

Place your hands on your hips, with the thumbs on the hip bone at the front and the fingers behind.

Bend your knees slightly. Turn your pelvis by moving your thumbs upwards and backwards slightly while your fingers move downwards and forwards.

What singers say

'I've learned that my whole body has to be involved in my singing. If my posture isn't good, I can't use my back to support the sound. Doing so means that pressure is removed from my larynx and the sound is not only freer and bigger but much easier to produce.'

Lois, 21

More posture exercises
Here are a few exercises that will enable you and your singers to compare good and bad posture, and the effects on their body and vocal production.

Tip: Before you work on these with singers, try them yourself so that you are familiar with their effects.

Relaxed or locked knees?
Stand up straight with your body balanced. Relax your shoulders, put your hands down by your side and relax your knees. Keep your head and spine straight, and your breathing steady and natural. Breathe in and out a few times.

Now lock your knees (push them back as far as you can) and breathe in and out a few times, as naturally as possible. You will begin to feel that your breathing has become restricted and that there is tension in the lower abdomen and up towards the throat. Unlock your knees once more, and breathe again to feel the difference. Try this when leaning your body weight to one side and locking one knee. You will find that this affects your breathing too.

Even leaning the body weight to one side and locking a leg will result in poor breathing and tuning problems.

The effect of balance and tension
In your bare feet, walk around the room singing a simple song. Now walk on tiptoe and do the same exercise. Can you feel your leg muscles stretching? Can you feel how your body has to adjust the balance and position of your head? You may also find that you cannot reach high notes as easily.

Try this exercise with another singer. While one of you sings, the other should listen to hear the difference in the timbre of the voice. Then swap over.

Shoes with a heel higher than 4cm force the body to re-adjust and balance itself. This can affect the quality of the voice.

Relaxing the shoulders
Tension in the shoulders limits the blood supply to the heart and makes you colder; it tightens the muscles in the throat and can lead to tension in the jaw, affecting the quality of the voice. The following exercise is a good way to avoid this. Raise your shoulders up as far as you can. Drop them a little; then drop them again to release tension. Compare the feeling of tense and relaxed shoulders.

In the workbook

- *Page 4* Self-assessment: Check singers' answers (marked on diagram) and discuss if necessary.

- *Page 5* Check singers' responses to the exercises and discuss if necessary.

Posture for advanced singers

Few people realize how much of an effect posture has on general health and well-being. For example, over a period of time bad posture can produce serious neck and back pain. We need to be aware of our posture at all times, not just when singing.

Tip: Ask your singers to think about posture when standing in a queue, such as at a bus stop or in a shop. An awareness of good posture will help the flow of blood and oxygen to the tissues throughout the body, releasing tensions and making them feel fitter and livelier to tackle the demands required for singing and everyday life.

Tip: Posture may lapse over the course of a rehearsal. Some brief physical exercise during choir practice, such as two or three slow stretches, or a little gentle jogging on the spot, will stimulate and maintain the energy required for singing.

By the time they reach Yellow level, singers have already made a long-term commitment to singing. The habits they will have acquired in *Voice for Life* will be an excellent basis for the future, but here are some further suggestions which may be of benefit both in the present and the long-term.

You could encourage your singers to consider some sessions of Alexander Technique. This aims to teach people to be aware of their bodies and posture. Many singers believe it has profound benefits.

What singers say

'I've had Alexander Technique lessons every week for the last 4 years in term time and I have noticed a huge difference in the way I hold myself to sing. It enables all my muscles to be free and work to their optimum'
           Jane, 17

In addition, singers may like to investigate Pilates, which can help change the way we move and how we align our bodies. Pilates incorporates features of many physiotherapy techniques and other movement disciplines therapies and offers a number of physical benefits: better posture, greater strength and muscle tone, a more efficient respiratory system, joint mobility, improved flexibility, and a boosted immune system, amongst others.

Details of both Alexander Technique and Pilates practitioners can easily be found on the Internet.

What singers say

'I had serious back problems which began when I was at university. These were caused over a period of time by bad posture during my singing and music making. Through physiotherapy and the introduction of Pilates technique I have been able to prevent the problems from recurring.

I have found that my body is stronger now and supports my voice better – and I know how to sing without allowing any tension to creep into my body. I no longer find that all my muscles ache after a long concert or rehearsal. I just wish I had known about the benefits of Pilates years ago, and understood what an effect posture could have on my whole body as well as my singing voice!'
           Andrea, adult

Good breathing is fundamental to good singing, affecting dynamics, phrasing, tone quality, tuning and musicality. It features throughout *Voice for Life*. The early levels introduce singers to the physical sensation of good breathing, and aim to make it a habit. At the higher levels, singers learn the mechanics of breathing, where to breathe in music and why, and to improve their breathing capacity. As you teach these things, you are also helping singers to make sense of what they are singing.

We all have different lung capacities and it can take a long time to master the art of breathing. All your singers will benefit from basic breathing exercises, so encourage them to have a vocal workout as often as possible. (Daily is ideal – but short sessions of around ten minutes are best.) Breathing exercises are included at each level.

 As a choir trainer, you will find some knowledge of anatomy is useful when you teach breathing. It is important to use the correct terminology. For example some teachers talk about using the stomach to sing, but this is misleading. The stomach has no part in singing; it is the diaphragm, and the abdominal muscles around it, that are activated when we breathe to sing. Understanding the movements of these muscles is fundamental to the teaching of effective breathing. Here are the basics:

Inhalation (breathing in)

As you inhale, the diaphragm descends (contracts), pulls the bottom of the lungs down, and creates a vacuum which causes air to enter. As air fills the lungs, the lower ribs expand outward, and the waistline also expands. (The diaphragm is the main muscle of inhalation. While its effects can be detected, it is not possible to feel or control it directly.)

Exhalation (breathing out)

As you exhale, the process is reversed: the diaphragm relaxes (and ascends), being pushed up by the abdominal muscles. This causes the lower ribs to contract inward, resulting in a contraction of the body around the waistline. The lower abdominal muscles must be allowed to relax fully. (There is more about the diaphragm on page 37.)

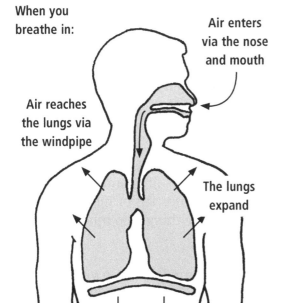

When you breathe in:
Air enters via the nose and mouth
Air reaches the lungs via the windpipe
The lungs expand
The diaphragm contracts and moves down

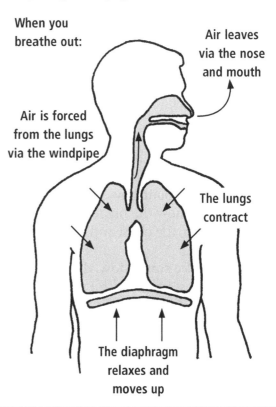

When you breathe out:
Air leaves via the nose and mouth
Air is forced from the lungs via the windpipe
The lungs contract
The diaphragm relaxes and moves up

To encourage good breath control

At White level, singers are introduced to a few basic principles: firstly, that to sing well the breath has to be controlled, and secondly that breathing must be relaxed. The workbook also emphasizes the links between breathing and posture.

Key points for White level breathing

Breathing is a natural reflex. This means that in normal life we do not need to think about it – it happens automatically. However singers need to think more about how they breathe, and learn to control it, because this affects all aspects of singing. When breathing to sing, singers need to:

- take in deeper breaths than when breathing 'automatically' and the air should be drawn lower into the body

- control the outward breath

- breathe in the right places in the music to make sense of the words and musical phrases (this is not formally addressed at White level but it may be useful to introduce the concept)

- keep the chest, shoulders and throat relaxed and open

When practising breathing it is very easy for tension to creep into the body. As you practise breathing with singers, look out for the following:

- shoulders that move up and down a lot – movement here should be steady and barely noticeable

- visible strain or tension in the throat and neck area

- heaving movement up and down in the chest

- noisy inhalation (intake of breath should be silent – if you can hear a noise, there is tension in the body)

Tip: Always include some breathing exercises in your choir's warm-ups. These will gently remind your singers to prepare the body for singing, and will also help increase their breath capacity and control. Try the following (these also appear on pages 8 and 9 of the White workbook):

1) 'Watch' your breath

'Watch' your breath without trying to control it. Just let it go in and out automatically. Think about how it feels. Try to relax. (Once singers are comfortable with this, ask them how the breath feels at certain points – the nostrils or mouth, the back of the throat, the chest and so on – but don't complicate things too much at first.)

2) Take some slow, deep breaths

Next, start to control the breath. Breathe in and out deeply, slowly and gently. Don't gulp air in or force it out. Keep watching yourself as you do this. Feel your chest rise smoothly as you breathe in, and fall as you breathe out. The rest of your body should stay still and relaxed, especially your shoulders. (It is important to emphasize relaxation here, as some singers can become tense when asked to breathe mindfully. Make your instructions calm and gentle, and the breathing should follow suit.)

3) Breathe and count

Next, breathe in slowly and count to three in your head. Then hold your breath for another three counts. Finally, count to three again as you breathe out. Do this a few times. Keep your neck and throat relaxed. (Once again, young or new singers may become tense when doing this, so emphasize relaxation.)

When singers can do this comfortably for three counts, try four. But be careful not to hurry this.

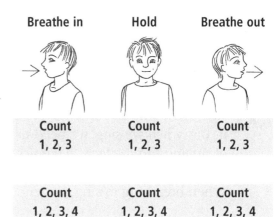

Breathe in	Hold	Breathe out
Count 1, 2, 3	Count 1, 2, 3	Count 1, 2, 3
Count 1, 2, 3, 4	Count 1, 2, 3, 4	Count 1, 2, 3, 4

4) Breathe and hiss

Repeat step 3, but this time, when you breathe out, make a gentle hiss or say 'shhhh'. Don't force the air out. Keep counting. Stay relaxed.

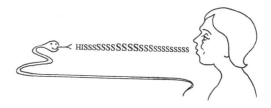

HISSSSSSSSSSSSSSSSSSSSSSS

5) Breathe and hum

Repeat step 4, but this time, when you breathe out, hum a low, quiet note. Make it as smooth as possible. Later, try this with 'vvv' and 'zzz'.

HUMmmmmmmmmmmmmm

Tip: Make sure you model good breathing for your singers so they can see what relaxed, controlled breathing looks like in others. If necessary, point out ways to improve posture during rehearsals and gently remind singers of the effects of good and bad posture on their breathing.

Most new singers should find these exercises reasonably straightforward, but if they encounter difficulties, it is probably best (at first) to move gently to something else and revisit them later. If singers come to associate these exercises with anxiety or 'trying too hard', tension can occur and may be hard to eradicate later.

Tip: Some choir trainers and teachers have a special signal that tells singers to take a very brief break – often just a minute. This can be an opportunity for everyone to 'gather their wits' and switch off for a short period before returning to the task in hand or moving on to something else. This isn't appropriate in all circumstances but you may find it helpful if you feel your singers are becoming tense.

In the workbook

- *Page 8* Posture self-assessment: Check singers' answers and discuss if necessary.

- *Page 8* 'Watch' your breath: Check singers' responses and discuss if necessary.

- *Page 9* Breathing checklist: Check and discuss singers' responses; give feedback if any aspect of breathing needs further attention.

To encourage good breath management and singing with an even tone
Light Blue level develops the skills learned at White level by means of an extended range of exercises (see page 7 of the workbook) and more opportunity for reflection about the effects of breathing on the quality of the voice.

Key points for Light Blue level breathing
Again, explain that breathing is a natural reflex. In normal life we do not think about it. But when we sing, we need to control the breath. Breathing is a fundamental part of singing and it affects dynamics, phrasing, tone quality and tuning. A few breathing exercises every day (like the ones below) will quickly improve a singer's technique. When breathing to sing, singers need to:

- inhale more deeply than when breathing 'automatically' and control the outward breath

- breathe in the right places in the music to make sense of the words and musical phrases (this is not formally addressed at Light Blue level but singers will have encountered this during rehearsals)

- keep the chest, shoulders and throat relaxed and open

When practising breathing, it is easy for the body to become tense. Singers may start to move parts of the body that should not be involved in the breathing mechanism. Check that your singers stay relaxed. Look out for the following signs of tension:

- moving shoulders – they should be more or less static

- heaving movement up and down in the chest

- visible strain or tension in the throat and neck area

- poor posture

Keeping these things in mind, try some of the following exercises (these also appear on page 7 of the Light Blue workbook):

1) Breathe in through your nose
Breathe out. Then take in a long deep breath through your nose. Hold the air gently, then allow the breath to come out through your mouth in a gentle sigh.

2) Breathe in through your mouth
When you can do (1) above without any tension in your throat or body, try breathing in and out through your mouth. Make sure your throat is open.

3) Controlling the breath with a hiss
Breathe in slowly through your nose while you count to three. Breathe out slowly through your mouth while you count to three, making a hissing noise.

HISSSSSSSSSSSSSSSSSSSSSSSSSSS

Breathe in and hiss out again. Increase the count to four, then five. If your neck and throat get tense, go back to a lower count and practise that a few times.

4) Controlling the breath with a hum

Breathe in slowly while counting three, then hum a low note while counting three. Make sure the note you hum is even in tone – the same volume from beginning to end.

Then increase the count to four, then five. Make sure that the humming remains even in volume each time.

5) Developing breath control and even tone

When you can produce an even hum for (4) above, do the exercise again but instead of humming, sing 'oo' or 'ah'. Keep the volume even each time.

Tip: Turn some of the exercises above into a game: can the choir count on one breath to a higher number at each rehearsal? Ask your singers to sit down when they have run out of air to see who has the best capacity and control. (But be careful to do this in a relaxed way that isn't too competitive – competition may cause tension!)

Encourage singers to consider how it feels while practising these exercises. Can they describe the physical sensation? Will they recognize that sensation again? This approach should increase their personal awareness so that they begin to remember for themselves how to breathe correctly without being reminded too often. Remember that young singers may not have the vocabulary for this, but you can help them to explore how good breathing feels.

Singers need to learn good breath control without allowing tension to creep in around the throat and neck. Do not pressurize singers (particularly young or inexperienced ones) to sing long phrases without a breath – it takes time to build a healthy awareness of breathing technique and to develop lung capacity. By demanding too much of singers with limited physical capacity, you may inadvertently introduce problems such as noisy breathing and tension in the throat.

Remember that nerves or anxiety may affect breathing. Try to create a supportive, relaxed atmosphere so that singers can develop their breathing without becoming tense. Positive affirmation and praise is the best way to encourage confidence.

Tip: Tension can be contagious, moving through a choir from singer to singer. If during a rehearsal you recognize that your singers have become tense, take a break from the music and practise some breathing and posture exercises.

In the workbook

- *Page 7* Breathing self-assessment: after singers have attempted all the exercises on this page, discuss the self-assessment points at the foot of the page

Breathing: Dark Blue level

To help singers develop good breath management, even tone and control of dynamics; to encourage understanding of appropriate places to breathe in music
At Dark Blue level, exercises and self-assessment help singers to become more aware of the mechanics of breathing, and to manage the breath to produce even tone and appropriate variations in volume. Page 7 of the workbook addresses when to breathe.

Key points for Dark Blue level breathing
As breathing is such a vital part of singing, every singer, no matter how experienced, needs to work on breathing technique and develop their lung capacity. Whatever you are working on with your choir, keep posture and breathing in mind. Remind singers that when breathing, the shoulders and chest should always stay relaxed. Try the following exercises with them:

1) The sensation of breathing
Place your hands around your waist and breathe in slowly. When you breathe in, you should feel your waist getting larger. When you breathe out, your waist should get smaller again. Do this a few times until you are used to the sensation. Make sure your chest and shoulders remain relaxed. Your shoulders should not rise as you breathe in or fall as you breathe out.

2) Silent breathing
Keep your throat relaxed when breathing – otherwise you will hear a noise when you breathe in. Do the above exercise again. Make sure that when you breathe in, your breath is silent. Concentrate on taking long deep breaths, keeping your body and throat relaxed.

Asking singers to take a big breath before a long phrase may result in a noisy 'panic' breath, causing tension and shallow breathing. Encourage singers to breathe calmly and deeply and, if possible, well before their entry. Be careful not to take in a noisy breath yourself: some choir trainers do this to get the choir to watch and come in together. If singers copy this, they will become tense and not breathe deeply enough.

Now try the following exercises from the workbook, ensuring that singers keep their shoulders, chest and throat relaxed:

3) Controlling the breath with a hiss
Breathe in slowly to a count of four, and out again slowly over a count of four, hissing like a snake. Then try again but count to five. Each time you repeat the exercise count to a higher number.

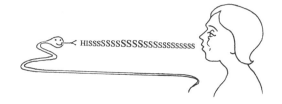

HISSSSSSSSSSSSSSSSSSSSSSSS

4) Controlling the breath with a hum
Breathe in slowly to a count of four, then hum a low note while counting to four. Repeat the exercise counting to a higher number, keeping the tone and volume even. Then do this again, sing the note to 'oo' or 'ah' instead of humming.

HUMmmmmmmmmmmmmm

Module A: Using the voice well

Explain to singers that breath control is closely linked to dynamics (variations in volume – singers will learn about these in Module B). Good breathing supports the voice when singing at all volume levels. Without good breath control it is not possible to sing loudly without singing from the throat (which produces a harsh sound like shouting, and can damage the voice if prolonged). If not adequately supported by sustained breath, quiet singing may sound thin, breathy and uneven.

5) Breath control and dynamics
Take a long deep breath, then sing a single long note to 'ah'. Start the note quietly, get gradually louder (crescendo), then gradually quieter again (diminuendo). Make sure that your change of dynamic is slow and that the breath comes out steadily. Try not to make a breathy sound or tighten your throat.

Tip: Ask singers to describe how different types of breathing feel. This increases their awareness of the sensation, which in turn will help them to breathe correctly without needing to be reminded.

Knowing when to breathe
As well as an ability to control their breathing, singers also need awareness of when it is appropriate to take a breath. This may take time to develop, as it requires mastery of a number of different musical, technical and physiological factors. From the outset, any participation in choral singing will make singers aware of the issue, but it is not formally addressed at White and Light Blue levels. At Dark Blue level, however, singers are required to start to make judgements about when to breathe.

Get to know pages 7 and 8 of the workbook. Singers may not yet formally understand these concepts, but will already have encountered some of them in rehearsals and performances. You might want to discuss them, or at least be sure that the important details have been understood. The key points are that choral singers need to:

- pronounce consonants at the same time
- co-ordinate their breathing with each other
- take advice from the choir trainer or conductor about where to breathe in the music
- learn how to 'stagger' the breathing on occasions to give the illusion of long, unbroken lines

Singers also need to be aware that at times they will need to make their own decisions about when to take a breath. Breathing needs to:

- fit with the words, and help them to make sense
- fit with the shape of any musical phrases
- follow breath marks shown in the music (but follow the conductor's advice as well)

'Tick' breath mark

'Comma' breath mark

In the workbook

- *Page 6* The sensation of breathing: Check singers are doing this correctly, and discuss the sensation with them.

- *Page 6* Silent breathing and Breath control exercises: Check, and discuss if necessary.

- *Page 6* Breath control and dynamics: Check (dynamic change should be slow and even), and discuss if necessary.

- *Page 7* Knowing when to breathe: *Away in a manger*
  There are only three correct breath marks, one in each of the first three lines, after the words *bed, head* and *lay*. The mark in the last line is best avoided, but would be acceptable. The others are inappropriate places to breathe. Check and discuss.

- *Page 8* Knowing when to breathe: Ticks suggest good places to breathe; asterisks suggest additional breathing points if needed. A breath is taken in the rest in line 3. Check and discuss.

This time there are no breath marks in the music. Put breath marks in the places where you think it is appropriate to breathe. Read the text aloud first to help you.

This is the day which the Lord has made, which the Lord has made: we will re-joice, will re-joice and be glad in it, will re-joice and be glad in it.

What singers say

'Knowing when to breathe! It's funny, I used to find it hard. But the more I practised my breathing technique, the easier it got. Partly I guess because I stopped panicking so much about running out of breath.

Megan, adult

'Our conductor made us read the words first before singing them. Once we understood the words, it was easier to know the breathing places.'

Nicholas, 14

To help singers understand the mechanics of breathing; to develop breath management, even tone and control of dynamics; to develop understanding of where to breathe in music; and to introduce the use of staggered breathing

Light Blue and Dark Blue levels stress the importance of careful, relaxed breathing. This should by now be a habit, but breathing technique needs constant work. At Red level, singers learn some of the physiological aspects of breathing, which helps them to exercise and develop the various muscles and organs.

Key points for Red level breathing

After completing Red level, singers will:

- understand the function of the diaphragm and associated muscles

- be able to identify parts of the body involved in breathing

- use various exercises to develop breath control and capacity, and understand how these link to the anatomy

As a choir trainer it is important to understand the material on page 29 of this book before working on it with singers. Below you will find the material from pages 6 and 7 of the Red workbook, together with further hints and tips to help you teach it.

Understanding the diaphragm

The diaphragm is a large muscular partition that separates the top half of the body (the chest and lungs) from the bottom half (the abdomen). It is attached to the lower ribs and falls and rises as you breathe. It is the main muscle you use when you breathe in. It draws air into the lungs, providing oxygen to the blood. (You can't actually feel your diaphragm – you feel the muscles around it moving.)

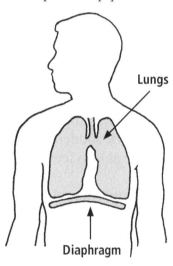

Lungs

Diaphragm

What happens when you breathe

When you breathe in, your diaphragm flattens. This pulls the bottom of the lungs down, which makes air rush down your windpipe into your lungs. As your lungs fill with air, they get bigger. Your lower ribs rise slightly, and your waistline gets wider.

When you breathe out, your diaphragm relaxes again, and the muscles in your abdomen push it back to its natural dome-shaped position. This forces air back out of your lungs. Your lungs get smaller again and your waistline gets narrower.

Tip: Suggest to your singers that they start by simply 'watching' the breath (see page 30) and, as they breathe, try to feel how the muscles in the chest, lungs and abdomen move. Exercise 1 on page 34 ('The sensation of breathing') will also help with this.

Point out to singers the alternative words for breathing in and breathing out – 'inhaling' and 'exhaling' respectively.

Practising breathing

Although the diaphragm plays such an important part in breathing, it is not possible to feel it or control it directly. It is the abdominal muscles that surround the diaphragm that help breath management when singing. As breathing is so dependent on muscles working efficiently, singers should do regular breathing practice for about ten minutes a day. Here are some exercises to help your singers.

Tip: As you work through these exercises with your singers, give them plenty of time to identify the different sensations and effects. Students who are new to this kind of work may well take a while to understand what you are asking them to notice.

1) Keeping a steady upper body

Use this exercise to help you feel the movements in the body that happen when you breathe. Exhale (breathe out), making a 'sss' sound or a whispered 'ah' until your lungs are empty. Can you feel the lower part of your rib cage contract (get smaller) while you do this? Now inhale (breathe in) deeply through your nose and feel how the rib cage naturally moves back out.

Do this again. This time, as you exhale, raise your arms almost as high as your shoulders – but take care not to raise your shoulders themselves. Then, lower your arms as you inhale. While you do this, your upper body should move as little as possible. Remember this feeling of having a steady upper body and keep it when you sing. Otherwise, the upper body tends to collapse towards the end of a phrase. This has a bad effect on the tone.

2) Exercising the diaphragm

Make a barking sound like a dog, or a short laughing 'ha' sound. It should be sudden and high-pitched. Repeat it five times. As you do, you will be able to feel the diaphragm rapidly contract and release.

3) Comparing relaxed and tense breathing

Drop your jaw slowly. Can you feel how this causes air to be drawn into your lungs? Note how the diaphragm falls and the lower rib cage expands. Do the same thing again, but this time breathe in noisily. This time, your body and diaphragm will become tense, especially the muscles in your neck.

When you take a breath before singing, try to breathe silently. This avoids tension in your throat and body. Breathe calmly and deeply, giving yourself plenty of time before you are due to start singing. This will give you time to look and think ahead.

Tip: If you ask singers to take a big breath before a long phrase, they may take a noisy 'panic breath' which causes tension and shallow breathing. Encourage them to breathe deeply, silently and, where possible, well in advance of their entry.

Also be careful not to take in a noisy breath yourself in order to get the choir to watch and come in together. This will result in the choir imitating that same action, creating tension and restricting the larynx.

Remind singers that if they feel dizzy or weak while practising, they should stop, sit down and relax. If the problem persists, you may need to help investigate the causes.

Tip: Certain singing positions restrict breathing. For example, when singing without music, some singers hold their hands behind their backs. Encourage them instead to keep their arms and hands relaxed by their sides. This encourages freer breathing. There is more lung tissue in the back of the body than in the front; the rib cage must be allowed to expand sideways, forwards and backwards. Demonstrate this to your singers with the following supplementary exercise (which is not in the workbook):

 4) Restricted breathing
Sing a short song or hymn with your hands clasped behind your back. Then sing the same music again with your hands relaxed, by your side: this should make it much easier to breathe freely and to remain physically relaxed.

 Tip: Remind singers that when singing from music, they should hold it so that they can see you over the top; to watch you conducting, they should need only to move their eyes, *not* their whole head. Remind them to relax their shoulders and keep the elbows away from the body – this will enable them to breathe freely as they sing.

 The following workbook exercises develop breath control. Encourage singers to sing straight through without taking any breaths. (If they can't do this, tell them not to worry. Advise that if they keep practising the exercises on the previous page a little each day, they will gradually find it easier to control their breathing, and will be able to get a little bit further through each time.)

 5) Breath control exercises
While singing this exercise, tell singers to imagine they are inflating a tyre in the lower back – they need to keep 'inflating' right to the end.

When singers are comfortable with the exercise above, try the next one, which will help breath control over a wider range of notes.

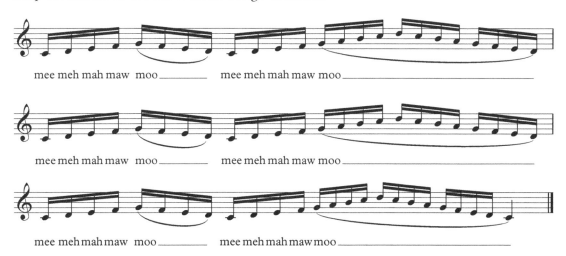

Knowing when to breathe

First formally encountered at Dark Blue level, this skill is further explored at Red level. On pages 9 and 10 of the workbook, singers can find out how to breathe in a way that makes sense of the text they are singing.

Encourage singers to read the text aloud before singing it, so that the sense of the words can inform breathing decisions. (It can also help to discuss the meaning of the words if they are unclear.) Some additional hints may be useful:

- It is usually best to breathe when there is a comma or full stop in the text.

- It isn't necessary to breathe at every comma – fewer breaths make longer, smoother phrases.

- It isn't good to breathe in the middle of a word (except during staggered breathing – see below).

Tip: Point out that not all musicians have the same views about when it is best to breathe in a piece of music, and there may well be several suitable places in a vocal line to take a breath. From time to time, when working on a piece, ask your singers where they think they should breathe. It is likely that you will get several different answers. If you have time, you could encourage singers to discuss their opinions.

However you should also make singers aware that, while their opinions are valid, when you (or another conductor or choir trainer) ask for a breath in a particular place, they should follow this instruction because you are seeking a particular musical effect that will only work if followed by every singer in the choir.

Staggered breathing

The material at Dark Blue is revisited on Page 10 of the Red level workbook as understanding of the concept needs to be more sophisticated now. Make sure that singers know: the *purpose* of staggered breathing (to create the illusion of a long phrase being sung without a break); the *technique* (to breathe on a vowel sound, not a consonant); and the *procedure* (to negotiate with other section members – and the choir trainer – when each individual should take a breath). You can help by identifying passages to practice the technique.

More about breathing

Singers take time to fully understand breath control, so monitor the development of individual singers within the choir and watch out for problems. If you expect very young singers to sing long phrases without breathing, this may well cause nervous tension – which in turn will produce poor breath control. Counteract this by allowing singers to stagger their breathing while they develop their lung capacity and their understanding of breathing technique.

Many professional singers are not able to fully achieve very long phrases without losing pitch and diction – they view it as natural to converse with colleagues (and conductor) as to where each individual will breathe in order to maintain intensity and the illusion of no break in the vocal line. Make sure you encourage the singers in your choir to do this.

In the workbook

- *Page 6* Labelling the diagram: Check answers in the illustration on the right.

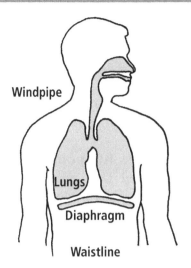

- *Page 6* Questions: The diaphragm moves **down** when you breathe in; the lungs get **smaller** when you breathe out.

- *Page 7* Keeping a steady upper body: Check singers are doing this correctly; monitor and discuss if necessary.

- *Page 7* Exercising the diaphragm: Check singers are doing this correctly; monitor and discuss if necessary.

- *Page 7* Comparing relaxed and tense breathing: Check singers are doing this correctly; monitor and discuss if necessary.

- *Page 8* Breath control exercises: Monitor and discuss if necessary.

- *Page 9* Knowing when to breathe: Sensible places to breathe are: bar 2; before bar 11; before bar 13. Inappropriate places to breathe are: bar 7; before bar 10. The mark in bar 3 is debatable – not incorrect but not entirely musical. Check and discuss.

- *Page 10* Knowing when to breathe: Ticks suggest appropriate places to breathe; asterisks suggest additional breathing points if needed. Check and discuss.

To help singers understand the mechanics of breathing and use this to prepare the voice for singing; to encourage singing with good breath support; to encourage use of the back muscles to strengthen the sound

By this level of *Voice for Life,* singers should be familiar with the function of the diaphragm and some of the associated muscles. You may need to remind them of the mechanisms discussed on page 29 of this book.

Key points for Yellow level breathing

The Yellow workbook develops control of the musculature surrounding the diaphragm and in the back, giving singers techniques, strategies and exercises to increase intensity and strength in the voice. For this to happen, more detailed understanding of the diaphragm is required now. Make sure that singers understand the following points:

- During inhalation, the dome-shaped diaphragm contracts and descends, pulling the bottom of the lungs down and causing air to rush in.

- As the lungs fill with air, the lower ribs expand outwards and the waistline expands.

- During exhalation, the diaphragm relaxes and rises, being pushed up by the abdominal muscles.

- As air leaves the lungs, the lower ribs contract inwards and the waistline contracts.

As the voice settles and develops, it is important not to over-support it with the diaphragm, since this can lead to a pressed or forced sound. It can also lead to constriction in the throat. To ensure that the throat is relaxed, try the following exercises as a prelude to choir practice:

1) Placing the voice in neutral

Stand up straight, with the feet slightly apart, and make a panting sound like a dog. The diaphragm will move up and down as described above. Make sure that the throat are mouth are relaxed. Try not to force the breath out, as this will dry out the vocal folds and could close the throat. Instead, aim for a gentle in-and-out movement of breath, using equal effort for inhalation and exhalation. This is the voice in neutral – its normal relaxed state.

Simple breathing is something that we do all the time without thinking about it. The exercise above uses this natural reflex. It is a good way to remove tension and prevents vocal fatigue. Encourage your singers to use it during their own practice so that they keep the throat relaxed – it appears on page 6 of the Yellow workbook.

2) The excited diaphragm

Having relaxed the throat, the following exercise prepares the diaphragm for singing. Place the voice into 'neutral' again. This time, do it in such a way that you bring a sense of excitement to the movement. Take in a breath, maintaining this feeling of excitement. With the 'excited diaphragm' working all the time, it should be possible to sing long, supported notes and phrases more easily.

Once you have achieved the previous exercise with your singers, try the following:

3) Using the excited diaphragm

Choose a comfortable note to begin the exercise below. Repeat both sets of vowels several times. Each time you repeat, move up or down a semitone. Singers may find the exercise tiring at first, but this demonstrates that the correct muscles are working. It should not feel painful or uncomfortable, however.

| oo | ee | oo | ee | oo | ee | oo | ee | oo | ee | oo | ee | oo | ee | oo | ee | oo |
| ah | ee | ah | ee | ah | ee | ah | ee | ah | ee | ah | ee | ah | ee | ah | ee | ah |

Having mastered these diaphragm exercises, encourage singers to prepare their voices for singing by using this level of excitement every time they sing. This not only makes the diaphragm work hard but will also help to imbue their singing with intensity. Now try the following exercise to build on this:

4) Breathing warm-up

This is a very good warm-up exercise. It is based on 'Placing the voice in neutral' but this time, each outward movement is vocalised and there is an inalation at every rest. Practise this using both 'ah' and 'oo' sounds. With each repetition, move the starting note up or down a semitone. Gradually increase the speed.

| ah | ah | ah | ah | ah | ah | ah | ah |
| oo | oo | oo | oo | oo | oo | oo | oo |

5) Singing with intensity

Choose one of the following phrases from Handel's *Messiah*:

- Baritones and basses: 'For behold, darkness shall cover the earth'

- Tenors: 'He was cut off out of the land of the living'

- Counter-tenors: 'Then shall be brought to pass'

- Altos: 'Behold a virgin shall conceive' or 'Then shall the eyes of the blind' (alto version)

- Sopranos: 'And the angel said unto them' or 'Then shall the eyes of the blind' (soprano version)

Singers should imagine that they are very excited but forbidden to make a sound (like trying not to laugh). They should keep that sensation in mind whilst singing the phrases (which should not be forced or overdone). They may feel as though they are trying to suppress the sound. As long as this suppression only happens in the diaphragm and not in the throat, they will be working hard to support the sound without singing *forte*, enabling a high degree of intensity.

As professional singers will tell you, singing quietly is harder work than singing loudly. This exercise helps singers to sing quietly without losing support (which can result in sagging pitch). Singers may all look somewhat overexcited until they get used to the idea! (The phrases from *Messiah* are simply suggestions. You may well feel other phrases are equally appropriate.)

Using and developing the back muscles

The back is covered in muscle and is therefore much stronger than the front of the body. By using the muscles in the back to support the voice, singers can employ a far larger range of muscles than just the diaphragm; this increases the power of the voice, and also helps avoid over-use of the diaphragm.

The muscles of the back

The main back muscles that support the voice are the *latissimus dorsi* and the *quadratus lumborum* (see diagram). The exercises below use these muscles, but you can use other muscles too (notably the *trapezius*, which runs from just below the middle of the spine to the neck).

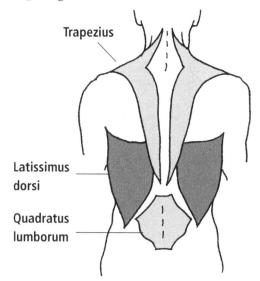

Trapezius

Latissimus dorsi

Quadratus lumborum

The exercises on page 8 of the Yellow workbook will help singers to strengthen the muscles of the back to support singing. They are reproduced below, with some tips to help you teach them.

These exercises are not dangerous, but approach them with care. After trying them, singers who are just getting used to working with these muscles should probably feel slightly tired, as at the end of any physical work-out. But be gentle and look for signs of discomfort, fatigue or dizziness. Encourage singers to tell you if they feel any of these symptoms: they may indicate technical problems (see opposite).

1) The sensation of using the back muscles

Exhale sharply. One of the functions of the *quadratus* is to cause this movement. If you used enough effort, the *latissimus* will have helped out too. Did you feel your back muscles tightening? Now bend forwards and rest your hands on your lower back. Try to feel your flanks (the fleshy area that runs down from your back across your hips). Now exhale sharply again. Did you feel the muscles working that time?

Tip: These sensations may be unfamiliar to your singers, so give them time to identify the muscle movements. Encourage them to do these exercises during practice at home.

2) Strengthening the back muscles

Choose a comfortable starting note. Repeat the exercise several times, moving up a tone each time. Before singing each phrase, exhale forcefully. It may seem strange to sing after exhaling, but this forces the back muscles to support the sound. Take care not to close your throat: the air needs to pass through without hindrance.

ha ha ha ha ha___   ha ha ha ha ha___   ha ha ha ha ha___ *etc.*
haw haw haw haw haw___ haw haw haw haw haw___ haw haw haw haw haw___
hoo hoo hoo hoo hoo___ hoo hoo hoo hoo hoo___ hoo hoo hoo hoo hoo___

Tip: You may need to help individual singers identify suitable starting notes for this exercise, according on their range and stamina.

Explain to singers that when doing this exercise, they should aim to reach the point where the back muscles feel just slightly tired. The more they practise, the easier it will become as the back muscles strengthen. As a consequence, they will be able to sing for longer with less effort, and will not keep running out of breath.

 If singers feel dizzy when singing this exercise, they may be using too much air and hyperventilating as a result. This may be because they are generally taking in too much air when they sing. Suggest they try not to take a big breath before the exercise, but breathe phrase by phrase instead. They should have expelled all the air by the end of each phrase, and simply take in enough breath to recover before the next one.

 Some singers, because they do not use the diaphragm or back enough, get used to supporting the voice with the throat. As a result they may sing habitually with a raised or locked jaw – which can have unwelcome effects on the vocal tone. As the diaphragm and back muscles take over the support role, you should encourage these singers to gradually release the tension in the jaw. Once the jaw and throat relax, the sound will improve.

 In the workbook

- *Page 6* Marking the diagrams: Check by referring to page 29 of this book.

- *Page 6* Placing the voice in neutral: Check singers are doing this correctly; monitor and discuss if necessary.

- *Page 7* The excited diaphragm: Check singers are doing this correctly; monitor and discuss if necessary.

- *Page 7* Using the excited diaphragm: Check singers are doing this correctly; monitor and discuss if necessary.

- *Page 7* Breathing warm-up: Check singers are doing this correctly; monitor and discuss if necessary.

- *Page 7* Singing with intensity: Check singers are doing this correctly; monitor and discuss if necessary.

- *Page 8* The sensation of using the back muscles: Check singers are doing this correctly; monitor and discuss if necessary.

- *Page 8* Strengthening the back muscles: Check singers are doing this correctly; monitor and discuss if necessary.

Tone and range: Introduction

 All human voices are different. The quality of the sound is affected by many factors, including the sex, size, shape, age and health of the individual, as well as more detailed and specific aspects of each singer's physiology and technique. It is debatable whether some voices are naturally physically better adapted to singing than others: but nearly all voices respond to careful training and can be developed into a musical instrument of considerable expressive power.

As a choir trainer, one of your main functions is to improve the voices of individual singers – which, naturally, will improve the sound of your choir as a whole. The 'Tone and range' section of *Voice for Life* focuses specifically on how to help individuals:

- find a suitable **register** (a comfortable place in the voice to sing)
- within that register, develop the **range** of notes the singer can sing comfortably and without straining
- improve the **tonal quality** of the voice, making it consistent and flexible throughout the range
- understand the **mechanics** of voice production so they can monitor and improve their own singing

Followed systematically, the activities, exercises and advice in this section of the book – in conjunction with the other elements of Module A – will help your singers to find a robust, versatile voice.

Before you start
If you have not taught voice production before, do not worry: the basics are provided here. (Bear in mind too that aspects of this topic are covered in more detail in *The Voice for Life Guide to Choir Training*.) Before you begin work with your singers, make sure you are familiar and comfortable with the introductory material on these pages, and the relevant content in the workbooks. Only then should you move on to the details for the specific levels which begin on page 51.

 Anatomy of the nose, mouth and throat
Some knowledge of the anatomy of the nose, mouth and throat is useful when teaching voice production. If you know the location of some of the items mentioned in the 'Tone and range' and 'Diction' sections, you will find it easier to help your singers.

The anatomical features mentioned in *Voice for Life* are shown in this diagram. Note that the **vocal folds** (see opposite) are not visible at this magnification – they are located within the larynx (see the more detailed diagram on page 70).

You may find it useful to refer back to this diagram as you work through the material below.

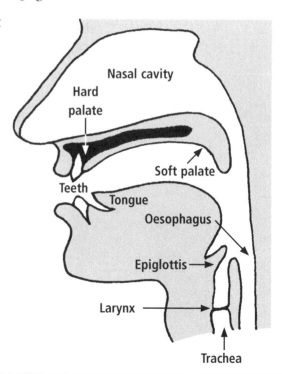

Voice basics

Sound is produced by vibrations of the **vocal folds**. (These are sometimes called the vocal cords, but the term 'folds' is more accurate because the muscles are made up of several different parts.) The vocal folds lie inside the **larynx** (voice box).

The **pitch** of the voice (how high or low it is) depends on the rate of vibration. For Middle C, the vocal folds vibrate 256 times per second; an octave higher is twice this rate. The rate of vibration depends on the length and thickness of the vocal folds, and how much tension they are placed under: as with a guitar string, the more tension, the higher the pitch. The tension is affected by the muscles of the larynx. (This information may be helpful to you, but may be less relevant to your singers, as it is hard to visualize or sense the process in a useful way.)

Tip: Don't be afraid to touch the larynx gently to feel its vibrations as you speak or sing; you can also feel it moving upwards as you swallow. Encourage your singers to do this too (the workbooks contain activities and guidance).

The **register** of the voice is the place where singing feels comfortable for each individual. Essentially the four main voice types in a choir – soprano, alto, tenor and bass – correspond to a vocal register, though some singers don't always fit easily into these categories at first. A singer's register depends on many things: age, size, sex and experience. The lower levels of *Voice for Life* contain exercises to help singers identify their register so that you can place them appropriately within the choir.

Within the register, singers will be able to sing a **range** of notes (between the highest and lowest pitches they can comfortably manage). Young or inexperienced singers may have a very limited range. (For the White level 'Tone and range' targets, a range of five notes is sufficient; for Light Blue, an octave.) Exercises in the workbooks help singers gradually and gently expand their range. (Note that many sources use the terms 'range' and 'register' practically interchangeably.) There is more preparatory information about register and range on the following pages.

The sound produced by the vocal folds is very quiet, but the vibrations are amplified by sympathetic vibrations in the **vocal tract** (the throat, the mouth and to some extent the nasal cavity) and other parts of the body too. This is called **resonance**. Cultivating a resonant voice is an important part of singing and there is plenty of help throughout *Voice for Life*. (For more about resonance, see pages 52 and 56.)

Tone is the word usually used for how singers use the vocal tract and associated resonance to modify the sound made by the vocal folds. Tone should be as consistent as possible throughout a singer's range so that every pitch is equally reliable. The workbooks contain many activities and exercises geared to enabling singers to monitor, evaluate and adapt the sound they make.

There are also various common impediments to good tone which, at various stages of development, affect some singers for various physiological, psychological and technical reasons. It is important to be aware of these: most of them are relatively easy to remedy but you do need to be able to point individual singers in the right direction. These are mentioned in the following pages in the various contexts where they are particularly likely to occur.

Tone and range: Introduction

Your role as a choir trainer
Initially you need to help new singers to find a register in which they can comfortably sing. Then move on to work on tone and range. There are exercises for all this in the workbooks, but you will need to help singers to: find a resonant sound; to listen to it, feel it and reproduce it. It is your job to:

- model a good vocal sound for your singers

- encourage them to recognize a good resonant vocal sound in themselves and in others

- spot singers' vocal problems and react to them promptly and calmly

- manage the layout of the choir carefully to enable each singer to achieve their full vocal potential

Modelling a good vocal sound
As a choir trainer, you must be able to demonstrate what you want your singers to do – to establish the sound, the pitch area, and the pace which you want the exercises (or indeed any music) to be sung. Sing to your singers, or get experienced members of the choir to demonstrate. (As much as possible, avoid using the piano when you work on tone and range – singers should concentrate on the vocal sound alone.)

Tip: Male choir trainers should be aware that children may struggle to copy the bass or tenor voice, as they may not instinctively transpose what they hear to an octave in their own range. If this is a problem, ask a few of the more established young singers to repeat what you sing at a higher octave for the others to imitate.

Encouraging recognition of a good vocal sound
When training singers to produce a good tone, you must develop two linked skills: sound production (and from the outset, encourage physical awareness of the making of the sound) and listening. Physical and aural awareness must go hand in hand. We constantly monitor our voices in two ways: inner hearing and physical sensation. The sound we produce when singing reaches the inner ear via the vibrating tissues of the throat, neck and skeleton. Singing needs to feel right and sound right.

The more your singers can recognize these physical sensations and reproduce them, the more successful their singing will be. Ask them to listen for good tone quality and to think about how it feels when they produce a resonant sound. This will encourage them to make the connections between the physical sensation and the production of good vocal tone. (Activities in the workbooks encourage this awareness.)

The physical sensation of resonance
Sing a moderate to high note with resonance (see page 56). Ask singers if they can feel a buzzing in their ears, and have them copy this sound at a pitch of their choice. Then sing the same note again, but with a breathy tone. Suggest they copy you. They will feel no buzzing. Point out that they should always aim for the former sensation.

Many young singers need to search for a resonant sound as the voice develops, and tuning sometimes suffers as a consequence. If this happens, it is very important not to discourage singers: they risk becoming withdrawn, and tension in the voice and unwelcome changes in the tone colour may occur. (If this becomes a problem, it can help to work on aspects of vocal technique in small groups from time to time.)

Looking out for problems

Developing singers always need guidance from a teacher or choir trainer. It is easy to develop bad habits between one lesson or choir practice and the next. In a large choir, you may not always find it easy to identify struggling singers. It can help to ask older, more experienced singers help you to listen out for problems. If you do this, make sure it is discreet, fair and in the spirit of improving the choir as a whole – do not let it become too obvious (or in any way accusatory or vindictive).

Managing the layout of the choir to enhance tone and range

Deciding who should stand where can be complex: different singers require different approaches. But moving singers around has advantages. For example it helps you to:

- avoid a young singer competing in volume with an older choir member (which can be discouraging for the former)

- encourage a singer with a breathy voice to produce a clearer tone by placing him or her next to someone with a clear voice

Yet it can have disadvantages too, because:

- placing a young singer with a breathy voice next to a strong powerful singer may encourage the former to take yet more breath, causing more technical problems

- allowing young singers to imitate more experienced ones, or to compete with the tone and volume of older singers, may cause them to force their voices, causing harsh sounds and poor tuning

In practice, as you become familiar with your choir, you will quickly learn what works and what doesn't. Whatever, get your singers used to moving around frequently so that they are not made anxious when you change their positions.

More about range and register

The range of individual voices varies greatly. With training, the range is liable to expand. (Conversely, a singer's range may contract with age.)

Most young children (up to about five) are comfortable in a small range of notes, around middle C to around the G above. Most 7- to 11-year-olds can sing easily from middle C to the C above; regular singers who are encouraged to develop their upper range will reach well above that. Before adolescence, few children have a range much below middle C, although occasional Bs and B flats should be possible.

The approximate ranges of the standard choral registers – soprano, alto, tenor and bass – are shown below. There is however plenty of music that extends above and below these limits. There are also plenty of singers who do not manage the full range of these registers; likewise some will sing comfortably beyond them.

In reality many adult female singers are really mezzo-sopranos, somewhere between soprano and alto; and many adult males are baritones, somewhere between tenor and bass. The decision as to which part a choir member will sing should not always be dictated solely by their vocal range. Other factors such as their vocal timbre and music reading ability should also be taken into account.

Mezzo-sopranos or baritones who sing only alto or bass parts risk losing their upper range through lack of use. Encourage all singers to use their full range when warming up.

A note about changing voices

Voice for Life is for all singers, whatever their age and stage, so the workbooks make only passing reference to what happens to the voice at adolescence. Just like any other singers, those with changing voices benefit from regular vocal exercise, but take particular care not to ask them to push the voice beyond its comfortable range (which could vary frequently at this time). There is more guidance on how to support adolescent changing voices in *The Voice for Life Guide to Choir Training*.

While an individual's voice is changing, help him or her to get used to it and to feel comfortable. It may help to focus less on the practical singing targets of *Voice for Life* and concentrate instead on the other modules. It is also unwise to consider singing exams like the RSCM awards at this time; an examiner can only assess the voice they hear on the day, and singers are unlikely to give their best if they're unused to a newly changed voice. Let the voice settle before attempting exams.

A note about vibrato

Vibrato is a slight, normally quick fluctuation of pitch. It develops naturally as part of a well-produced voice. There is no need to train vibrato with special exercises; if singers concentrate on forming good technique as outlined in this book, vibrato will appear as the voice matures. It can then be deliberately used for expressive purposes to colour, warm and enrich the sound. Its extent will depend on the size and quality of each individual's voice, as well as its owner's temperament and taste.

If you have young female singers in your choir, allow them to enjoy the warm, vibrant tone of their developing voice and its vibrato. Fearing that this will lead to a big 'wobbly' voice commonly associated with opera singers, some young women try to avoid acquiring vibrato. But doing this can inhibit their vocal development and lead to vocal problems later in life.

Likewise some choir trainers, in search of a 'pure' soprano sound, actively discourage this vocal development. This may encourage young women to tighten the throat to maintain an unwavering sound, thereby causing constriction which harms the tone. You should try to let vibrato happen until it is fully developed, at which point singers have more control over it and can use it at will.

Poor vocal technique may result in excessive uncontrolled vibrato (also known as tremolo). Common causes are lack of control of the breath through the vocal folds or constriction of the throat. These can both be helped by improving breath support.

To encourage use of the voice in a variety of ways; to help singers locate the larynx; to help singers identify and feel resonance; to help singers find a comfortable place in the voice to sing and gently test the limits of the vocal range

 At White level, the tone and range activities encourage new singers to explore the basics of voice production. In the workbook, this section is called 'Voice exercises' rather than the more formal 'Tone and range'.

 Key points for White level tone and range
It is normal for young voices to be quiet and breathy, and for the vocal range to be very small. With young singers, it is vital to:

- make sure singers are warmed up and relaxed before singing starts

- focus on enjoying the physical and mental sensations of singing

- avoid too much insistence on 'progress' or pressure (to increase volume, for example): this can have a negative, demotivating effect

- stress the benefits of regular vocal exercise

 Tip: Before everything else you must establish good posture habits and basic breath control, as outlined earlier in this book. If these are in place, and you (and other singers) make beginners feel a valuable part of the choir, you should find that they naturally find more volume and resonance. Regular singing in choir (and between rehearsals as well) will help young voices to grow in strength, range and agility.

You will also be surprised how much your singers will pick up by listening to other more experienced singers around them. Encourage beginners to talk to other singers.

Once singers have warmed up with breathing exercises, they will be relaxed, alert and ready to exercise their voices. The activities below – which appear on page 10 of the workbook – will make singing easier and more enjoyable.

 1) Voice scribbling
Move your finger up and down in the air as if you were scribbling, and follow it with your voice. Use a humming sound or 'ooo', and move up and down as high or low as feels comfortable.

Move your finger slowly at first, then speed up. Start quietly, and get louder if you can. You could do this in pairs, singing your partner's scribbles. Remember to stay relaxed.

 2) Using the voice in different ways
Ask singers to make different sounds with their voices: whisper their name, quack like a duck, say 'hello' in sing-song voice, bark like a dog, imitate a police car siren, gasp in surprise, and so on. These loosen up the voice, extend its range and aid relaxation. Encourage singers to enjoy the different sounds their voice can make – but look out for signs of unwelcome tension. The aim is to remain relaxed at all times.

The physical sensations of singing
Page 11 of the White level workbook introduces some of the physical aspects of voice production and resonance. Work through these activities and exercises gently with your singers. It may help to have more experienced choir members assist the beginners with some of this.

 Where does the voice come from?
Your voice comes from a part of your throat called the voice box or larynx (say '*LAR-inks*'). It contains tiny flaps called vocal folds. When your breath passes over the vocal folds, they vibrate inside your throat and make the sound of your voice.

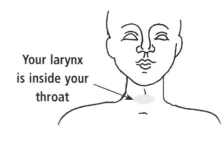

Your larynx is inside your throat

 1) Feeling your larynx working
To feel where your larynx is, gently place your hands or fingers on your throat. If you speak or hum, you will feel your larynx vibrate. You can also feel your larynx move upwards when you swallow.

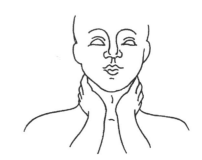

 The sound made by your vocal folds alone is very quiet indeed. But the vibrations in your larynx make other parts of your body vibrate too. This makes the sound louder. Singers call this **resonance**.

 2) Feeling resonance
You can feel resonance in your face and body. While you hum, gently touch areas of your face such as your jaw, cheeks, nose and forehead. Can you feel the vibrations?

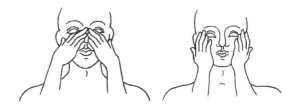

You may need to do this a few times to get used to it. Try touching with your fingertips or the palm of your hand. Don't press hard or you won't feel anything.

Next, gently touch your chest and stomach while you are singing, and feel the sound vibrating here too.

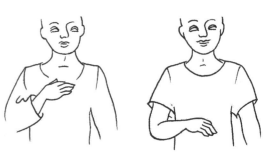

 Tip: Young singers may not understand at first what it is they are trying to feel. For instance they may not recognize vibration (or even know the word). You may need to find creative ways of explaining this.

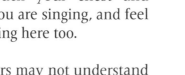 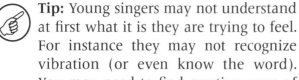 If singers appear baffled or uncomfortable during these activities, do not insist on continuing them. Instead, revisit them frequently – beginners will gradually come to recognize what is involved.

Pitch and range

Page 12 of the White level workbook contains activities and exercises (shown below) to help young singers with the concepts of pitch and range.

Once again, take these slowly and, if possible, try to involve more experienced members of the choir to work with beginners.

1) High and low

Encourage your singers to listen to other singers, either in your choir or on recordings. You may suggest some music to listen to, or identify suitable members of the choir. Start with high and low voices separately. If you do this during choir practice, you will be able to direct the listening more effectively, pointing out the contrast between high and low voices

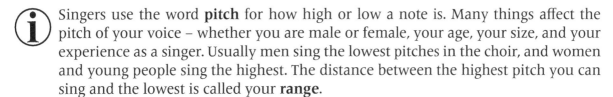

Singers use the word **pitch** for how high or low a note is. Many things affect the pitch of your voice – whether you are male or female, your age, your size, and your experience as a singer. Usually men sing the lowest pitches in the choir, and women and young people sing the highest. The distance between the highest pitch you can sing and the lowest is called your **range**.

To find your range, first hum a pitch that is comfortably in the middle of your voice. Then slide up and down as far as you can comfortably go. Never force your voice beyond its range without help from your choir trainer or teacher.

Exercises to increase range

The best exercises to increase vocal range are sirens, which are covered in more detail in the Light Blue level section (page 57). Encourage singers to build on the exercise above, humming first and then using *ah* and *mee*. At this level, it doesn't matter at all how high or low the siren goes; just take it to the comfortable limit of the voice. Be careful when choosing a starting note – a lot of inexperienced singers will naturally start very low in their range (within a third of their bottom note).

Make the higher notes easier using lip trills. To do lip trills, keep the lips loose and make a *brrr* noise (as if blowing bubbles underwater). With a little practice singers will be able to do this first on a single pitch, then on a slide or scale. Use it to slide up a fifth from your starting note, and back again; then repeat a step higher.

Because lip trills relax the face and neck, they help singers to the reach the top end of their range more easily. If singers find it hard to sustain the trill, this may well be because there is tension in the face and neck (which results in a 'raspberry'), or because there is not enough breath to keep the lips vibrating. Refer back to the section on breathing (page 30) if you need to.

Exercises to aid pitch recognition

Pitch recognition and pitch matching are of course vital elements of choral singing but some new singers – especially but not exclusively younger ones – may need a bit of encouragement. Here are a few ideas:

Younger singers may respond well to pitch recognition games involving movement. Play or sing some notes, and suggest they make a 'tall shape' or point upwards when they hear a high note. When they hear a low note, they should make a 'small shape' or point to the floor. You can gradually introduce gradations for this so that they begin to distinguish between ever smaller differences in pitch by more nuanced degrees of high and low gesture. (This also ties in with 'Voice scribbling' on page 51.)

This will start to develop the mental link between 'visualized' high and low and heard pitch – this will be vital when singers start to learn to read music. You can also use the siren exercise on the previous page to help this, as follows. Start on a comfortable note as before; then draw a wiggly line with a finger in the air. Ask singers to follow the pitch contour you draw. Start with small fluctuations, and gradually get wider.

You could take this further by drawing the shapes on a board or paper – an echo of the neumes that preceded staff notation. Likewise you could ask singers to draw – either in the air or on paper – the contour of a line or phrase that you sing.

To encourage singers to make the link between what they hear and what they sing, play or sing some short, simple phrases and ask singers to identify and reproduce the last note in each one. Begin with very short phrases that move by step within a small range; gradually increase the length and complexity. Then ask singers to identify and reproduce more than one note in each phrase – the last two for example. The phrases can be from well-known tunes or things you make up.

Inexperienced singers often find it harder to match pitch against an instrument than against a human voice. As much as possible, demonstrate these exercises (and everything else) by singing, rather than playing.

At White level, it is not important that singers can differentiate interval leaps exactly, but they should be able to tell whether successive notes move up or down, and distinguish small intervals from big ones. The theory in Module B will help with this.

Pitch matching

If singers find it difficult to match pitch, ask them to sing any note. Sing this pitch yourself, then move up a step, encouraging them to match you. Matching pitch is not automatic for everyone, but almost everyone can learn to do it with time and patience. (Never write any singer off as 'tone deaf': true amusia is very rare indeed, and many people who consider themselves to be 'tone deaf' have in fact just never learned pitch matching, and have instead learned to be fearful.)

If you are a tenor or bass, some young beginners might find it hard to adapt to the fact that the notes you sing will be an octave below theirs. Don't stop singing to them (if you do, they will not learn to follow you) but do consider getting in a more experienced upper-voice 'interpreter' to help them find the correct pitch. If need be, use a keyboard to help you out – but try not to rely on this.

Voice development

Page 12 of the workbook also contains three hints or activities to help singers focus and strengthen the voice. Each of them requires some additional notes of caution which (for simplicity's sake) are not shown in the workbook but appear here below each one. Bear these in mind when monitoring and assessing singers.

- Open your mouth wide when you sing, or the sound will get trapped inside. From time to time, sing in front of a mirror to check your mouth is wide open.

Singers should take care not to open the mouth too wide, as this tightens the jaw and pushes down on the larynx. The mouth shouldn't open more than is comfortable; you should usually be able to get one or two of your own fingers between your teeth; any wider is probably straining and stretching too much.

- When you sing, make as much space inside your mouth as you can. Imagine you are biting an apple. Keep your tongue flat and your throat relaxed.

Singers should take care not to push the tongue back or make it rigid; a yawn will help to open up the space at the back of the mouth.

- Exercise your voice regularly and do your practice. Once a week at choir rehearsal probably isn't enough to give you the strength you need.

Look out for signs of tiredness in your singers. If they appear fatigued, don't encourage them to try to 'sing through' it. Little and often is the best way to increase vocal stamina.

In the workbook

- *Page 10* Voice scribbling: Observe, check, and discuss if necessary

- *Page 10* Using your voice in different ways: Observe, check, and discuss if necessary

- *Page 11* Feeling your larynx working: Observe, check, and discuss if necessary

- *Page 11* Feeling resonance: Observe, check, and discuss if necessary

- *Page 11* Voice checklist: Observe, check, and discuss if necessary

- *Page 12* High and low: Can singers identify high and low notes?

- *Page 12* Find your range: Observe, check and monitor

- *Page 12* Voice development: Observe, check and monitor

To help singers understand more about vocal anatomy and resonance and find a comfortable register; to encourage singing with even tone over an ascending and descending scale of an octave (at a pitch chosen by the singer)

 The Light Blue workbook consolidates and expands the activities at White level, moving towards a more systematic approach to pitch, tone, range and register. The key material here is on pages 8 and 9 of the workbook.

 Key points for Light Blue level tone and range
Vocal sound is made in the larynx and resonates in parts of the face and body. The word singers use to talk about how a voice resonates and other qualities is **tone**. Activities in the workbook encourage understanding of this. Further exercises enable the identification of each singer's **range** – the distance a singer's highest and lowest comfortable notes – and begin to look at ways of expanding it.

 Tip: When working on tone in the early stages, do not worry too much about exact pitching. Sliding from one pitch area to another helps new singers find where their voice resonates in different parts of their throat, mouth, head and chest.

The numbered exercises below are taken directly from the workbook, interspersed with advice about how to use them with your choir. As much of this material relies on physical sensation, it is important that you encourage singers to follow the activities carefully.

 1) How your voice works
Your voice starts in a part of your throat called the **larynx** (say *LAR-rinks*). It contains tiny flaps of skin called **vocal folds**. When your breath passes over them, they vibrate. Put your hands or fingers gently on your throat while you speak or sing to feel these vibrations. They create the sound of your voice.

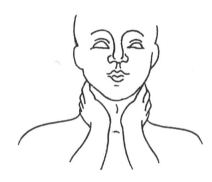

2) Resonance
The vibrations in your larynx make other parts of your body vibrate too. This makes the sound louder. Singers call this **resonance**. Try touching other areas of your face and body (such as your cheeks, jaw and nose) while humming. Can you feel the vibrations in some of these places?

 The main areas of resonance are the throat, mouth, nose, head, chest and stomach. Experiment with different sounds like high-pitched sirens (see below), or low growling. With each sound you make, feel the vibrations in different parts of your body.

Tone

Singers use the word **tone** to talk about how a voice resonates and how even it is. Encourage singers to listen to many different voices and to try to describe them, however briefly. Identifying different tone qualities becomes increasingly important later in *Voice for Life*, but even at this stage it is important that singers begin to recognize good tone quality.

Tone depends on many things, like posture and breathing; if need be, refer singers back to these sections of the workbook for exercises to help with these. Tone is also affected by how comfortable the voice is when singing, so discourage singers from any singing activity that introduces tension to the voice, such as trying to sing notes that are too high or low for them.

The following exercises will help singers find a range in which it is comfortable to sing. For some people, this may initially be just a few notes in the middle of their voice; for others it may be an octave or more. Again, this depends on many factors including a singer's age, sex, size, experience and level of relaxation.

3) Finding a comfortable note

Laugh energetically ('ha! ha! ha!'). Now do this again, but this time, hold the 'ah' sound of the final 'ha!' The note you are now singing will be in a comfortable part of your voice. Repeat this exercise regularly. As you develop as a singer, you will find that the note at the end of your laugh will change.

On page 8 of the workbook, singers are asked to identify their comfortable note and to write it down on a stave provided. You may need to help pre-reading singers with both the identification of the note and its notation. The process is important: not only does it provide an accurate reference point for future use, but it also validates the singer's voice and acknowledges that you are going to develop it.

Tip: Bear in mind too that not all singers will be fluent music readers at this stage. It is likely that you will need to teach the exercises below by ear (although it is also useful to refer singers to the notation as this aids developing reading skills).

Page 8 of the workbook also explains the words 'pitch' and 'range', both of which you will need when working on these exercises. It may be useful to check – particularly with younger singers – that they have properly understood these concepts.

4) Increasing your range using sirens

Using *Ah*, *Mee* or *Hmm*, make siren sounds. Start with the note you found on page 8. Slide up to a higher note, back down to your starting note, down to a lower note, then back up to where you began. Gradually make the siren cover a wider range. Keep the sound even and the notes smoothly connected.

Tip: At first, use slides of no more than three notes wide but gradually extend these towards an octave, keeping the tone sustained from one pitch area to another in the voice. Keep the sound even and the notes smoothly connected.

Sirens and slides can be used at all levels of singing to help connect notes throughout a singer's range. Remember that all singers need to exercise their vocal muscles (just as an athlete needs to work on the fitness and strength of their muscles) or they lose the ability to reach notes at the top and bottom of their range. The following exercises, reproduced from page 9 of the workbook, focus on range development.

5) Finding and developing your range

 Start with the note you found on page 8. Sing the three-note pattern below to *Ah*, *Mah* or *Yah*. After you sing it, move to the next note up. Keep going up as long as you can sing comfortably. Don't force your voice beyond this point.

Finding and developing your range (contd)

 Next, do the same thing but instead, move to the next note down, still using *Ah*, *Mah* or *Yah*. This time keep moving down for as long as you can sing comfortably. (The example below does not appear in the workbook.)

 Tip: When listening to these exercises, make sure that they are sung legato and that the vowel sounds remain constant throughout. If the singing is not smooth, or the vowel sounds change, it may indicate poor breath control or tension in the throat.

6) Producing a good tone

 Hum a note, then open your mouth to a vowel sound: *Hmm–ee* for example. Sing up and down a five-note phrase (phrases are explained on page 10) using this vowel. Then sing the same exercise using a different vowel. When you hum, the sound should be resonant. You should feel vibrations behind your lips. When you open your mouth for the vowel, keep the sound in the same forward position.

 Tip: Much of the work on tone will concentrate on the middle of the singer's range where the voice is comfortable. But at the same time you need to extend the pitch and tone range to higher and lower registers. Exercises like those on the preceding pages can be gradually moved further up or down the register, enabling you to work on the same patterns in different parts of the voice, and to build on existing experience.

For the Light Blue pitch and range targets, your singer must sing a one-octave scale with even tone. To prepare for this, use the exercises above to develop range. Then practise one-octave scales like the one below.

Training for the scale target: hints and tips

 When you do the test, make sure that you choose a scale that lies comfortably with the singer's range. Bear in mind that, as the choir trainer and assessor, you can work on this exercise as often as necessary until you feel it appropriate to sign the target box. As singers progress towards achieving the necessary fluency and evenness of tone, you may hear inconsistencies. These are listed below, with some remedies.

If the tone or volume of the scale is uneven, encourage singers to practise it using a hum. This will bring the tone forward and encourage a good legato. Singing the scale using a lip trill will encourage even breath support and relaxed top notes.

You may hear a very noticeable change of tone (to a much lighter sound) at one point in the scale. This may indicate that the scale crosses a natural break in the singer's vocal registers known as the *passaggio*. Registers are not fully explored in *Voice for Life* until Red level, but you can begin to strengthen this area with gentle siren exercises. For the Light Blue scale target test, though, it might be sensible to try a scale starting on a lower or higher note to avoid this break.

Encourage good intonation by practising the scales with all the notes detached from one another, so that every pitch has to be accurately focused. Listen for any notes that slide up or down to the required pitch. Give your singer a good internalized sense of the role of each note of the scale by practising the scale with a rest or clap replacing one degree of the scale – particularly the dominant (fifth note) or submediant (sixth note), as these highlight particular aural relationships which aid intonation.

In the Light Blue level workbook

- *Page 8*   How your voice works: Observe, and discuss if necessary
- *Page 8*   Resonance: Observe, check and discuss if necessary
- *Page 8*   Finding a comfortable note: Check and assist as necessary
- *Page 9*   Increasing your range using sirens: Check and assist
- *Page 9*   Finding and developing your range: Check and assist
- *Page 9*   Producing a good tone: Check and assist
- *Page 9*   Singing a scale of one octave: Practise, check and assist

Tone and range: Dark Blue level

To help singers develop the register and range found in Light Blue; to encourage singing, with even tone and resonance throughout, a scale of at least an octave
Exercises in the Dark Blue workbook aid the production of a bright, resonant tone; singers learn how to position the tongue and 'place' the voice to optimize tone.

Key points for Dark Blue level tone and range
Normally, singers should aim to produce as resonant and bright a sound as possible. In order to sing with a bright tone:

- the tongue should be raised at the back, not flat, the tip not too far back in the mouth

- the larynx should not be too low

- singers should avoid singing down the nose

These last two points are not formally addressed in the Dark Blue workbook but they may already be causing complications for singers. See pages 71–74 for more details.

Once again, it is important to work through these exercises and activities systematically, as they introduce new sounds and sensations which singers may take a while to absorb. The workbook exercises are reproduced below, with some hints and tips.

1) Positioning the tongue
Say the word 'sing'. On the 'ng' part of the word, can you feel the back of your tongue gently touching the roof of your mouth? You should also be able to feel the sides of your tongue touching your upper molars (the teeth at the back of your upper jaw).

Now find a comfortable note and slowly sing 'ng' followed by the vowels in the example below. Feel your upper molars with the sides of your tongue throughout, but don't force your tongue against your teeth.

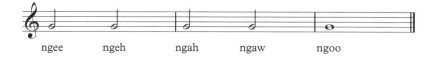

ngee   ngeh   ngah   ngaw   ngoo

Now try the exercise below, using 'ng' and each of the vowels. Move up or down a semitone with each repetition.

ng_____ ee_____

Repeat with:
'ngeh' 'ngah'
'ngaw' 'ngoo'

Practise these several times until you are used to the position of the tongue. Keep your jaw relaxed – check that it can move freely up and down and from side to side. The tip of your tongue should feel as if it is resting behind the lower front teeth.

If the tongue is too flat, or if the tip of the tongue moves too far backwards, singers will produce a dark, swallowed sound. Having worked on raising the rear of the tongue, check that its tip has not moved back inside the mouth. It should feel as if it is resting behind the lower front teeth (see the diagram on page 46).

Module A: Using the voice well

Note too that when raising the tongue, some singers tighten the jaw at the same time, causing unwelcome tension. As you practise this exercise, check that singers can move their jaws up and down, and from side to side freely.

 Tip: The production of good vowel sounds (see the section on *Diction*, page 77) helps to develop a full, bright tone, as well as aiding intelligibility and intonation.

 ### 2) Producing a good tone
Hum a note, then open your mouth to a vowel ('hmm–ee' for example), and sing up and down a five-note scale. (See below.) While humming, the sound should be resonant. You should feel vibrations behind your lips. When singing the vowel, you should feel the vibrations in the same position. Try this with other vowels too.

hmm	ee_____	hmm	ee_____	hmm	ee_____
hmm	eh_____	hmm	eh_____	hmm	eh_____
hmm	ah_____	hmm	ah_____	hmm	ah_____

 Tip: As before, exercises to develop tone tend to focus on the middle of the range. But you also need to extend the pitch and tone range to higher and lower registers. (For the Dark Blue pitch and range targets, your singer must sing a one-octave scale with even tone and resonance throughout.) The exercises above can be gradually moved further up or down the register, enabling you to work on the same patterns in different parts of the voice. The exercises below develop consistency throughout the range.

 ### 3) Slides and sirens
Starting on any comfortable note, make a sliding siren sound, three notes wide (as shown below). Slide from the lower note to the higher note and back again. Make sure the tone is even and the notes are connected smoothly. Use various different vowel sounds. Start each siren a semitone higher than the last. Gradually extend the width of the siren from three notes to four, to five, up to an octave.

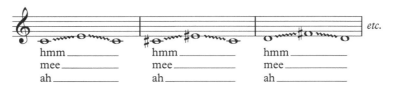

hmm_____	hmm_____	hmm_____
mee_____	mee_____	mee_____
ah_____	ah_____	ah_____

 ### 'Placing' the voice
There are two important qualities when learning tone production: keenness of ear and the ability to hold onto the right sound once it has been found. This is not just about remembering the sound, but also about remembering how it felt *physically* to create it. 'Placing' the voice is a useful way of recalling the physical sensation of sound production. This topic is introduced on page 10 of the workbook (as shown below). Go slowly at first: singers who are new to it may need a fair amount of help.

 ### 4) 'Placing' your voice
Think of your face as having different levels or areas. Imagine placing notes there as you sing. This helps you make the same sound again, and control your tone. For example, imagine placing your higher notes in your forehead. Imagine slightly lower notes around eye level, middle-range notes around the top teeth, and low notes around your chin and bottom jaw. Focus the sound into these different areas.

Placing will vary according to register. For example, for sopranos high E and F can be placed in the forehead, C and D around the eye level, G and A around the top teeth; and low A, B and C between the chin and bottom teeth. Focusing the sound into these areas helps singers to find the resonance required for a pure, clear tone. Remember that the sound is not actually being made in these places, it is just a sensation of vibration. With this in mind, try the exercises below with your singers:

 ### 5) Voice 'placing' with low notes
Sing this exercise starting on a note that is low in your range. Imagine placing the sound near the bottom teeth, moving slowly to the top teeth and back down again.

nn_____ oo_____ nn_____ oo_____

 Tip: Now ask your singers to try this again, this time imagining the notes starting at eye level and moving up to the forehead. They should notice a difference in how the sound feels. It will have little or no resonance when placed in this position, because in order to produce a resonant sound, notes at the bottom of the range need to be placed differently from notes at the top of the range.

6) Voice placing throughout your range (i)
Sing this exercise starting on a note that is low in your range. Sing through several levels in the face as quickly as you can as you move up and down.

ee_____ eh_____ ah_____

7) Voice placing throughout your range (ii)
Start on a fairly high note. Place the sound around nose or eye level when you begin. As you reach the lower notes, allow the sound to travel to the bottom teeth before going back up again. Relax your jaw on the first and last notes so the 'ee' doesn't sound too harsh. Keep the tip of the tongue behind the lower teeth.

nee_ nah_ nee_ nah_   nee_ nah_ nee_ nah_ nee

 Tip: Singers should choose a starting note that is in the middle of the voice in order to reach the lowest note. Suggest they place the sound around nose or eye level when they start, then, as they reach the lower notes, allow the sound to travel to the bottom teeth. Remind them to:

• keep a relaxed jaw for the first and last notes so that the 'ee' doesn't sound too harsh

• keep the tip of the tongue behind the bottom teeth

Additional exercises

The following exercises do not appear in the workbook but are particularly useful at this level for improving tone and range. You can use them during rehearsals with the choir as a whole, or when training individual singers.

8) Widening the throat

When working on this exercise, suggest singers should imagine that the vocal folds form a tube about 2cm in diameter, and they should widen it to 3cm or even 4cm as they sing towards the 'ee' vowel. (If it helps, use your hands to create that tube shape in front of you; draw your hands apart as you sing so that you can see the circle growing larger. Singers can try this too.)

noo   naw   nah   neh   nee

9) Silent laughing

Another method of widening the throat is to laugh silently; this will widen the inside of the larynx (the opposite of swallowing). When this is achieved, singers will not feel any particular sensation except one of release. Do not confuse this with stretching, which is not appropriate here. Can singers hear how the sound has grown in strength?

In the Dark Blue level workbook

- *Page 9*   Positioning the tongue: Observe, and discuss if necessary
- *Page 9*   Producing a good tone: Observe, check and discuss if necessary
- *Page 9*   Singing a scale of one octave: Practise, check and assist
- *Page 10*   Slides and sirens: Check and assist
- *Page 10*   Voice placing with low notes: Check and assist
- *Page 10*   Voice placing throughout your range (i and ii): Check and assist

What singers say

'As a teenager, I used to get really impatient if I couldn't reach notes at the extremes of my range. It's like ... human nature to want to get to the notes you can't sing, isn't it?. But my teacher kept telling me just to wait, and to practise, dand to wait, and to practise. She told me to be gentle with my voice. And of course she was right - eventually my voice just 'grew'. Not only in range, but in power and consistency too.'

Emma, adult

To help singers understand the mechanics of sound production and to develop the range and resonance of the voice; to help singers understand the different registers of the voice and how to access them; to enable singers to sing an ascending and descending scale of at least an octave on any vowel, with consistent resonance throughout, placing sounds correctly

At Red level, singers should be independent and confident. It is now time to develop and refine their technique so that they take full control of their voices. Exercises and activities in the workbook enhance knowledge, technical skills and vocal awareness.

Key points for Red level tone and range

Vocal sound is produced in the larynx by vibrations of the vocal folds. Encourage singers to touch the throat to feel the larynx vibrate as they speak or sing (see page 56): they should also be able to feel it move upwards as they swallow. The vibrations of the vocal folds cause other parts of the body to resonate, which projects the sound outwards. The main areas of resonance are the throat, mouth and nose. (Singers should know these things by now – but it does no harm to revisit them.)

Resonance is also affected by the shape and size of the space inside the mouth. It is important for singers to be able to raise their soft palate when they sing as it creates more resonating space. The diagram on page 46 will help you to locate the hard and soft palates. The following exercises (on page 11 of the workbook) will help your singers to find the soft palate and lift it:

1) Finding the soft palate

With your tongue, feel the roof of your mouth. The hard part near the front is called the hard palate. Further back there is an area of soft muscle tissue called the soft palate. If you yawn, you can feel the soft palate rising, creating a space at the back of your mouth. Singing with the soft palate raised allows the sound to resonate more fully. One way to raise your soft palate without yawning is to imagine your back molar teeth lifting up into your head. Practise this and remember how it feels.

2) Experimenting with the soft palate

Sing a note in the middle of your range with an 'n' sound and with your lips slightly apart. Use your hands to feel the sound resonating in your throat, mouth, neck and chest. Focus the resonance in your nose and head and feel it buzzing there.

Take a breath, sing the note again with the 'n' sound, and now raise the soft palate. Then open your mouth and sing 'ee'. Can you hear how much brighter and stronger the sound has become?

The importance of vocal exercise

Remind your singers often that exercise is vital to the development of the voice. Singing once a week in choir practice is not enough to strengthen the muscles required to support the voice. As little as ten minutes exercise a day in the early stages of voice development will enable a singer to maintain a good healthy voice in the long term. (Ask your singers to compare themselves to an athlete or swimmer and ask how many hours of training this might involve each week.)

Tip: You may find it useful to identify for singers exercises they can do in their own time – and try to check from week to week that they have actually done these.

The registers of the voice

The earlier levels of *Voice for Life* focused on finding the 'natural' register (a place in the voice that feels comfortable for singing) and producing a resonant sound. At Red level, singers find out about different registers in their own voices, how to move freely from one register to another, and how to maintain the strength, resonance and agility of the voice. This important material begins on page 12 of the workbook.

 Understanding the voice and its registers

Singers usually talk about the voice as having four registers: chest, middle, head and falsetto. These names relate to different vocal ranges and the area in which the voice is placed.

- Notes in the **chest register** (or **chest voice**) are in the lower part of the voice. The vibrations are felt mainly in the chest. Your speaking voice is also in this register

- Notes in the **middle register** are in the middle part of the voice. The vibrations can be felt in the lower or upper parts of the mouth.

- Notes in the **head register** (or **head voice**) are in the upper range of the voice. Vibrations are felt in the middle and upper parts of the head.

- Falsetto occurs when the vocal folds are stretched with no counter-tension in the muscle inside the vocal fold itself. This results in a light sound. It is obvious in men; in women and children it is often the sound heard at the top of the range before this has been developed into fuller, more vibrant singing. See page 75 for more about falsetto.

As the voice develops, it is important to learn to sing in all registers. Each register has different and complementary characteristics, which provide singers with a rich palette of vocal colours. There is overlap between each of the registers, and singers need to be able to move smoothly between them. Healthy singing requires a mixture of the head voice with the lower registers.

 If the head voice only is used right down to notes lower in the voice, there will be little or no strength to the sound. Likewise, if a singer cannot access the head voice and only uses the chest voice and middle register, then the upper notes will be harder to reach. This can result in shouting and a forced tone. Use of the chest voice in this higher range is often called 'belting'; produced incorrectly, it can lead to serious vocal health problems.

To develop a resonant sound throughout the range, all the different registers and vocal colours need to be explored. Many of the exercises in this guide have a range that covers all the registers. Make sure you take them to the extremes of the range and concentrate on making an even sound throughout, aware that although each register has different characteristics, it is possible to transfer smoothly between them.

The exercises overleaf will help your singers to do this. In addition, they will help to develop quality and control as well as building up strength in the voice. Read the following section carefully before attempting it with your singers.

Tip: At this level, some of the physical and psychological processes involved in sound production and register recognition are very subtle: you may not always find it easy to articulate them to your singers. The descriptive imagery accompanying some of the following exercises can help singers find the right sound as they practise; but you may find other ways of doing this. Anything that enables singers to envisage what is happening vocally, aurally or physically can help develop a good vocal technique.

Always ensure the voice is warmed up before starting these exercises. First do some simple siren sounds (see 'Slides and sirens' below), then silent laughing (see page 63) to open the throat, followed by a few descending scales.

Before you start, remind singers of the basics of voice placing that they learned at Dark Blue – that it helps to remember where sounds vibrate and resonate within the head and body in order to be able to reproduce good vocal sound time after time. Point out too that they will need to move smoothly between registers of the voice so that the sound doesn't change suddenly as they move from one to the other – and that the following exercises will help with this.

 1) Slides and sirens
Starting on any comfortable note, make a sliding siren sound, three notes wide (as shown below). Slide from the lower note to the higher note and back again. Make sure the tone is even and the notes are connected smoothly. Use various different vowel sounds. Start each siren a semitone higher than the last. Gradually extend the width of the siren from three notes to four, to five, up to an octave.

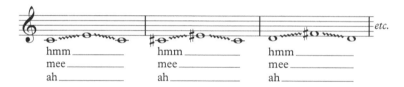

 2) Placing the voice (i)
Sing the exercise below, starting on a note in the middle of your range. Sing slowly and steadily, breathing in between each note and placing it carefully.

Think of the area of your face where you will feel the vibrations, and widen the throat as you sing through each note. Sing the exercise several times, starting a semitone higher each time.

 3) Placing the voice (ii)
For the exercise below, choose a starting note that is fairly high in your range. Place the sound in your forehead and allow it to travel upwards as the pitch gets higher, but don't force the sound. If it feels uncomfortable, stop the exercise and ask your choir trainer to find you a different starting note.

Try to keep a light quality in the sound. To do this, you could try putting your arms out in front of you with your hands together, and drawing your hands apart slowly as you sing the exercise.

nn____ ah_____ ah ah ah ah ah ah ah

4) Moving between registers (i)

For the next exercise, choose a starting note that is fairly low in your range. With your hands, imagine you are drawing a circle on each side of your head, moving from the back of your head, up and over towards your face and back round. Do this while you sing the exercise. This will help you travel from one register to another with no bumps in the sound.

ah____

5) Moving between registers (ii)

Choose a comfortable starting note for the following exercise. Place the lower notes around the lower teeth and the high notes in the forehead. Think as quickly as you can about these changes of position. However, take care not to disconnect the notes from one another – there should not be a bump or a complete change of tone.

Try sliding between the notes first. Once you can smoothly connect the notes, sing the exercise again without the slide, but keeping the sense of connection between the notes.

ee ah ee ee ah ee ee ah ee

Tip: If your singers struggle to connect notes smoothly in these exercises, do more 'Slides and sirens' to remind them how it feels to connect the registers of the voice. (This can also be a useful way to enable singers to access the higher notes in their range, whilst keeping the tone even and 'connected' between registers.) When you return to the exercise in question, the notes should be more evenly joined.

If they continue to struggle, they may be worrying about singing individual pitches too precisely, which results in bumpiness. Encourage them to slide between the notes of the exercise they are singing without worrying too much at first about the tuning of each note. Once they achieve a smooth transition between notes in the exercise, they should stop the sliding and simply imagine that they are doing this to maintain their focus on connecting the registers of the voice.

6) Agility in the voice (i)

For this exercise, make sure your vowel sounds are resonant. Don't allow the energy to collapse once you have sung the highest note: continue it through to the end of the phrase. Imagine inflating a tyre around the base of your back. This should give you the supporting muscular energy that you need.

soh pah soh pah so soh pah soh pah so soh pah soh pah soh
yah yah yah yah yah yah yah yah yah yah yah yah yah yah yah

7) Agility in the voice (ii)

Choose a comfortable starting note for the next exercise. Sing it several times, starting a semitone higher each time. Sing with good vowel sounds and lots of agility.

ah_____ eh_____ aw_____ ee_____ ah_____ eh_____ aw_____ ee

Tip: Don't let the tone get heavy as the pitch descends; aim for a bright, resonant sound all the way down. Encourage singers to feel a sense of lift through each phrase. If you're conducting, you could reinforce this with your own gestures.

Discourage singers from exaggerating face shapes on the changes of vowel. Keep the lips well forward and the neck muscles relaxed.

8) The nasal twang

To increase the strength of the notes in your lower register without damaging your voice, you can use a nasal 'twang' sound. Try the exercises below:

Starting on a note in the middle of your range, sing 'qua' down a scale, with a nasal twang sound. (Imagine you are about to sing the word 'quack'.) Notice that the mouth is quite closed for this sound. Then loosen your jaw and try to get the same buzz to the sound. Repeat the exercise, starting a semitone lower.

qua qua qua qua qua qua qua qua   qua qua qua qua qua qua qua qua

9) The nasal twang in the low register

As you pause on the final note of the next exercise, drop your jaw. Make sure the sound does not change as you do this. Watch yourself in the mirror. Note how the position of your face changes from being wide and open to long and relaxed.

qua qua quack   qua qua quack   qua qua quack

Make sure that singers don't force this: they should only let the jaw drop as far as it will naturally go when it is relaxed. Watch out for any signs of tension in the neck or jaw, and correct them immediately.

Tip: Note that here, 'nasal' implies resonance in the area known as the 'mask'. 'Twang' is not produced from the nose, but by narrowing and shortening the vocal tract. To check that the sound is not being produced from the nose, get singers to pinch their own nose as they sing – the sound shouldn't change.

Although nasal twang is a useful way to develop the strength of the lower register, singers should not use this sound in all their singing. Particularly during classical and choral singing, singers should aim for a sound that is open and less nasal, by opening and lengthening the vocal tract. The exercise below (reproduced from page 14 of the workbook) will help with this.

 10) Producing an open sound in the low register
Allow the jaw to drop open on 'yah', remembering the feeling you had on the last note of the previous exercise.

mee   moh   yah   mee   moh   yah   mee   moh   yah   *etc.*

 In the Red level workbook

- *Page 11* Self-assessment panel: Discuss if necessary

- *Page 11* Finding the soft palate: Observe, check and discuss if necessary

- *Page 11* Experimenting with the soft palate: Observe, check and discuss if necessary

- *Page 12* Self-assessment panel: Discuss if necessary

- *Page 12* Slides and sirens: Check and assist

- *Page 13* Placing the voice (1): Check and assist

- *Page 13* Placing the voice (2): Check and assist

- *Page 13* Moving between registers (1): Check and assist

- *Page 13* Moving between registers (2): Check and assist

- *Page 14* Agility in the voice (1): Check and assist

- *Page 14* Agility in the voice (2): Check and assist

- *Page 14* The nasal twang: Check and assist

- *Page 14* The nasal twang in the low register: Check and assist

- *Page 14* Producing an open sound in the low register: Check and assist

To ensure that singers sing with resonance throughout the vocal range; to ensure the jaw is relaxed and the larynx is not pushed or crushed downwards; to help singers to blend registers; to encourage singing with a variety of tone colours

 By Yellow level, singers will be confident and independent, making their own choices about voice production and style. Pages 9–13 of workbook contain exercises and strategies (reproduced below with teaching tips) to develop the voice and increase its flexibility.

Key points for Yellow level tone and range
Vocal sound is produced by vibrations in the larynx (voice box). The larynx is at the top of the trachea (windpipe), and is made of cartilage. The parts of the larynx that vibrate are the vocal folds, which lie horizontally across the thyroid cartilage. Understanding and controlling the physiology of voice production is vital if singers are to unlock their full vocal potential.

The diagrams below show the parts of the neck and throat that are involved in voice production. As you do the exercises below, it may help you to refer back to them to remind yourself of the different parts and what they are called.

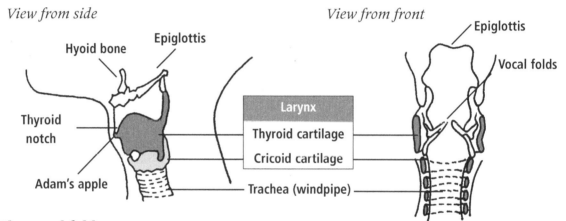

View from side

Hyoid bone
Epiglottis
Thyroid notch
Adam's apple

View from front

Epiglottis
Vocal folds

Larynx
Thyroid cartilage
Cricoid cartilage

Trachea (windpipe)

The vocal folds
The vocal folds are sometimes called vocal cords, but as they are made up of several parts, 'folds' is more accurate. They are about as long as the width of a finger nail. For them to work properly, the larynx must be able to move up and down and tilt freely. If it becomes crushed or fixed during singing, the sound will be badly affected.

A fixed larynx will lead to a hardness of tone which (in the long run) takes a lot of energy to produce and is unpleasant to listen to. If it is fixed too high, a strangled sound will result (this is a problem common in tenors and some young singers). A larynx that is fixed too low can produce a 'hooty' or swallowed sound. The exercises in this section will help your singers to neutralize the muscles under the jaw and throat, which releases the larynx.

 Tip: Throughout these exercises, watch for singers who push the chin down when they sing. This will crush the hyoid bone and push the larynx downwards, with the effects described above. But watch too for singers who push the chin too high – this has other bad effects on the voice.

 Before you attempt the exercises below with your singers, make sure they understand that they should do them slowly and gently. If they feel the slightest discomfort they should stop, rest and consult you. Never push singers through this section.

1) Finding the larynx

Study the diagrams above and find the thyroid notch with your index finger. This is the V-shaped indentation at the top of the Adam's apple (a projection of the thyroid cartilage). It is usually more prominent in men.

Gently place your thumb and middle finger either side of this notch and move them backwards along the top of the thyroid cartilage. You'll notice that they rise and then fall as they follow the shape of the cartilage. About a centimetre back you will feel two small 'horns' sticking up. On top of this sits the hyoid bone, sometimes called the tongue bone because the base of the tongue is attached to it.

Remember this construction because it is important that the hyoid bone is always free when singing. If the tongue pushes down on it, the sound produced will be rather unnatural and swallowed. Similarly, if you have 'fixed' the hyoid bone with the muscles in front of it, you will produce a tight sound.

Try holding your hyoid bone between your thumb and index finger and see whether you can move it from side to side. Be very gentle! It should move easily and freely about one centimetre in each direction. Having checked that the hyoid bone is flexible, try moving the whole larynx from side to side (again, be gentle).

Tip: If the larynx is too high, the vocal sound will be strangled; too low and it will be 'swallowed'. To ensure that the position of the larynx is correct, singers must learn to neutralize the muscles under the jaw and around the hyoid bone. This 'releases' the larynx. The exercises below (starting on page 10 of the workbook) will help.

2) Releasing the larynx

Produce a hollow 'ghur' sound, either speaking or on a pitch of your choice. Raise the back of your tongue against your soft palate so the 'g' is produced at the back of the throat. (If you are unsure where your soft palate is, roll your tongue back along the roof of the mouth from behind your teeth. With the tip of your tongue you will first feel the bony hard palate and then the fleshy soft palate.) Watch this in a mirror. The hollow vowel which follows should make your larynx drop dramatically.

Tip: Some teachers liken this sound to the noise a sea lion makes! If singers struggle to produce it, try finding this on the Internet. A singer who achieves this sound has successfully used a muscle called the *sternothyroid* to pull the larynx down from underneath, rather than using the hyoid bone to force the larynx down from above.

Begin the exercise below at a comfortable pitch for you, but near the bottom of your range. Repeat several times using the 'ghur' sound. Once you have mastered this, move onto a gentle, continuous 'vvv' sound.

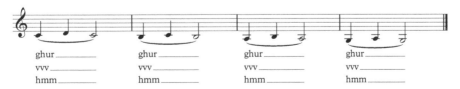

ghur _____   ghur _____   ghur _____   ghur _____
vvv _____   vvv _____   vvv _____   vvv _____
hmm _____   hmm _____   hmm _____   hmm _____

Next, repeat the exercise using a hollow humming. Let a little air escape first to create space at the back of the throat and neck. Whilst producing the 'vvv' sound or when humming, the larynx should stay reasonably low.

Singers should normally aim to produce a resonant, bright sound, but on occasions a darker timbre may be required. This is achieved by positioning the larynx fairly low. However, this requires practice to ensure that the tone does not become either hard or shallow. The next exercise will help with this:

 3) Lowering the larynx to produce a dark tone
Try the following exercise, based on the 'ghur' exercise above. Again, choose a fairly low starting pitch. This time, join the 'ghur' onto an 'oo'. The 'ghur' will lower the larynx before you open onto the 'oo'. This 'oo' should be dark in tone because the larynx is low, the throat is open and, therefore, the vocal tract is lengthened. Some people like this darker sound. It can be useful in sombre pieces such as Rimsky-Korsakov's *Our Father* or the 'Lacrimosa' from Mozart's *Requiem*.

It requires practice to ensure that this dark tone does not become hard or shallow. As long as it is achieved as explained above and the hyoid bone is not pushed down, it will not become hooty or swallowed. Do not fix the larynx down – a larynx which is fixed or forced into a low position is as bad as one which is fixed too high.

 Tip: Bear in mind that while you may require singers to use a dark tone on occasions, normally they should aim to produce a resonant, bright sound. Brightness aids good intonation and enables the natural clarity and energy of the voice to emerge. To achieve this, singers need to remain relaxed and focused.

 Refining technique and troubleshooting
As singers develop, their progress may be accompanied by the acquisition of bad habits which can harm their sound and may even damage the vocal mechanisms. Pages 11–13 of the workbook contain a number of exercises and strategies to help singers refine their technique and troubleshoot problems. These are reproduced below with a few additional tips to help you.

 4) Relaxing the throat and jaw
Aim to sing with a relaxed throat and jaw at all times. If you find your throat is tight when you sing, try these exercises to help widen and relax your throat:

Try laughing heartily – a real belly-laugh – without making a sound. Imagine you want to laugh, but are in a place where you must not make a sound. Do you feel a widening in the throat? A silent sob or cry has the same effect. You should feel a release of tension, not a stretch.

 Tip: Singers may find this tricky at first, but encourage them to persist. They are learning to harness what is usually an involuntary emotional and physical response, during which the throat naturally widens. It provides support around the voice and will help to ensure a full, open tone.

Singers may find it easier to approach throat-widening from the perspective of the next exercise, which helps to widen the throat by tapping into the same natural reflex action described above. It is based on 'Placing the voice in neutral' (see page 42), but this time singers must vocalize on the outward movement and inhale at every rest. Choose a comfortable starting note.

hah   hah   hah   hah   hah   hah   hah   hah

Having learned to widen the throat, singers must learn to control the movement of the soft palate and the position of the tongue. Otherwise the tone may become nasal and harsh, preventing a full, bright sound. This is a common problem, as singers often constrict the throat and direct the sound down the nose when trying to reach higher notes.

As well as being unpleasant to listen to, singing with nasal tone can cause other problems. It is much harder to produce sound when singing down the nose because the effort is divided in two (between the nose and the mouth). This requires extra breath pressure and in turn causes tightening of the throat. This may lead to physical problems with the voice.

However, singers may be unaware that they are producing nasal tone: it can be hard to identify internally. The following three exercises (reproduced from pages 11 and 12 of the workbook) help singers to identify and eliminate a nasal tone.

5) Discovering if you sing with a nasal tone

It is not always easy to know if you are singing with nasal tone. One common sign is tickling in the throat after you have been singing high in your range.

To identify what a nasal tone sounds and feels like, sing the sound 'ng' (like the end of the word 'sing') on any comfortable note. Notice how, when you do this, the tongue is raised and the soft palate lowered. All the sound is directed down the nose. Pinch your nose, and the sound will stop.

Now sing 'ah' instead, and then pinch your nose. Does the sound change at all? If so, you are producing a nasal sound when you sing. The next exercises will help you to eliminate this problem and produce a full, bright tone. Try using the following exercise to eliminate the problem:

6) Eliminating a nasal tone

Choosing any comfortable note, sing 'ng' and then move without a break to 'ah'. You should be using the elevated tongue position described in 'Releasing the larynx' on page 71. The soft palate has to be raised up from the tongue to let the sound travel forward to the mouth. Try pinching your nose now. If you have lifted the soft palate efficiently, the sound should not change.

What singers say
'Practice? It's like ... sing, listen, feel, think, change. Again and again and again and again. And then some more.'

Sean, adult

If you find this exercise tricky, try using a hard 'g' between the 'ng' sound and the 'ah'. Place the 'g' on the hard palate so that the sound equates to 'ngGah'. The hard 'g' should throw the sound forward.

 To help with this, try the following exercise. Choose a starting pitch comfortable for you, and move the starting pitch up or down a semitone with each repetition. Concentrate on singing with the sound at the front of the mouth, not coming down the nose.

ng ah _____ ng eh _____ ng ee _____ ng aw _____ ng oo _____

 Tip: If singers are worried about whether or not they are singing with nasal tone generally, ask them to pinch the nose periodically while singing the vowels (but not while singing the 'ng' at the beginning of each pattern or the sound will stop altogether). If they can feel vibration, or if the sound changes, the soft palate has dropped. Tell them to try not to worry about this; simply keep working at the exercises above and it will improve in time.

 Another important way to eliminate a nasal sound is to ensure that the soft palate is properly raised: this restricts airflow to the nose. The following exercise will help with this.

7) Raising the soft palate

Choose a starting pitch comfortable for you, and move the starting pitch up or down a semitone with each repetition. Make the 'b' sound at the end of each note energetic and prominent. Again, make sure you bring the sound to the front of your mouth.

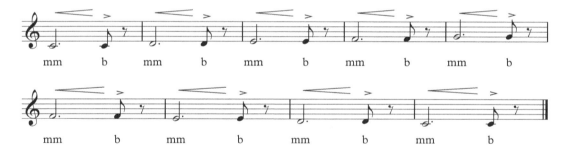

mm   b   mm   b   mm   b   mm   b   mm   b

mm   b   mm   b   mm   b   mm   b

 Tip: This should feel like a yawn. The 'mm' sound is nasal (if you pinch your nose while making it, the sound will stop) and allows air up into the nasal area. Singers should be able to feel the difference as they make the transition to the 'b'. If they find the sudden change difficult, first try moving from 'mm' (or another nasal consonant like 'nn' or 'ng') to a vowel, checking there is no nasality on the vowel. This will begin to exercise the correct muscles, and the change should become easier in time.

What singers say

'In some ways, the better you get at singing, the harder it gets. There's always something new to try, something to improve, something you want to change. Your judgement improves, so you get more self-critical. That's great ... but you have to learn to like your voice too! Love it, even.'

Gabrielle, adult

Falsetto

By Yellow level, singers will have fully explored their range and experimented with different registers and techniques. They will have a variety of approaches to singing and may want to extend these. For some, accessing the falsetto voice will provide a useful addition to the vocal palette. Here are some hints.

The word *falsetto* comes from the Italian word *falso*, meaning 'false'. This implies that the falsetto sound is unnatural; however, it is an essential part of every voice. Nearly all singers have some sort of falsetto voice, but in women and children it tends to be rather breathy and difficult to project, and therefore of limited use.

For men, however, falsetto can be very useful as it can improve the tone of the entire voice, particularly the higher register. It is easy to hear because it is different from the usual or 'full' voice. For tenors, using falsetto is important while the voice is developing. There is also some evidence that developing falsetto in boys as their voices change helps to develop a stronger upper register in the mature voice. The following exercises – on page 13 of the workbook – are for men only.

Tip: Bear in mind that you will need to assist singers with this individually. Help each one to find a suitable starting note which tests higher notes but doesn't over-stretch the voice. Never encourage singers to push too far – exploration of this new vocal facility should be gentle and unhurried.

9) Accessing the falsetto voice

Experiment with high notes to find your falsetto voice (ask your choir trainer or teacher to help you with this). Having located the sound, sing the following exercise with your falsetto voice. Choose a comfortable starting note. Repeat the exercise using the five pure vowels listed in 'Diction' on page 79.

wah wah wah wah wah wah wah wah wah wah wah wah wah wah wah wah

Producing the correct falsetto sound

The falsetto sound may be weak and rather breathy at first, but with practice it will become stronger. It should not be harsh. If it is gentle and rounder, the singer should notice a slight upwards movement of the hyoid bone and larynx, but there should be no tension. (Encourage singers to record their falsetto voice and listen to it: this will help them to become accustomed to the sound and how it feels.)

It is important to get the correct, released sound, as this will help to provide space above the larynx and in the throat. If the sound is strangled, it is because the larynx is being pulled up by the wrong muscles in the jaw. The movement of the hyoid bone and larynx should not be restricted (see page 71). Don't allow the muscles to restrict or squash the larynx in any way. If a singer can only seem to produce a strangled falsetto sound, try the following exercise:

10) Avoiding a strangled sound

Repeat the exercise shown opposite. This time, precede each vowel with a 'b' (e.g. bah, bah). Next, repeat the exercise using a rolled 'r' (e.g. rah, rah). You could also combine these to create a 'brrr' sound to precede each vowel.

In the Yellow level workbook

What singers say

'By slowly cutting out the nasality in the sound and reducing breath pressure, an easier, more balanced sound began to emerge in my voice.'

Nicholas, adult

'I found that freeing up my falsetto helped my singing enormously. I can access an easier tone in my middle register: a brighter sound that had more height to it. It has also helped me to develop a mixed tone on high notes.'

Jerome, adult (tenor)

A singing voice can be beautiful in its own right, but singers must also communicate a text. Vowels and consonants are the tools used to make this happen; in every piece they must be moulded and adapted to give conviction to the performance and bring the music to life. In singing, the optimal production of vowels and consonants in a stylistically appropriate way is called diction. Working with singers on their diction has two main benefits:

- It develops a full range of tone (from the vowels especially)
- It enables the singing of texts with expression, meaning and clarity

The diction targets in *Voice for Life* require increasing understanding of how vowels and consonants should be produced for maximum effectiveness. Your role as a choir trainer is to develop and assess your singers' diction in different ways. It is never too early to establish certain general points, as outlined here.

Some general points about diction

Few of us use our mouths sufficiently when either speaking or singing. When starting work on diction, it can be helpful to focus on the speaking voice. Encourage singers to enunciate their words carefully in everyday speech, since good habits are likely to be transferred to the singing voice. (It is also important that you model good diction yourself, whether speaking or singing.)

Beautiful tone inside a closed mouth will never project. When singing, the mouth should be well open and shaped to support the vowel and the tone, but not forced. Ask your singers to imagine when singing that they are communicating with somebody on the other side of the room, hall or church.

Remind singers that very often when a choir or soloist sings, listeners will not have the words in front of them; clear diction is vital if the text is to be heard and understood.

Tip: It can help to model good and bad diction while standing some distance from your singers. Can they understand you when you speak from the other side of the room, hall or church? Can they understand each other if asked to do the same thing?

Diction at the different levels of *Voice for Life*

There are no formal diction targets for White level. At this stage it will be enough to encourage singers to pronounce their words clearly (with large, bright, open vowels and crisp consonants) and address some of the general points made above.

At Light Blue, Dark Blue and Red levels the approach to diction is similar, delivered by means of the exercises and activities which are outlined on the opposite page. Most of these continue into Yellow level but these advanced singers are also expected to understand vowel and consonant production in more analytical detail.

For full details of what is required level by level, consult the individual workbooks. Each of these contains the relevant information and exercises to be studied at any given stage. There are some general approaches to diction training on the next page, followed by more specific information about each level.

Diction

Tongue-twisters

Tongue-twisters are a good way to work on diction and to get singers' mouths moving at the beginning of a rehearsal. There are various examples of these throughout the workbooks for singers to practise, listed here in order from easier to more difficult:

- Red lorry, yellow lorry
- Copper-bottomed coffee pot
- The tip of the tongue and the lips and the teeth
- He mourns the aroma of Verona's arena
- She sells sea-shells by the sea shore
- The six thin things, the six thick things

Pick a tongue-twister and ask singers to speak it at first. The aim is to say the words as quickly as possible without compromising clarity. (You may wish to start slowly and build up speed.) Remind singers to keep open mouths, and to use the jaw and facial muscles as much as is necessary. (Tongue-twisters exercise more than the tongue!)

Next, try singing tongue-twisters. You could combine them with exercises from other parts of Module A such as 'Breathing' and 'Tone and range'. For instance, ask singers to move a tongue-twister up and down a scale, either singing the entire phrase on one note, then proceeding to the next, or singing each word to a different note.

Phrases

Point out to singers that when written and spoken, words are grouped into sentences to make them easier to understand. Similarly, in music, notes and words are grouped into phrases. Phrases should be clear and even. The are often sung in a single breath; make sure your singers know where to breathe to make sense of the words; see the information on breathing from Dark Blue level (page 35). You will need to explain the phrases in each piece you sing.

Understanding vowels and consonants (from Light Blue level onwards)

First, check that singers can distinguish vowels and consonants. Most young singers will know the difference between the vowel and consonant letters of the alphabet but in this context it may be helpful to point out that:

- consonants require movement of, and contact between, any or all of the lips, tongue, teeth or other parts of the mouth
- vowels are formed by the shape of the mouth and throat alone

Once this distinction is made, you can proceed to develop each type of sound as detailed below.

What singers say

'You take vowels and consonants for granted until you start to think about how many different parts of the mouth have to move to make them properly!'

Sabine, adult

Vowels

All the vocal exercises in *Voice for Life* use a particular selection of vowels, shown in the panel opposite, which have been chosen to help develop resonance. Encourage singers to identify the sensation of singing these vowel sounds.

Ee	as in	**me**
Eh	as in	**leg**
Ah	as in	**father**
Aw	as in	**door**
Oo	as in	**moon**

Normally, singers should produce as resonant and bright a sound as possible. This will not only enable them to sing intelligibly, but will also aid intonation. Producing good vowel sounds will enable them to develop a full, bright tone (see pages 60–61).

Consonants

While pure vowels are necessary for the production of a resonant, bright and well-projected sound, these also need to be connected to clear consonants. Right from the outset of *Voice for Life* you should insist on crisp, well-articulated consonants in both singing and speaking. Encourage singers to think carefully about how each consonant is made with the lips, mouth and teeth. Can they explain how a particular word or group of words is formed in the mouth by a chain of minute movements?

Projecting consonants

Ask singers to whisper the words of a well-known song or hymn with enough energy for you to understand them at the back of the hall or church. Next, ask them to sing the same song *piano* but with the consonants *forte*. They will probably find this unnatural because most people do not speak this way. Point out how much energy it takes to sing like this; but that this is how to make sung consonants clear.

Comparing voiced and unvoiced consonants (from Dark Blue level onwards)

There are two basic groups of consonants: voiced and unvoiced. Unvoiced consonants contain no vocal sound, only air movement: voiced consonants contain a neutral vowel sound which is created in the vocal folds. The table of voiced consonants with (where they exist) their unvoiced equivalents can be found on page 12 of the Dark Blue workbook, and is reproduced here:

Ask singers to move from a voiced consonant to its unvoiced equivalent and back again, noting the difference between the two; the voiced consonant requires vocal sound; the unvoiced one merely involves an escape of breath.

Voiced consonant	Unvoiced equivalent
B	P
G	C or K
D	T
V	F
J	CH
Z	S
Voiced consonants with no unvoiced equivalent:	Unvoiced consonants with no voiced equivalent:
L, M, N, W	H, X

Flexibility of the mouth

Go through each pair of voiced and unvoiced consonants and notice how each transition requires a slightly different use of the tongue, lips and teeth. Next, repeat them in rapid succession, gradually increasing the speed. Point out to singers just how flexible the mouth, lips and tongue need to be to do this properly.

Diction

Singing voiced and unvoiced consonants
Voiced consonants are those to which we can give a definite pitch – for example, the consonant 'm' can easily be sung to a definite pitch when humming; but it is much harder to do this with the letter 's'. Singers will probably understand this instinctively but you may find it useful to help them make the distinction by singing a few unvoiced consonants followed by their voiced equivalents.

Energetic consonants
Ask singers to sing through the list of consonants, assessing how much volume they can get out of each one, and noting the effort required to do this. With this louder, more energized sound, they should evaluate how hard they feel they are working in relation to their normal practice. Can they give these strong consonants an effort level on a scale of 1 to 10? They should aim for that level when they sing in a choir.

But make singers aware that consonants can be overdone. They should not interrupt the legato line; instead they should be added within the line to energize the vowels. Encourage your singers to practise singing difficult phrases of their repertoire on a single vowel to begin with, in order to achieve legato; then add in the consonants without losing the smooth line. Sensitivity and artistry is a requirement here.

Tip: Remember that the acoustic of the building must also be considered. Large and small rooms have their own characteristics. These often change once the seats are filled. Encourage your singers to listen to how these characteristics change so that they can adjust their diction as necessary and settle into a performance quickly.

Starting and ending words with consonants
In singing, the continuing vocal line is produced by the vowels; consonants punctuate and energize this but should not interrupt it. When a consonant follows a vowel, singers should maintain the resonance as long as possible before quickly moving the mouth and tongue to form the final consonant. After a consonant, the mouth should open immediately with the tongue shaped to produce an appropriate, resonant vowel. Encourage singers to try this with a range of vowels and consonants.

Moving between vowels and consonants (from Red level onwards)
When singing, the production and shape of vowel sounds is not always instinctive; it may require careful analytical thought if words are to be enunciated clearly. Encourage singers to identify the vowels they need to produce in the middle of words. The words in the panel below (from 15 of the Red workbook) focus on the vowels listed on page 79; you (or singers) can add more of your own if you wish. For each word, singers should:

- decide which vowel they need to produce after the consonant and model its shape (can they say the word in slow motion?)

- sing it with short consonants and long vowels, making the latter as resonant as possible

Loop	L	oo	p
Need	N	ee	d
Blend	Bl	eh	nd
Lark	L	ah	k
Lord	L	aw	d

Strength of consonants

At higher levels, singers need to develop strong consonants and learn how to control their production in order to regulate diction well. Using the words in the panel on the previous page (or your own selection), singers should experiment with the strength of the consonants (remembering that the vowel sounds must not lose their quality):

- singing very quietly, keeping the consonants clear
- singing quietly but with the vowels as loud as possible
- singing loudly, keeping the consonants clear
- singing loudly, with the vowels as loud as possible

Tip: In this context, make singers aware that different types, moods and styles of music require different relationships between the volume of vowels and consonants. Singers should consider what is appropriate for each particular piece. An effective strategy here is to have singers listen to recordings and comment on (and reproduce) the vowel–consonant relationships in different types of music.

Flexibility of vowels and consonants

Using the same list of words, breathe in with the mouth prepared in the shape of the vowel for your chosen word. When you sing the word, move the tongue and/or lips quickly to form the consonant, then immediately back to the vowel for its length. In the same way at the end of the word, keep the mouth shape the same and only move the tongue/lips to form the final consonant. It is sometimes necessary to shorten a note for neatness, creating time to breathe and ensuring that the next word starts cleanly and without sounding rushed.

Diction for advanced singers (Yellow level)

While the targets do not specifically test the topics below, singers need to be aware of them, use them and display the appropriate attention to detail to meet the required standard for the assessed performances. There are a number of additional diction tips on page 16 of the Yellow workbook; make sure singers have absorbed these.

Starting notes with a vowel

'Onset' is the technical term for the start of a note. There are three ways to start a note using a vowel: **aspirated** onset, **glottal** onset and **simultaneous** onset. In normal singing, simultaneous onset is desirable. In order to understand this, singers need to be able to recognize all three types of onset.

In an **aspirated** onset, air is expelled before the vocal folds are engaged. To demonstrate this, ask singers to choose a note in the middle of the voice and sing 'ah,' but start the sound with an extended 'h' (this is called an aspirate). The result is quite breathy and the onset (the point at which the note starts) is hard to control.

In a **glottal** onset, the sound starts with the vocal folds together. The air is trapped until the folds are opened, after which the air passes over them to create the sound. To demonstrate this, ask singers to begin a vowel note with a hard attack, such as might emphasize the first letter of the word 'arm'. The result can be quite jerky and the onset can stick out. (The glottal onset is also known as a glottal stop.)

Diction

 In a **simultaneous** onset, the air and the vocal folds start moving at the same time. Ask your singers to sing 'ah' once again, this time without either an aspirate or a glottal onset. At first they may find it difficult to begin words without either the aspirate or glottal onset. The following exercise will help to improve their ability to sing with this level of control:

 Improving the simultaneous onset
Having identified what the simultaneous onset should feel and sound like, suggest that singers approach it by gently singing long vowel syllables:

- starting with an 'm' at the front

- then, removing the 'm' but adding a delicate 'h' aspiration

- finally, removing the 'h' and singing just the vowel itself

By repeating this on different vowels in different parts of the voice, singers will increase their ability to begin notes cleanly and in tune.

 Diphthongs
A diphthong is a combination of two vowels in succession. For example, the word 'day' consists of the vowel sounds 'eh' and 'ee'. In normal speech the tongue moves smoothly from one sound to the next to produce a single syllable. But in vocal music, a diphthong may be set to a long note. This makes it necessary to consider the two vowels: should they be of equal length or should one be longer than the other?

Usually, in words that contain a diphthong the first vowel should be as long as possible. The second vowel should be placed as close to the end of the note's length as possible, but not so close as to blur any final consonant. To demonstrate how to approach diphthongs, try the following exercise:

 Experimenting with diphthongs
Ask singers to try singing a word containing a diphthong in the following ways:

- as in (1) below: with each vowel sound of equal length

- as in (2) below: with the first vowel very short and the second as long as possible

- as in (3) below: with the first vowel as long as possible, changing to the second vowel as close to the end of the note as possible

Singers should normally aim to achieve the third effect. Encourage them to practise this using many different diphthongs, in order that they become aware of the sound and sensations of good diphthong technique.

Diction level by level
Below is a summary of what singers are expected to encounter at each level of *Voice for Life*, and details of how to assess the targets and workbook activities.

 White level
There are no formal diction targets at White level.

 Light Blue level
Singers must sing with clear diction, producing good pure vowels and clear consonants.

Encourage singers to open the mouth more than when they speak, and to use the tongue and teeth more to pronounce letters. This may feel strange at first, but it helps the voice to project (reach the listeners properly) and keeps diction clear. When assessing, make sure that singers sing clearly enough for listeners to understand what they are singing, and open their mouths wide enough to project the sound.

 In the Light Blue workbook

- *Page 10* Vowels and consonants: Check that singers can sing the vowels in the panel to a scale or a siren exercise, maintaining the sound and shape of the vowel without changing

- *Page 10* Tongue twisters: Check that singers can sing tongue twisters on successive notes of a scale

- *Page 10* Projection of consonants: Check and discuss if necessary

 Dark Blue level
To sing with clear diction producing good pure vowels and clear consonants.

 In the Dark Blue workbook

- *Page 11* Tongue twisters: Check that singers can sing tongue twisters on successive notes of a scale

- *Page 11* Vowels and consonants: Check that singers have correctly identified the five vowel letters; and that they have sung the vowels in the box to a scale or siren exercise, maintaining the sound and shape of the vowel without changing

- *Page 12* Comparing voiced and unvoiced consonants: Check that singers can move easily between voiced and unvoiced consonants: discuss if necessary

- *Page 12* Energetic consonants: Check that singers understand the principle here

What singers say
'Our conductor once told us to imagine we had to make our consonants heard in the next street! We laughed, but we knew what she meant.'

Elliot, 14

Diction

Red level

Singers must understand the need for clear diction and how to use it appropriately according to the style of music being performed, and demonstrate this in rehearsals and performances.

In the Red workbook

- *Page 15*   Tongue twisters: Check that singers can sing tongue twisters on any notes you specify; check the singer's own tongue twister in the box – can they say or sing it?

- *Page 15*   Projecting consonants: Check and discuss if necessary

- *Page 15*   Smooth lines: Check and discuss if necessary

- *Page 15*   Moving between vowels and consonants: Can singers do this with each word in the panel, and with some of your own (or their own)? (See page 79 for details)

- *Page 15*   Strength of consonants: Can singers produce words in each of the four styles listed?

Yellow level

Singers should sing with clear diction to create appropriate style and expression, and display a range of diction skills when they perform. Singers are encouraged to think very analytically about how they produce vowels and consonants.

In the Yellow workbook

- *Page 14*   Clear consonants and smooth lines: Check all stages of this exercises and discuss if necessary

- *Page 14*   Moving between vowels and consonants: Can singers do this with each word in the panel, and with some of your own (or their own), using the chest register? Are the vowels resonant? (See page 79 for details)

- *Page 15*   Strength of consonants: Can singers produce words in each of the four styles listed?

- *Page 15*   Starting notes with a vowel: Can singers produce notes with **aspirated** onset, **glottal** onset and **simultaneous** onset?

- *Page 15*   Simultaneous onset: Check the exercise and discuss; have singers completed all the exercises on the page?

- *Page 16*   Experimenting with diphthongs: Check that singers have correctly understood the exercise and can reproduce diphthongs as specified in the third example

What singers say

'Your mouth needs to work really hard to get vowels to sound right. You really have to concentrate.'

Elliot, 14

The performance element of *Voice for Life* requires singers to think carefully about singing in public. From Light Blue onwards, the targets require singers to prepare music for a performance which is assessed by the choir trainer. The performance tasks become gradually more demanding as the levels progress. Below is some general advice about working towards the performance targets. Specific information about each level begins overleaf.

 Teaching, testing and assessing performance skills
In essence, for their performance targets singers need to bring together everything they have learned elsewhere in *Voice for Life* – especially Module A. This means that they should display good posture, breathing, command of tone and range and diction, bringing everything together in a convincing whole. Assure them that if all these other elements are in place, performance will be straightforward.

If possible, make sure the test happens in a familiar and relaxed environment. Make sure you are familiar with, and adhere to, your organization's safeguarding policy and practices regarding supervision and one-to-one contact with children. For safeguarding reasons, the venue should not be a private home.

Up to Dark Blue level, it is up to you whether you ask singers to perform for you alone or to the rest of the choir as well. The latter may be more nerve-wracking but is also a good indicator of how a singer deals with the public situation. However this is not a requirement and different singers may respond differently.

Practise with singers how they should stand and behave when they perform for the test. Encourage good posture: the test process may lead singers to make themselves as small as possible! Even if it isn't your choir's custom, suggest that singers memorize their performance music and maybe even perform without a copy. While this isn't a formal requirement at any level of *Voice for Life*, it is a good discipline and a useful memory exercise.

When assessing the tests, bear in mind the criteria listed at each level (these are shown on the following pages). Look for confidence and competence, in the context of the age and stage of the individual.

At the end of the test, thank the singer and give constructive feedback about their singing. In some cases, you may want to hear them sing again before you sign the target box: the voice may need time to develop, or a particular aspect of the piece may need more work. Inform singers that this is a possibility *before* they take the test; but also try to avoid this situation by making sure that singers are fully prepared in advance.

What singers say
'I was always really scared of stuff. I hated doing things in public. But – well, singing is different. I know that if I've practised it then I don't really need to be nervous. Of course I'm always a little bit anxious before a concert – our conductor says that's a good thing. But singing has made me less worried about other things, more confident. Happier.'

Anne, adult

Performance

White level

There are no formal training materials or assessments for performance at White level. The targets require singers to sing with focus and concentration, and in time and in tune with other singers. The important things they need to know are:

- when to start and stop singing
- when to take breaths
- what notes and words to sing
- how loudly or quietly to sing
- how quickly or slowly to sing

The targets also state that singers must be able to follow the conductor at key moments in a piece, like the start and end. If your choir isn't usually conducted (for example, if you are both choir trainer and accompanist), they will still need to know how your choir manages these key performance moments.

Tip: Help singers to learn to follow these cues by limiting the verbal instructions you give at these points in rehearsals; for example, don't count the choir in audibly when practising – you won't be able to in performance! Sometimes it's a subtle nod of the head from the accompanist or an experienced singer; whatever it is, make sure your choir can all see the cue without looking away from the congregation or audience.

In the White workbook

- *Page 13*   Conductor checklist: Check and discuss responses

Light Blue level

Singers must perform a verse of a song or hymn they have prepared in advance. During the performance, listen for the following things:

- good even tone
- clear diction and projection
- continuity of notes in phrases

Help your singer to choose a piece they know well, that lies in a suitable range. Encourage the singer to practise at home, preparing for the performance by:

- speaking the words (and ensuring the singer understands them)
- vocalising the tune to a single vowel sound or hum

What singers say

'I was really nervous before my performance. But I just tried breathing and concentrating and it was OK. I felt proud when I'd done it.'

Edith, 12

In the Light Blue workbook

- *Page 11*   Help the singer to choose their verse for performance and note it in the box

- *Page 11*   Check that the singer understands the practice points and what to listen to when practising

- *Page 11*   When the singer is ready, arrange a time for the performance; and give feedback after it

 Dark Blue level

Singers must perform a song or hymn they have prepared in advance. A small portion of this should be unaccompanied. Encourage singers to practise their piece using the strategies on page 13 of the workbook: sliding between each note; or singing without words (to 'ah' or humming). During the performance, listen for the following things:

- clear diction and projection

- good intonation throughout, even when unaccompanied

- continuity between notes in phrases

- good, even tone

 In the Dark Blue workbook

- *Page 13*   Help the singer to choose their verse for performance and note it in the box

- *Page 13*   Preparing for your performance: Check the singer understands the practice strategies; check the seven tick-boxes

- *Page 13*   When the singer is ready, arrange a time for the performance; and give feedback after it

 Red level

Singers must sing a short solo or solo line (which they have prepared in advance) in a service, concert or other public event. This may or may not be unaccompanied. Encourage singers to practise their solo in their own time using the strategies and checklist on page 16 of the workbook. During the performance, listen for the following things:

- clear diction and projection, and uninterrupted melodic lines

- even tone throughout, and ease of movement between registers

- good breath control, with breaths taken at appropriate points

- good intonation throughout, even when unaccompanied

Performance

In the Red workbook

- *Page 16*   Help the singer to choose what to sing, and where and when, and note it in the box
- *Page 16*   Preparing your solo: Check the singer understands the practice strategies; check the 12 tick-boxes
- *Page 16*   Give feedback after the performance

Yellow level

For the Yellow level performance targets, singers must sing:

- three contrasting solo pieces with a range of over an octave (optionally, any or all of these may be sung from memory)
- a solo or solo line (which they have prepared in advance) in a service, concert or other public event

Encourage singers to practise in their own time using the strategies on page 17 of the workbook. During the performance, listen for the following things:

- clear articulation and projection, and uninterrupted melodic lines
- even, resonant tone throughout the range
- an ability to move smoothly and with agility between the different registers of the voice
- good breath control – demonstrated by dynamics, focused tone and good intonation
- the use of different vocal colours

You may find it useful here to refer to the syllabus for the RSCM Gold Award (see page 9 for details), which gives a more formal checklist of the skills and qualities required of singers at this level.

In the Yellow workbook

- *Page 17*   Help the singer to choose what pieces to sing, and where and when, and note them in the box
- *Pages 17–18*   Preparing for your performance: Check the singer understands the practice strategies
- *Page 18*   Give feedback after the two performances

What singers say

'The performance targets were hard work because there was a lot of music to learn. But I just kept on practising. My choir director was really good and we made sure together that I was ready for everything. We even had a small audience when I sang my three solo pieces, which made it a bit of an event! After that I felt quite happy singing the solo in church a few weeks later.'

Philip, adult

Module A: Using the voice well

What singers say

'My choir usually sings in church services, so the first time I sang in a concert in a hall, I was quite surprised when everybody clapped. I mean, I was surprised, but I really loved it. It's great when people clap. It means they like it.'

Evie, 12

MODULE B

Musical skills and understanding

CONTENTS

Module B: Introduction

Module B: Musical skills and understanding

This module is concerned with the principles and practical applications of music notation, terminology and theory. The general aims of Module B are:

- to help singers learn to read and understand music

- to help singers apply that learning and understanding through all practical encounters with music

- to encourage singers to become self-sufficient musicians who are able to read, understand and interpret music notation and directions in rehearsal and performance

Each of these aims is assessed by means of the targets for each level, which are listed on pages 96–100 and at the back of each workbook.

How Module B is organized

Each level of Module B builds systematically on the previous one. As they move through the scheme, singers encounter different topics in different degrees of detail, so that by the time they complete Yellow level, they should understand:

- Pitch notation (including clefs and leger lines)

- Duration notation (note and rest values in various contexts)

- Pulse and rhythm notation (including a range of simple, compound and complex time signatures)

- Scales, intervals, keys, accidentals and modes

- Chords, voicings, inversions, harmonic structures and cadences

- Different score layouts and their navigation and interpretation

- Signs, symbols and performance instructions and directions

These topics are of course interlinked, and you will often address them simultaneously rather than sequentially. They are not all covered in the same depth at all levels but they are developed systematically through the scheme. (There are occasional alerts in the text if a topic demands knowledge of something from earlier in the book.)

How to use this part of the book

This part of the book contains advice and practical exercises to help you train singers in the module with confidence. First, read the introduction which begins on the opposite page. Then, from page 101, the material for each topic listed above is presented level by level, so you can easily see what to cover at each stage. Within each section, for each level, you will find in the following order:

- Key points of what is presented in the workbook for that topic (for further details, refer to the workbooks themselves)

- Tips (shown by the icon on the left) to help you teach that topic

- Keys to the workbook exercises and activities (material quoted verbatim from the workbooks is shown on a grey background)

- Occasional more general advice about a particular topic, or ways of checking singers have fully completed the assessment tasks

Why music theory?

Musical skills and understanding should grow together; as singers make technical progress with the voice, they need to develop a theoretical framework to support their singing. Singers who can read and write music are better able to learn, remember, understand and communicate it. They are musically independent and are also likely to have a better grasp of stylistic nuance.

On a practical level within your choir, singers who read music will normally learn repertoire more quickly and deeply. Those who do not read will slow you down as you will have to teach pieces by rote. This will also have the negative effect of frustrating singers who can read, as they may feel held back while they wait for others to learn their music. While this situation can and should be managed, the best solution is definitely to have as many readers as possible in your choir.

Readers are also likely to be stronger and more confident singers and will support the others. This is a mixed blessing. Accomplished readers can really power a choir along; but try to encourage non-readers to improve their reading skills rather than letting them rely on their reading colleagues.

Although in the short term it may feel easier to teach by rote, particularly if concert and service deadlines are looming, learning to read music has significant long-term benefits for individual singers and the whole choir. It reduces learning time, increases understanding and musicality, and leaves more time to polish performances.

And ultimately, while many successful singers do not read music, readers have more options. Many music roles need a high standard of musical knowledge and ability – these include professional choirs, session work or deputizing for other singers, and teaching, work in choral direction, or examining. These are just some of the avenues that may be considered by advanced singers – and from which non-readers are excluded, however well they sing.

Your own theory skills as a choir trainer

Choir trainers need a good grounding in music theory. If you are not confident about it, the workbooks present the fundamentals in a logical, easy-to-grasp format. By working through them carefully (including the activities) you will gain the skills and confidence you need to teach theory. Make sure you have absorbed each section fully before you work on it with your singers. (Even confident theorists should read the workbooks in order to understand how the material is presented to singers.)

Tip: If you still feel you need more support, consider asking senior choir members to help younger singers with the theory tasks in *Voice for Life*, possibly as part of their Module D targets. If you identify senior singers with theory skills, you can make use of these in various contexts during rehearsals. If there are no singers in the choir who can fulfil this role, think about recruiting a music teacher for occasional sessions with singers to help with the theory targets.

This book shows you how music theory is taught in the *Voice for Life* scheme. It does not pretend to be a comprehensive guide to the subject. Useful resources to help you learn theory are listed at **www.rscm.com/vfl** – the *Voice for Life* web pages.

Module B: Introduction

 Starting theory with your singers
Our voices are part of us. To play a musical instrument, we have to associate physical actions with specific notes; but for singers this process is largely natural, instinctive and invisible. Inexperienced singers joining your choir will already know and sing a large number of songs, probably in a variety of styles. They may already have mature, well-developed voices. They may sing very well without understanding what the music would look like on the page, or how it is put together.

In short, it is all too easy for singers to get by without a grasp of theory. If they already learn and perform adequately by ear, theory may feel like a frustrating backward step. You need to make reading a desirable asset: if you encounter reluctance, use some of the arguments on the previous page.

 From the outset, always refer theory to practice. Any music symbol, term or concept should be experienced by the choir not only on paper but also as sound. If you neglect this, you risk theory becoming dry and irrelevant. Work in both directions: as well as asking singers to sing what they see, from time to time try notating (or, better still, asking them to notate) what they sing or hear.

For example, singers should be able to show their understanding of intervals by naming the interval between two notes played on the piano, and later by sight-reading music containing that interval, and perhaps by writing it down. Or you could suggest they relate the appearance of a dynamic marking to how it feels in the body to actually sing at the appropriate volume.

 Theory takes time. Be patient with your singers. Some will grasp theoretical concepts quickly; others may take longer. Different people learn in different ways, so you need to teach it in different ways too. Try to present theory as a way of solving musical problems – which it is – rather than a learning process in its own right. And make the most of any theory which your singers have already learned in other contexts.

 Strategies for teaching theory
Much knowledge and understanding of theory can be developed during rehearsals. It is surprising how much singers absorb simply by following music as they sing. Young singers learn to associate the notation on the page with the sounds they hear and sing in much the same way as, when learning to read text, young readers begin to associate spoken sounds with words on the page.

So you can start almost by stealth. Just make sure your singers regularly *see* music, even if you don't always formally ask them to read it. Give them the opportunity to follow music while listening to how it actually sounds when played or sung. At White level, singers are not expected to read notation – but they are required to be familiar with what music looks like and to understand the basics of how it works. The more your singers use music, the less intimidating they will find it.

 Tip: In rehearsals, ask singers about aspects of the music. What do the dynamics mean? Can they clap the rhythm of a short passage? What key is it in? If you name a note, can they find it in the score? If you sing a phrase from the music, can they find it in the copy? Of course not all singers will manage this, but they will quickly learn from more experienced singers and benefit from your explanation of the answers.

If singers become afraid of singing a wrong note, they will quickly stop trying to read music and rely instead on the singers around them. Be supportive when you ask singers to read. Encouragement is vital. Never scold or ridicule wrong notes. First praise what was good; then ask singers if they know where they went wrong. Always give them another opportunity to improve. And always reinforce theory by relating what they sing – and any errors they may have made – back to the notation.

 Musicianship – hand in hand with theory
The Voice for Life Guide to Musicianship is packed with advice and resources about sight-reading and aural tests, with specific reference to the practical musicianship targets in Module B. But these skills are not just a way of getting music off the page. They are theory in practice: real musical situations to which singers have to apply theoretical knowledge. Theory helps reading – but reading helps theory too. Ideally, practical musicianship skills develop in tandem with growing knowledge of theory.

Encourage sight-reading. It is good for a choir to get used to singing new pieces (or sections of pieces) without stopping. You can do this without the words, choosing a suitable vowel sound. This builds confidence and the ability to keep going regardless of mistakes. It also encourages singers to listen to how their individual part fits with the other vocal or accompaniment parts – another crucial theory aid.

 Tip: When you run sight-reading sessions, have singers assemble the elements of a piece step by step. For example, first ask them to clap the rhythm. Once this is secure, look at the melody – what note does it begin on? Where will they find this note – does the accompaniment help them to pitch it? Will the accompaniment be playing their part or is their part completely independent? Is the melody step-wise? Are there any bars that look particularly tricky, perhaps with large intervals?

Once they have considered questions like this, try singing the section to 'la' or any comfortable vowel sound. Then add the words. As their competence increases, be prepared to change your pace of teaching to match their confidence!

Give your choir the chance to sight-read music of an appropriate level unaccompanied. This makes singers less reliant on an accompaniment, and will help their rhythm and ensemble (some choirs get very good at singing a fraction of a beat behind the keyboard, or one confident singer). Prepare the music with the choir first: point out areas that might be problematic, and use their knowledge of theory to find solutions.

 Here are a few extra helpful sight-reading strategies, in order of complexity:

- Ask singers to follow a piece of music while you play it to them – can they indicate in the score where you stop playing?

- Mix up the parts – make sure that all your singers are standing next to someone singing a different part. This is also a good test of whether the choir members really know their music!

- Ask more advanced singers to teach their section the notes of an unfamiliar piece.

- Ask senior singers to take a part of the choir practice, teaching all the sections of the choir their notes.

Module B: Targets

 For completeness, all the targets for Module B are listed below – those for theory first, followed by those for aural tests and sight-reading. This book contains materials about teaching theory; detailed resources and information about how to develop aural and sight-reading skills can be found in *The Voice for Life Guide to Musicianship*.

Note that the requirements are cumulative, so that, for example, a Red level singer should have mastered the theory and musicianship skills in all previous levels.

 White level

To complete Module B, singers must:

- know how to identify their part in a score
- find their place in a musical score (using bar numbers if necessary)
- understand common music symbols, including repeats, breath marks and pauses
- understand the most basic dynamic markings listed on page 29 of the workbook

For the aural tests, singers must be able to:

- match the pitch of a note played on the piano (within an appropriate range)
- sing five notes that move up and down by step
- identify which of two notes is higher or lower in pitch
- sing back a simple one-bar melody with a five-note range. The key chord and tonic note will first be sounded and the pulse indicated. The melody will be played twice.
- clap in time to a familiar song or hymn

There are no formal sight-reading tests for White level.

 Light Blue level

To complete Module B, singers must know and understand:

- the pitch names of the notes of the treble clef
- the basic note values and their equivalent rests: quaver, crotchet, minim, semibreve
- the concept of scales and the pattern of the diatonic scale
- the concept of accidentals
- the key signatures of C, F and G major
- the concept of bars and simple time signatures
- the basic dynamic markings listed on page 32 of the workbook

For the aural tests, singers must be able to:

- sing back a simple melody. The key chord and tonic note will first be sounded and the pulse indicated. The melody will be played twice.

- clap back a simple rhythm. The pulse will first be indicated and the test played twice.

- sing, unaccompanied, a major scale (ascending and descending) of one octave. The key chord and tonic note will first be sounded.

- clap the pulse of a passage of music in two or three time. The passage will be played twice, and on the second playing the singer should tap the beat and stress where the strong beat falls. The singer should then indicate whether it is in two or three time.

For the sight-reading tests, singers must be able to:

- clap, or sing on one note, a simple rhythm from sight

- sing a simple step-wise melody from sight on any vowel. The key chord and tonic will first be sounded.

 Dark Blue level

To complete Module B, singers must know and understand:

- the common note values and their equivalent rests, including semiquavers and dotted notes

- the pattern of the harmonic minor scale and concept of the relative minor key

- key signatures up to three sharps and flats (both major and minor)

- the characteristics and names of basic intervals (unison, octave, major/minor third, perfect fourth and perfect fifth)

- the concept of a chord, the construction of a triad and the difference between major and minor triads

- the performance directions listed on pages 28–29 of the workbook

For the aural tests, singers must be able to:

- sing back a short melody. The key chord and tonic note will first be sounded and the pulse indicated. The melody will be played twice.

- clap back a short rhythm. The pulse will first be indicated and the test played twice.

- identify a triad as major or minor on hearing it played twice

- look at two bars of music and do the following:

  - name the key (up to three sharps or flats – major keys only)

Dark Blue level *cont.*

- name the pitch of the first note in their own vocal part

- on hearing the chord, sing the first note

- sing an interval above a given starting note (major/minor third, perfect fourth and perfect fifth)

- tap the pulse of a passage of music in two, three or four time. The passage will be played twice and on the second playing the singer should tap the beat and stress where the strong beat falls. The singer should then indicate whether it is in two, three or four time.

For the sight-reading tests, singers must be able to:

- clap (or sing on one note) a rhythm including dotted notes, from sight

- sing from sight a short melody on any vowel, demonstrating an awareness of dynamic level. The key chord and tonic note will first be sounded and the pulse indicated. The set piece may be in any key up to three sharps or flats and include dotted note values and leaps of thirds, fourths and fifths.

Red level

To complete Module B, singers must know and understand:

- the pitch names of notes in the treble and bass clefs, including those on leger lines

- time values of notes and rests, including tied notes

- key signatures up to five sharps and flats (major and minor)

- compound time signatures

- the characteristics and names of major, minor and perfect intervals up to an octave

- the notes of major and minor arpeggios in keys of up to five sharps and flats

- the performance directions listed on pages 28–29 of the workbook

For the aural tests, singers must be able to:

- sing back a melody. The key chord and tonic note will first be sounded and the pulse indicated. The melody will be played twice.

- sing, unaccompanied, a major or minor arpeggio of one octave (ascending and descending). The key chord and tonic note will first be indicated.

- look at a short excerpt of music and:
  - name the key signature (major and minor keys)
  - name the pitch of any note in the first chord
  - on hearing the first chord, sing any note in their vocal range at the request of the choir trainer
- sing any major, minor or perfect interval (up to an octave) above a given starting note
- tap the pulse of a passage of music in simple or compound time. The passage will be played twice and on the second playing the singer should tap the beat and stress where the strong beat falls. The singer should then state whether the passage is in two, three or four.

For the sight-reading tests, singers must be able to:

- sing from sight a simple anthem or song with words, demonstrating an awareness of dynamics, phrasing and expression. The key chord and tonic note will first be sounded. The set piece may be in simple or compound time, in any key up to five sharps or flats, and include dotted and tied notes.

 Yellow level

To complete Module B, singers must know and understand:

- all key signatures, major and minor
- the difference between melodic and harmonic minor scales
- double sharps and double flats
- the characteristics and names of all intervals up to an octave, including diminished and augmented intervals
- the difference between primary and secondary chords, and how chords relate to a given key
- the difference between primary chords in root position, first and second inversion
- added-note chords (e.g. chords with added sixth, seventh, ninth)
- the function of a cadence; the names and characteristics of perfect and imperfect, plagal and interrupted cadences
- the complex time signatures 5/4, 5/8, 7/4 and 7/8
- the concept of modes
- the performance directions listed on pages 34–35 of the workbook

Module B: Targets

For the aural tests, singers must be able to:

- look at a short excerpt of music and:
    - name the key signature (any key)
    - name the pitch of any note in the first chord
    - name the first chord and the inversion
    - name the relation of the chord to the key
    - on hearing the first chord, sing any of the notes in their vocal range at the request of the choir trainer

- sing any interval up to an octave above a given starting note

- sing a minor scale (harmonic or melodic, at the singer's choice) ascending and descending of one octave. The key chord and tonic note will first be sounded.

- identify the cadence (perfect, imperfect, plagal or interrupted) at the end of an extract of music

- identify the time of a passage in in 5/4, 5/8, 7/4 or 7/8. The passage of music will be played twice. The singer should then state the time signature.

For the sight-reading tests, singers must be able to:

- sight-read fluently a piece of moderate difficulty. The set piece may be in any key or time signature, and may include triplets, duplets, dotted notes, music in changing time signatures and syncopated rhythms.

White level
Ability to read notes is not required at White level, but singers do have to interact with printed music and the targets require familiarity with elements of notation. (Explain to new singers that they do not need to read music at the outset, but will learn to do so as the scheme unfolds.) At this level particularly, it is important that singers understand each point before you move on to the next. Follow this part of the workbook page by page, as the material has been carefully designed.

From the start, *Voice for Life* relates the sounds singers make and hear to the symbols they see on the page (see page 54). So page 14 of the workbook uses a familiar tune ('Three Blind Mice') to introduce the ideas of **pitch** (how high and low notes are) and **duration** (how long or short they are). It represents both these concepts in graphic form, then in notation (making the point that the latter is more efficient).

Tip: Repeat this activity with parts of other well-known songs. Can singers identify the highest and lowest notes? Show them as a graphic? Put some of the pitches on a staff?

Key points that beginner singers need to know about pitch notation are:

- Music is written on groups of five lines called a staff or stave
- You read the notes from left to right, as you do a book
- Notes can be written on the lines or in the spaces between them
- The higher a note is on the staff, the higher its pitch

In the workbook

- *Page 15*   Pitch puzzle – correct answers are shown below

Pitch puzzle
Draw a ring round the highest note on this staff, and a square round the lowest note.

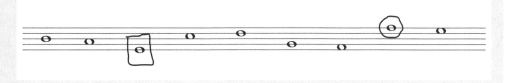

Note anatomy
Page 16 of the workbook introduces the anatomy of individual notes (notehead, stem, tail) and notes linked by beams, making the following key points about duration:

- Notes with hollow noteheads and no stems last longest
- Notes with stems are shorter than ones without
- Notes with solid noteheads are shorter than ones with hollow noteheads
- Notes with tails are shorter than notes without tails
- The more tails, the shorter the note

Tip: Encourage beginner singers to identify the different parts of notes in printed music. You could ask them to circle hollow or solid notes, notes with tails, or ones with beams. These activities accustom young singers to examining printed music and looking for details, without as yet asking them to turn those details into sound.

However you could also play or sing back to your singers bars or phrases containing notes they find – and encourage them to copy these by singing. This will begin to forge the link between notational symbols and the sound they make.

 In the workbook

- *Page 16*   Long and short notes – check that singers have correctly combined notes, stems and tails

 Clefs

Page 17 of the workbook explains how notation reflects high and low notes:

- Each staff contains a range of pitches

- The range is shown by a special sign at the start, called a clef

- There are two main clefs, the treble clef and the bass clef

 Tip: With beginners in particular, it can help here to discuss the concept of high and low sounds. Young singers may confuse sounds that are low in their own range (but actually quite high relative to other voices or instruments) with genuinely low sounds. Don't restrict the examples to music – encourage singers to think about sounds all around them, many of which have a pitch of some sort.

 In the workbook

- *Page 17*   High or low – violin, singing children and flute are high: the rest are low

 Pulses, beats and bars

Via a number of observations and activities, all related to 'real' music, pages 18–22 of the workbook explore the fundamentals of rhythm and its notation:

- Most music has a repeated 'heartbeat' called a **pulse**

- Each individual sound of a pulse is called a **beat**

- The pulse is often counted in regular groups of beats called **bars**

- Music is made up of long and short notes counted against a pulse. A pattern of long and short notes is called a **rhythm**.

- Music notation shows: the number (usually two, three or four) of beats to count in each bar (the **time signature**); where the bars begin and end (**barlines**); and the length of each note or rest

- The pulse can be fast, slow or in-between. The speed of the pulse is called its **tempo**.

Like many other music education resources, *Voice for Life* distinguishes between a pulse (a regular repetition) and a beat (a single iteration of that pulse). But many people use 'beat' to mean both a repeated pulse and a single iteration of it. You may have your own view on this, but young singers will benefit from consistency here. Using the two different terms is generally easier for beginners to understand.

 Tip: Beginners need time to grasp rhythm theory. They may never have considered it before; the 'numbers' involved are different from school maths; and they have to think analytically about time and duration as well as physically feeling it. Be patient. Make sure that singers have done and understood all the relevant workbook activities. It is also vital to relate the concept of tempo (page 20 of the workbook) to how you actually mark time when conducting. For young singers in particular, your beat must be very clearly articulated.

 Rests

At White level, singers are not required to understand rests in detail but they are expected to be able to identify them in printed music. The symbols for one-beat, two-beat and whole-bar rests are shown on page 22 of the workbook. Encourage singers to look for these in various scores.

 Tip: Young singers in particular tend to 'switch off' when they see rests. The 'Rest test' on page 22 explores what singers can profitably do when not actually singing. Of course it is most important to count carefully and follow the conductor; but singers can also usefully prepare for their next entry by regulating their posture and breathing. In this context, you may wish to revisit the relevant material in Module A.

 In the workbook

- *Page 18*   Counting and clapping – make sure singers have:
    - tapped or clapped along to various pieces of music
    - played the clapping game at the foot of the page and sung 'Three Blind Mice' (top of page 19)
- *Page 19*   Three questions about mice – you clap *once* while you sing the word 'Three', *once* while you sing the word 'blind' and *twice* while you sing the word 'mice'
- *Page 20*   Write a rhythm – check that each bar contains four crotchet beats
- *Page 20*   Speed test – check and discuss singers' answers
- *Page 21*   Clap and count in 3/4
- *Page 21*   Four questions about 3/4 – there are *four* bars of music; bar *three* has exactly the same rhythm as first one; there are *seven* one-beat notes; *four* notes are joined by beams (two groups of two)
- *Page 22*   Check singers can identify the rests on this page in printed music, and tell you how long each one lasts
- *Page 22*   Rest test – the only good ideas are 'Check your posture', 'Watch the conductor' and 'Breathe evenly'. All the others are bad. You may need to discuss singers' responses.

Finding your way around

Pages 23–28 of the White workbook explain how printed music works and how to navigate it. Again the emphasis is on practical activities – make sure your singers see and experience proper music as often as possible. (Even non-readers gain a surprising amount from following a printed copy.) The key elements of notated music are shown on page 23 of the workbook, as follows:

- Singers usually sing from printed music called a **score**

- A score contains a number of different staves, often grouped into **systems** to make it easier to read

- The number of staves in a system depends on the number of voices and instruments taking part in the piece

Tip: Ask singers to count the number of staves and systems in pieces of printed music. Encourage them to look at how the parts and voices are grouped together.

In the workbook

- *Page 23* Symbol search – check each item has been circled correctly in the score, and (if necessary) check singers' understanding by asking them to identify further examples

Singing from a score

Page 24 of the workbook shows how **soprano** (or **treble**), **alto**, **tenor** and **bass** parts appear in both **open** and **closed** scores. Singers are asked to find their own part at the beginning of a score, and, on page 25, to follow a part through two systems. (It may not be obvious to young singers that they have to follow the music from one system to the next, not from one staff to the next.)

You should already have allocated parts to singers based on their range and abilities (see the advice on range on page 49). Make sure all your singers know which part they are supposed to be singing, and where their line is in the score.

There may be circumstances in which singers do not know which part they sing. (You may not yet have decided formally to place them in a particular section; or the choir may consist only of uncategorized children's voices.) For the purposes of these exercises, if singers ask you which line or part to follow, choose the one that is nearest to their own voice.

Tip: As well as the music on page 24, wherever possible you should use actual scores for these exercises. Ask singers to follow a single line through a piece from start to finish. They can do this in several different ways, depending on their ability (so this works well with singers of different levels):

- While listening to a recording of piece of music, they can follow a particular part in a score (ask singers to follow their own part at first, then to follow a different one)

- They can read the words of a score as they follow a part

- If they have learned a piece by rote, suggest they follow the score while they sing (this is particularly helpful as they will begin to recognize the way the notation matches what they are singing)

- The 'Score study' worksheet on page 26 (reproduced on page 223 of this book) summarizes all these activities

Do not hesitate to use the same score several times. Every time singers examine a score for new features or instructions, or approach it in a different way, they learn more about it and become more familiar with notation.

In the workbook

- *Page 24*   Check singers have correctly circled the part they sing on both the open and closed score

- *Page 25*   Check singers can correctly follow their own part (you could ask a more senior choir member to help here)

- *Page 25*   Check singers can follow any part you specify (again, a more senior singer could help here)

- *Page 26*   Ensure that singers have correctly completed a few copies of the worksheet for different pieces – discuss if necessary

Other ways of finding your way around
Page 27 of the workbook looks at other navigational aids: bar numbers, different types of barlines, and upbeats. Once again there is no substitute for looking at real music. The practical aim here is to enable singers quickly to find any point you specify in the music, thus wasting less time in rehearsal.

Tip: During rehearsals, give singers plenty of practice finding their place in the music. (Try asking more experienced singers to help younger ones.) Within reason, vary your starting points when rehearsing. This keeps singers alert but also gives them vital practice at score navigation; it also makes them aware of other singers' parts. Think of the number of ways you can express a starting point:

- 'The upbeat to bar 15'

- 'After the double bar on page 3'

- 'At the 3/4 section'

- 'From 'Dwellers all in time and space' on page 4'

- 'The tenor entry in bar 9'

Don't hurry this at first. Giving young singers time to reach their goal calmly will have long-term benefits. You can also play a version of 'Bar number volleyball' (page 27 of the workbook) with your singers, moving from one choir member to another.

In the workbook

- *Page 27*   Bar numbers – check singers have correctly identified bar 45 (after the double bar in the second line)

- *Page 27*   Upbeats – check the correct note has been circled ('praise' at the end of bar 3)

- *Page 27*   Observe a few rounds of 'Bar number volleyball' or try playing it with the whole choir

Signs and symbols

Page 28 of the workbook addresses the special navigational symbols and instructions used when a piece doesn't go straight through the score from start to finish – **repeats** and other signs. You should ensure that singers are familiar with each of the elements on this page, once again in the context of actual scores.

Tip: When beginning a new piece, explain any repeats to your choir carefully and, if possible, check that these instructions have been understood by reference to the score. Do this as simply as possible, using the text of the piece and the barlines as landmarks rather than, for example, individual note names (which non-reading beginners may not understand).

Once singers are proficient with this, try asking them to show you how to navigate the score from start to finish. This can be done in a variety of ways. Singers can:

- read the text from the score, with repeats (repeated when reading) where they are indicated

- follow their part with a finger from start to finish, indicating repeated sections as necessary

- if they are confident, sing their part through including any repeats

In the workbook

- *Page 28*   Repeat exercise – bars 2, 3, 4 and 5 should be underlined.

- *Page 28*   Symbol search repeated – if necessary ask singers to do this for you with a score you show them.

More signs and symbols

As they progress through *Voice for Life* singers are expected to know and understand an increasing range of signs, symbols and performance directions. At White level, singers need to know:

- basic symbols and terms for dynamics and dynamic changes

- a few extra instructions like the pause symbol and breath marks

Full details can be found in the workbook on pages 29 and 30 and also in the Reference section on page 35.

Tip: By this stage, beginner singers may begin to feel slightly overwhelmed by all the things they have to remember – with some justification. Bear in mind that at White level engagement with notation is largely preparatory to the formal music reading that begins at Light Blue. While you want to be sure that everything has been understood, try to retain a spirit of exploration and fun.

The more you can make these activities into games, and the more you can continue to relate them to real musical experiences, the better. And don't forget to demonstrate to singers what notation actually *sounds* like. This is vital.

 In the workbook

- *Page 29*   The correct order of loudness is:

- *Page 30*   Sign time

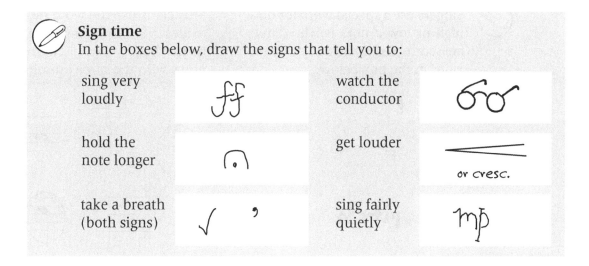

Sign time
In the boxes below, draw the signs that tell you to:

sing very loudly	*ff*	watch the conductor	(glasses)
hold the note longer	(fermata)	get louder	(crescendo) or cresc.
take a breath (both signs)	✓ '	sing fairly quietly	*mp*

What singers say

'If you just look at music when you are singing, even if you don't understand it, it starts to make sense after a while. At first I used to get lost, but now it's much easier to follow.'

Ella, 11

'When I joined the choir, I was worried because I couldn't read music. With the help of the conductor and some other singers, I learned quite quickly. It's less scary than it looks.'

Carl, 14

Light Blue level

Without a grasp of the concepts introduced at White level, singers will struggle with Light Blue. When they begin the level, even if they are unable to read notation, they need to understand what it tells us. Light Blue introduces formal reading skills not just as an end in themselves, but also as the basis of theory topics like counting and rhythm; intervals, scales and keys; and their associated notation – all of which are introduced at this level.

Use the 'Music basics' on pages 12–13 of the Light Blue workbook to check whether singers beginning the level have all the information they need. Singers' responses to these informal activities (which are designed not to feel like intimidating tests) will tell you if they are ready for Light Blue theory. Responses do not have to be 100% accurate, but singers who have significant difficulty will need further training, possibly with reference back to White level.

In the workbook

- *Page 12*   Upper boxes – check the answers below

Singers use a special word for how high or low a note is. The letters are scrambled up below. Write the word in the box below.

p   h
c
t   i

pitch

Musicians use the word **duration** to describe how long notes last. In the box below, circle the two notes with the same duration.

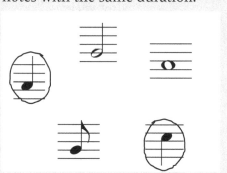

- *Page 12*   Lower boxes – the four main types of voice are **Soprano, Alto, Tenor** and **Bass**; check that the singer has correctly indicated the part that he or she normally sings in the choir

What singers say

'Reading music really helps me to understand what I'm singing. Understanding notation helps you get inside the music in a way that you never do when you only sing by ear.'

Frances, adult

'Now that I can read music, I can learn new pieces much more quickly than before. I feel independent. I'm trying to help other people in the choir with this now because the more people read, the less time we waste.'

Richard, adult

• *Page 13*   Upper boxes – check the answers below

 Connect each of the labels below to a sign or symbol on the music. One of them has been done for you.

Odd one out 1
Music contains signs called repeats which tell you to sing part of the music twice. Circle the sign here which is *not* a type of repeat.

Odd one out 2
Music contains signs which tell you to jump to another part of the piece. Circle the sign below that does *not* tell you to do this.

Odd one out 3
Circle the word below that is *not* the name of a part of a note.

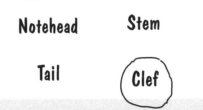

Odd one out 4
Circle the sign below that does *not* tell you how loudly to sing.

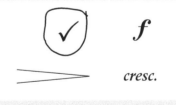

In the music below, draw a line under the bars you have to sing twice.

Traditional French carol

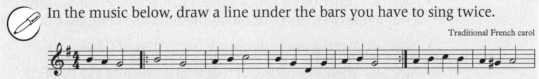

Notes and their names

Pages 14–16 of the workbook explore:

- how notes are named
- how they are shown in notation
- how clefs 'fix' the range of the staff
- how leger lines show notes that are too high or low for the staff

Tip: When helping singers with this section of the book, you should frequently explore the links between note names, notation and sound. Letters and graphics are not music. Without their aural context, names and symbols mean little – especially to younger singers. Make the connections in all directions: sound to name, sound to symbol, name to symbol, and vice versa. Play or sing notation frequently; and as often as is practical, ask singers to write down what they hear.

Opinions vary as to the wisdom of teaching treble and bass clefs at the same time. It is often assumed that most singers will learn the treble clef first, and the bass will follow. (At first, singers only need the clef of the part they sing, and learning just one may be easier than learning two.) If you have beginner basses in your choir they will need the bass clef first (though in practice they may already have encountered the treble). The exercises in Module B are suitable for both treble and bass readers.

It can help to find out whether singers have other music lessons. If they do, they may already be familiar with notation and also have basic keyboard skills. Some choir trainers find this helpful, making frequent reference to a keyboard when teaching pitch theory; others feel this distracts singers from learning to sing from notation. *Voice for Life* doesn't assume or insist on keyboard skills, but acknowledges that some singers may benefit from translating pitch theory to the keyboard. This can help to:

- 'fix' note names and notation to actual pitches
- create visual and physical references for notation and sung pitches
- aid intonation and 'aural imagination'

In the workbook

- *Page 14* Going up, F comes after E; going down, B comes after C
- *Page 15* Note name reminders – check singers' responses (Not all teachers find these phrases or acronyms useful – but many beginners expect to learn them!)
- *Page 16* Letter box – check singers can accurately match the letter names to their position on the staff. The composer is BACH.
- *Page 16* Word game – the words are EGG and CAGE
- *Page 16* There are plenty of words here, such as FEED, DEAF, BADGE, FADED, CABBAGE, BAGGAGE. Check singers' responses. Can they sing what they have written or play it on a keyboard? If not, you could play their word-notes for them.

How long notes last
Pages 17–18 of the workbook revisit the equivalent material at White level but in rather more detail: at Light Blue, singers learn the names of notes of different durations and their equivalent rests.

 Tip: Try to relate some of this material about duration to the clapping games on page 18 of the White level workbook. Can singers clap (or sing, or play) four-, two- and one-beat notes over a steady pulse? Again, it is important to establish a link between what the symbols look like and how they sound.

 In the workbook

- *Page 17*   Check the answers below

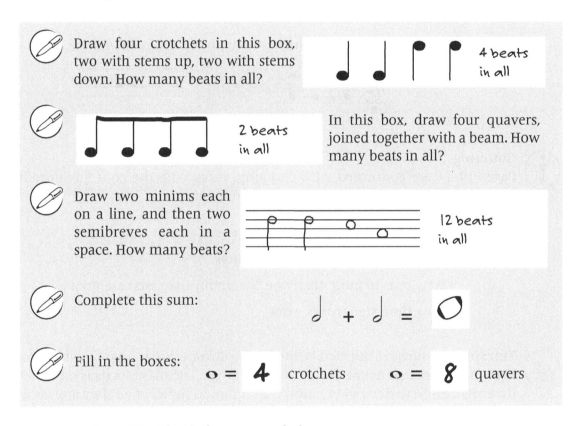

- *Page 18*   Check the answers below

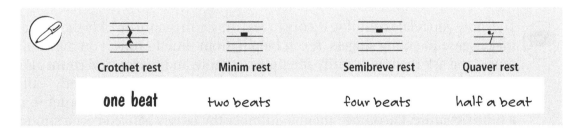

- *Page 18* – Minim and semibreve rests: some teachers tell young singers that the semibreve rest lasts longer because it has more 'energy' to cling to the line above it; while the minim rest is shorter because it has less 'energy' and has to sit on the line

• *Page 18*   Check the answers below

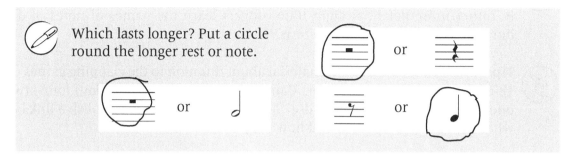

Which lasts longer? Put a circle round the longer rest or note.

• *Page 18*   Check accuracy of crotchet and quaver rests
• *Page 18*   Check the correct rest has been used, as below

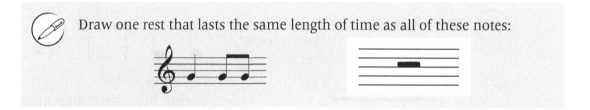

Draw one rest that lasts the same length of time as all of these notes:

 Counting

Pages 19–21 are concerned with counting, expanding the concepts introduced at White level. This section of the workbook looks at:

• how beats are counted and written in groups called **bars**
• how bars are separated by **barlines**
• how rests of more than one bar (multi-bar rests) are notated
• how **time signatures** work

 Tip: Singers who have finished White level will know what time signatures look like; Light Blue goes into detail about how they work. The main focus is on crotchet (/4) time signatures, so draw your singers' attention to these when they appear in music they sing. Page 19 also refers in passing to 2/2, which has minim beats. At this stage, this is really to show that both top and bottom numbers can change, but you could usefully point out the minim beat in any 2/2 pieces that the choir encounters.

 The more you relate counting theory to real music, the more quickly the concepts will make sense to young singers. It can help if, from time to time, you play unfamiliar music and ask them to identify the time signature and to clap and count along. You may find that you need to do this a lot before singers catch on properly – they may be naturally reticent and they may not know what to listen for in order to identify a time signature. Encourage them to number the pulses between each strong one to count the beat groups.

An understanding of time signatures is fundamental to practical musicianship, so it is tested extensively in the Module B aural tests. You will find further advice about connecting the theory of counting with the practice on pages 17–22 of *The Voice for Life Guide to Musicianship*.

In the workbook

• *Page 20*   Check the answers below

 On the stave on the right, write the time signature for music with two crotchet beats in a bar.

Here, write the time signature for music with three crotchet beats in a bar.

Here, write the time signature for a piece that has two minim beats in a bar.

 In a piece with this time signature, how many beats are there in a bar?

Draw one note which lasts for a whole 4/4 bar.

 In a piece with this time signature, how many beats are there in a bar?

Draw one note which lasts for a whole 2/4 bar.

• *Page 20*   Check singers' answers in the write-in box: can they clap and count along to their chosen songs?

• *Page 21*   Check the bars have been correctly filled, as below

• *Page 21*   Make a rhythm – check that all four bars have been filled in with the correct number of beats to match the time signature chosen by the singer; can the singer clap and count the rhythm he or she has created?

Intervals

Pages 22–24 of the workbook bring together the concepts of pitch (and differences between pitches) and note names. Singers learn:

- that the distance between notes of two different pitches is called an **interval**, and that intervals differ in size from **steps** (adjacent notes) to **jumps** (notes separated by a number of other notes)

- that intervals have different names depending on the number of steps they contain

- that it is important to practise intervals so that the muscles get used to how to sing the differences between pitches

- the names, sounds and 'distances' of five different intervals: **semitone**, **tone**, **fourth**, **fifth** and **octave**

Tip: These are vital theoretical concepts, but remember they are, above all, sounds. Make sure singers hear, sing and see different intervals often so that the ears, voice and eyes get used to their sound, feel and look. Establishing these ideas properly here – particularly the difference between tones and semitones – will pay off later.

In the workbook

- *Page 22* Check singers can 'draw' the shape of 'Three Blind Mice'; can they do the same with other well-known tunes?

- *Page 22* Check the pattern of dots, as below

Three blind mice! Three blind mice! See how they run! See how they run!

- *Page 22* The largest interval in 'Three Blind Mice' is between the words 'mice' and 'See'. Check this in the write-in box and on the music (the last note of bar 2 and the first note of bar 3). Can the singer reproduce this interval?

- *Page 23* You sing *five* notes to get from C to G as shown here. Can singers sing this and find it on a keyboard (if you use one)?

- *Page 23* You need *four* notes to sing by step from C up to F; an interval of four notes is called a **fourth**

- *Page 23* Can singers add their own examples of songs that start with a fifth and a fourth? Check these and ask to hear them sung.

- *Page 24* Check and discuss the three write-in boxes

- *Page 24* Singing by step – check, sing and discuss tones and semitones in 'Three Blind Mice'; sing some tones and semitones

Scales

Pages 25–27 introduce scale theory via the following principal facts:

- A **scale** is a chain of notes that moves step by step, normally between two notes an octave apart.

- Most scales use steps of two different sizes – tones and semitones.

- One of the most common scales is called a **major** scale. It uses a special pattern of tones and semitones.

- Scales can go down as well as up.

Tip: As often as possible, make the connection for your singers between these 'theory scales' and what they sing during warm-ups. Light Blue singers will be learning to sing major scales for the Module A 'Tone and range' targets, so will be familiar with them in the voice: understanding the intervallic structure can only help this.

The major scale feels very 'natural' for most singers as it is the basis of so much Western music, so it is unlikely that you will need to teach the actual pitches. The aim of this section however is to have singers understand the theory of the major scale so that eventually they can apply it to any given key.

Many different approaches can help singers internalize the idea of 'degrees' of a scale. The workbook suggests singing major scales to the numbers 1 to 8 going up, and 8 to 1 coming down. You may also want to use sol-fa, which names pitches according to their position in a scale. Theorists use names for pitches in a scale based on their relationship to the key note or **tonic**. These are listed on page 52 of the Yellow workbook.

Staircases

From Light Blue level, scale and key theory are explored in the workbooks by means of staircases. While this is not unique to *Voice for Life*, the systematic use of this concept throughout the scheme helps singers to grasp the structure of complex scales in all keys. It gives them the analytical skills to work out scales, keys, key signatures, intervals and accidentals for themselves without too much rote learning, making key theory more instinctive than is sometimes the case in other resources.

The staircase graphics in the workbooks also map to the keyboard (so black keys on the keyboard are shown in grey on the staircases). Singers may find that using a keyboard helps with pitch and interval identification, and it is certainly useful for more advanced scale theory. If you are uneasy yourself about how scales work on the keyboard, the staircases may help you to familiarize yourself with this.

Most of the staircase activities are presented as graphic puzzles. Some singers may be able to do these without listening to the sound they make, but don't encourage this; insist that singers sing the scales, hear the intervals and work out the pitch names (using a keyboard if preferred). This is particularly true in the early stages – the intervallic structure must be felt and embedded as well as read and understood.

In the workbook

- *Page 25* Check the answers in the write-in boxes and discuss if necessary; ask singers to sing the scale and pitches from it, too; for the last question, ask singers to sing the semitones

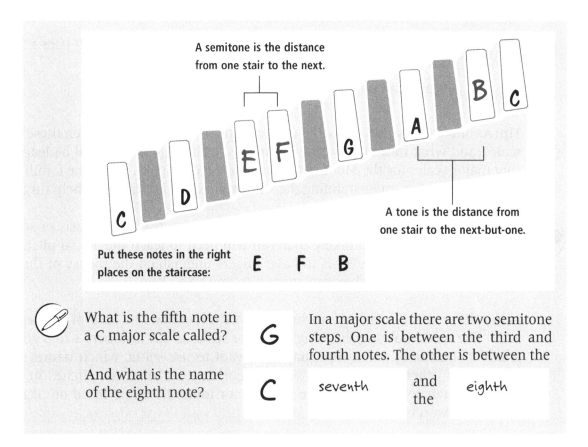

A semitone is the distance from one stair to the next.

A tone is the distance from one stair to the next-but-one.

Put these notes in the right places on the staircase: E F B

What is the fifth note in a C major scale called? **G**

And what is the name of the eighth note? **C**

In a major scale there are two semitone steps. One is between the third and fourth notes. The other is between the *seventh* and the *eighth*

Sharps and flats

Page 26 further explores the pattern of tones and semitones in a major scale, making the following fundamental points:

- All major scales follow the same pattern of tones and semitones (tone, tone, semitone, tone, tone, tone, semitone)

- In order to create major scales based on any note other than C, special notes called sharps and flats are necessary to put the tones and semitones in the right places

The workbook uses staircase puzzles to create the scales of G major (using F sharp) and F major (using B flat). Once again, make sure singers hear the results – encourage singing and playing. (If young singers are unable to sing the full range of a particular scale, be careful not to force them beyond their range. Either ask more experienced singers to demonstrate, or use a keyboard.)

Tip: At this level you may need to revisit the idea of tones and semitones quite frequently to be certain that singers have fully understood the concept of steps of two different sizes. Make the point that while the names of the notes in a scale may change, the pattern of tones and semitones does not.

In the workbook

- *Page 26*   G major staircase – check notes are correctly placed (see below); ask singers to sing the scale; where are the semitones?

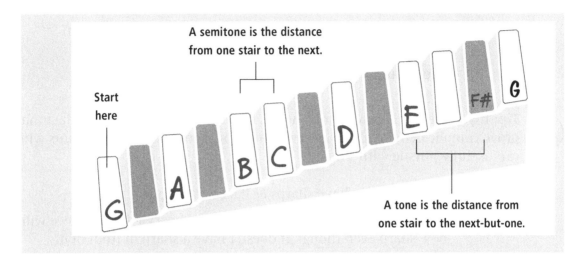

- *Page 26*   Sing, think, write – check singers can find the solutions aurally as well as by counting

  - The note a fifth above G is D

  - The note a fourth above G is C

  - The note a fourth below G is D

- *Page 27*   F major staircase – check notes are correctly placed (see below); ask singers to sing the scale; where are the semitones?

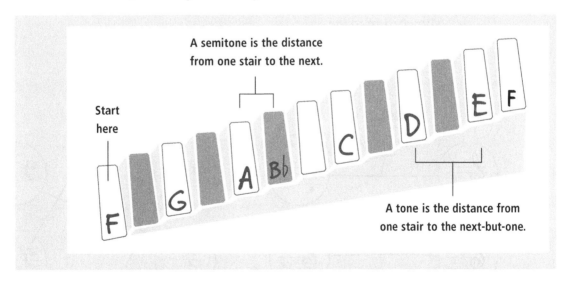

- *Page 27*   Sing, think, write – check written and sung responses

  - The note a fifth above F is C

  - The note a fourth above F is B flat

  - The note a fourth below F is C

  - You sing the note E on number 7

Understanding keys

Page 28 of the workbook explains the basics of key and tonality:

- If a piece uses the notes of a particular scale, we say it is in the **key** of that scale.

- If that scale needs sharps or flats, these are shown in a **key signature** at the start of each staff.

- The starting note of a scale is called the **tonic** or key note.

 Tip: If you are familiar with this theory, it is easy to lose sight of the fact that it can prove complicated for young learners. The workbook makes a few points which you can usefully pursue with singers:

- Key signatures have sharps *or* flats, never both.

- If the key signature shows F sharp, then every F in that piece will be F sharp even though it doesn't have a sharp in front of it.

- A piece in C major has no sharps or flats, so the key signature has no sharps or flats.

 In the workbook

- *Page 28* Check the answers in the upper box. The tonic of E major is E. The tonic of B flat major is B flat.

- *Page 28* Check the scale in the lower box. This exercise revises the key signatures of G major and F major, so check the key signatures and the construction of the scale. Don't miss the opportunity to have singers sing their scale, or as much of it as they can manage.

- *Page 29* Linked keys – check the answers as shown:

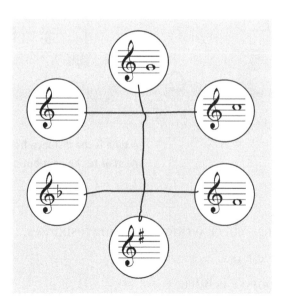
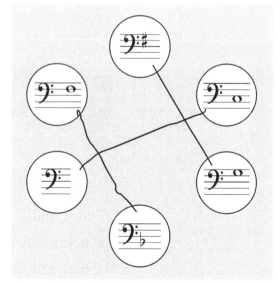

Understanding accidentals

Pages 30–31 explore notes that are not included in a key signature:

- Sharp, flat or natural signs placed immediately before notes are called **accidentals**.

- A **flat** sign immediately before a note tells you to sing the note a semitone lower.

- A **sharp** sign immediately before a note makes it a semitone higher.

- A **natural** sign tells you to sing the normal version of the note.

- Accidentals can be modified or neutralized within a bar.

Tip: You may need to revisit the idea of semitones. If you sing or play a note to your singers, can they sing the note a semitone higher or lower? Singers must develop an aural imagination of what accidentals do to the sound of notes. Use real music too. Ask singers to find sharps and flats in scores, then discuss and demonstrate what they do to the music.

Be aware that the term 'accidentals' is often used loosely to mean any sharp, flat or natural sign. In *Voice for Life* the term refers more strictly to signs used to modify notes outside a key signature.

In the workbook

- *Page 30*   Check natural signs are correctly written

- *Page 30*   Check write-in boxes, as below; can singers sing the note before and after its modification by the accidental?

Make this note into G sharp by adding an accidental.

Look carefully. What is the name of this note? Make it into a B natural.

The note is B flat.

Add a key signature to make this note a semitone higher.

Now make it a semitone higher by adding an accidental instead.

In the workbook

> • *Page 31*   Check write-in boxes, as below

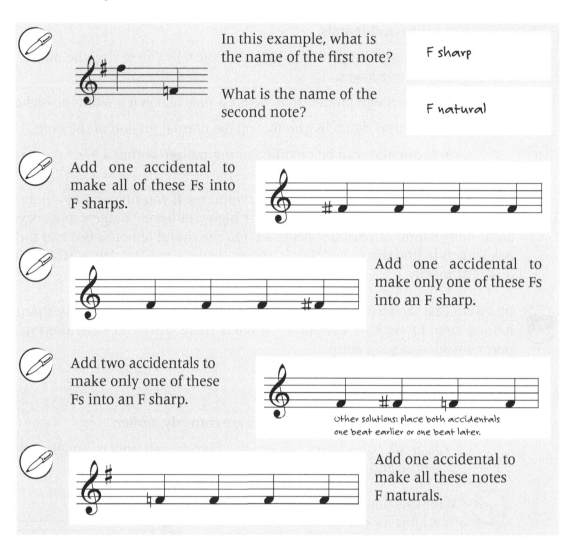

Dynamics

At Light Blue level singers are expected to remember all the signs and symbols they learned at White level. These are summarized on pages 42–43 of the Light Blue workbook. Pages 32–33 explore dynamics in rather more depth than at White level.

Tip: At this level, singers may be so preoccupied with the notes that they neglect to read other signs and symbols. So from time to time it can be useful to concentrate on dynamics alone: perhaps find a passage with plenty of volume changes, teach it by rote and then encourage singers to follow the dynamics, not the notes, as they sing.

Encourage singers to 'feel' dynamics by singing them. If possible, they should start to associate dynamic markings with the physical sensations involved in changes of volume. As before, singers are expected to know the following principal dynamics:

Try asking singers to sing one phrase several times, each at one of these dynamics.

In the workbook

- *Page 32*   Check write-in boxes, as below

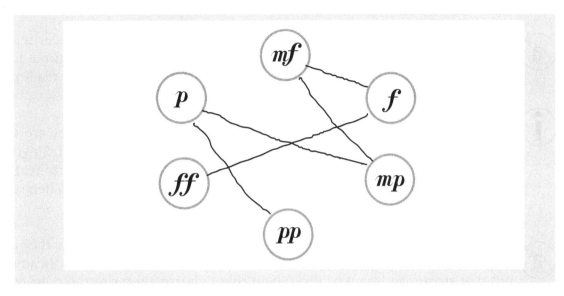

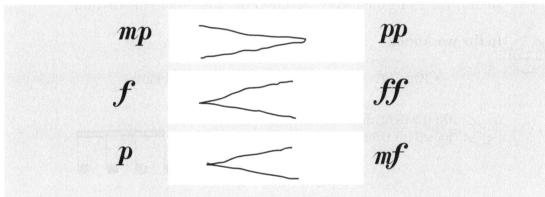

- *Page 33*   Check write-in box below and ask singer to clap or tap the rhythm observing the dynamics

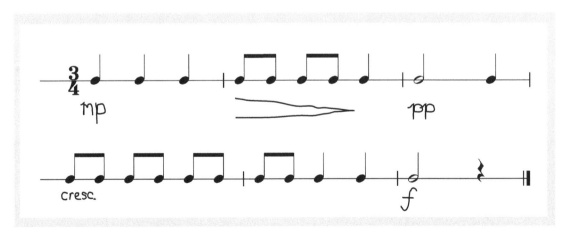

- *Page 33*   Check that singers have added dynamics to the earlier puzzle, and clapped it observing the changes in volume

Dark Blue level
The Light Blue basics of duration, pitch, interval and key are expanded considerably at Dark Blue. By the end of this level singers will have most of the building blocks of music literacy, in preparation for the more advanced theory in Red and Yellow.

 Tip: The development of reading should go hand in hand with broader repertoire and opportunities to sing more complex music. As long as you continue to relate what singers read to what they sing and hear, you are developing their reading skills.

 Semiquavers
Page 14 of the workbook introduces semiquavers, showing: how they are written, grouped and beamed; how long they last; and how they are counted. Singers may already be familiar with how semiquavers look and sound from repertoire. Practise counting groups of semiquavers against a crotchet beat. Some teachers use the counting syllables 'one-a-and-a' for each semiquaver.

 Tip: If possible, ask singers to find semiquaver notes and rests in scores they already sing. (This isn't easy: they will need to spot note-heads, tails and double beams. Point out that stems can go up or down, and that tails are always to the right of single stems.) Then sing the pieces, paying close attention to the rhythm.

 In the workbook

- *Page 14* Check the write-in boxes (see below)

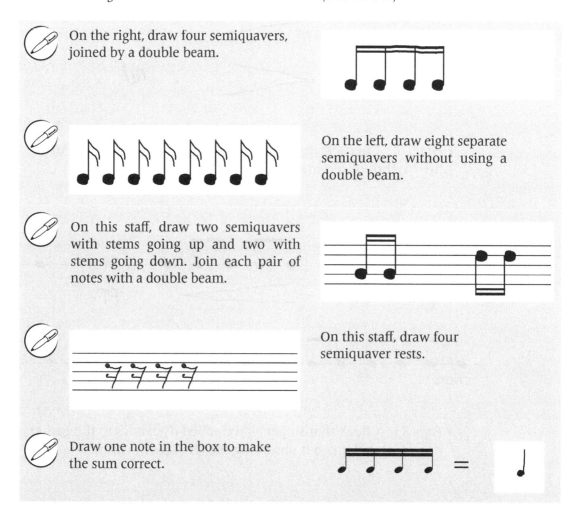

Page 15 of the workbook explains that a dot to the right of a note makes it last half as long again. Only dotted minims (a minim plus a crotchet) and crotchets (a crotchet plus a quaver) are required at Dark Blue. The principle is extended to rests too. Page 16 contains puzzles and activities to test that the principles have been grasped.

 Tip: Young singers may take time to fully grasp the idea of dotted notes. Make sure you relate it to music that they already know by clapping, counting and singing. It can help to use the word 'and' when counting quavers in between crotchet beats.

 In the workbook

- *Page 15*   Check the write-in boxes (see below)

 How many crotchet beats are there in a dotted minim, or a dotted minim rest? Write the answer in the box on the right.

There are **3** crotchet beats in a dotted minim or dotted minim rest.

 Put some dotted minims in the spaces (not on the lines) on this staff. Try some with stems going up and some with stems going down. Some have been done for you.

Put some dotted crotchets on the lines of this staff, some with stems up and some with stems down. The dot goes just *above* the line, to the right of the note head.

- *Page 16*   Make a rhythm – check that all four bars have been filled in to match the time signature chosen by the singer; can he or she clap the resulting rhythm?

- *Page 16*   Add the rest – check rests have been inserted correctly (see below); can the singer clap this rhythm?

 Add the rest
Fill in the gaps in the rhythm below with rests. Add a rest each time you see a *.

Dark Blue level: Intervals

The Dark Blue workbook explores intervals in more depth and introduces major and minor thirds. At this level, knowledge of intervals is tested for the first time outside the workbook activities: the aural tests require recognition of all the intervals covered so far. So it is important that you ensure your singers are secure with the theory here.

Tip: Make sure that singers sing, hear and read intervals in the context of real music, and that they experience the physical sensation of moving from one note to another. The workbook activities combine singing, listening, thinking and writing.

Before introducing the new intervals, page 17 of the workbook briefly revises the concept of and the five types that singers should already know. (If you feel a singer is insecure with this, refer back to pages 22–24 of the Light Blue workbook.)

In the workbook

- *Page 17*   Check the write-in boxes (see below), and that singers can sing the intervals as described

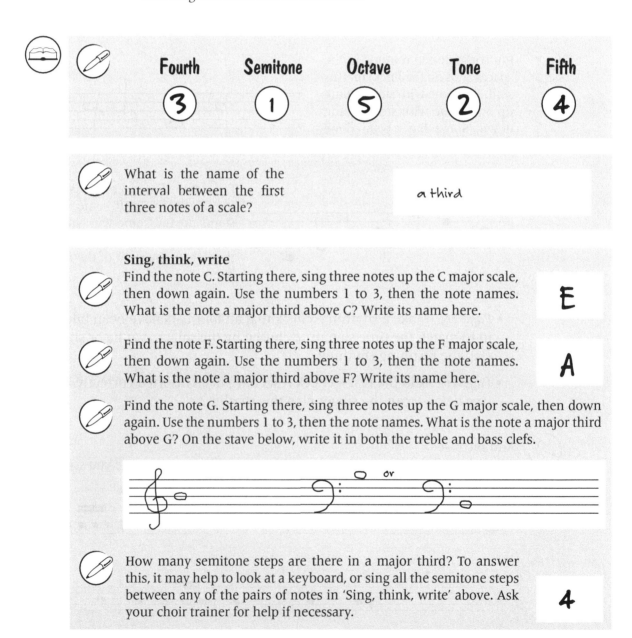

Fourth Semitone Octave Tone Fifth

(3) (1) (5) (2) (4)

What is the name of the interval between the first three notes of a scale?

a third

Sing, think, write

Find the note C. Starting there, sing three notes up the C major scale, then down again. Use the numbers 1 to 3, then the note names. What is the note a major third above C? Write its name here.

E

Find the note F. Starting there, sing three notes up the F major scale, then down again. Use the numbers 1 to 3, then the note names. What is the note a major third above F? Write its name here.

A

Find the note G. Starting there, sing three notes up the G major scale, then down again. Use the numbers 1 to 3, then the note names. What is the note a major third above G? On the stave below, write it in both the treble and bass clefs.

or

How many semitone steps are there in a major third? To answer this, it may help to look at a keyboard, or sing all the semitone steps between any of the pairs of notes in 'Sing, think, write' above. Ask your choir trainer for help if necessary.

4

Page 18 of the workbook explores the differences between major and minor thirds. As this is a vital concept in so much subsequent theory, make sure your singers understand it fully. The essential theoretical difference is:

- a major third is made up of four semitones
- a minor third is made up of three semitones

Tip: Concentrate on the sound. Encourage singers to count, sing, play on a keyboard, and experience the physical sensation of singing these different intervals. Follow the directions in the workbook, picking out the notes on a keyboard if necessary.

In the workbook

- *Page 18*   Check the write-in boxes (see below) and also that singers can sing these intervals and the songs they choose

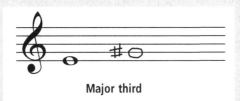

Major third

On the staff on the left, write a note that is a major third higher than the one shown.

On the staff on the right, write a note that is a minor third higher than the one shown.

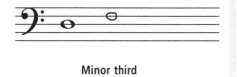

Minor third

 It can be easier to remember an interval if you think of a well-known tune that begins with it. Think of a tune that begins with a major third and one that begins with a minor third, and write their names here.

Major third

Oh when the Saints go marching in *

Minor third

Greensleeves *

* There are, of course, many other examples. See how many singers can find and sing.

- *Page 18*   Check responses and discuss (these are the same note, so there is no interval between them)

 What do you notice about these two notes?

   Or these?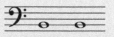

More about intervals

Page 19 of the workbook explores some additional ideas that will become important later in the scheme:

- Some intervals do not have major and minor forms; for example, the fourth, fifth and octave, are described as **perfect**

- Intervals can be measured in either direction – from a higher note to a lower one, or from a lower one to a higher one

Tip: There is no substitute for singing examples of these intervals in different directions. Ask singers to measure intervals by singing major scales to note names and to numbers, as shown at the top of page 10 of the workbook. The practical activities in *The Voice for Life Guide to Musicianship* will help with this too.

In the workbook

- *Page 19* Check singers can sing perfect fourths and perfect fifths, using the methods in the second paragraph

- *Page 19* Check singers can sing and name the notes in the write-in boxes (see below)

Sing G, then name the note a perfect fifth above it. **D**

Sing C, then name the note a perfect fourth above it. **F**

Sing D, then name the note a perfect fifth above it. **A**

- *Page 19* Stave mazes – check answers below. Bear in mind singers will need to use flats to complete the treble clef example.

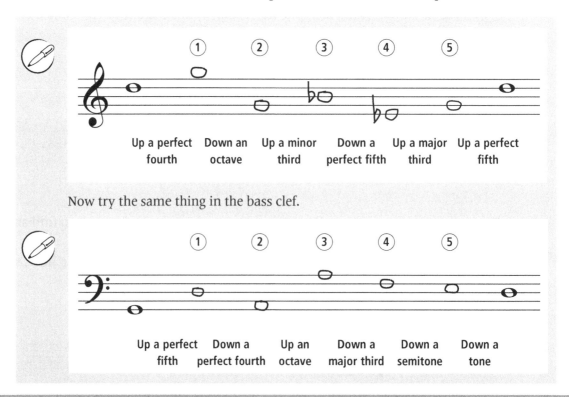

Up a perfect fourth   Down an octave   Up a minor third   Down a perfect fifth   Up a major third   Up a perfect fifth

Now try the same thing in the bass clef.

Up a perfect fifth   Down a perfect fourth   Up an octave   Down a major third   Down a semitone   Down a tone

Minor scales

Most singers will already have encountered music in minor keys, but Dark Blue level is the first time in *Voice for Life* that they must recognize and construct minor scales and triads (both as part of the workbook activities and in the aural and sight-reading tests). Only the **harmonic minor** scale is required, explained on page 20 as follows:

- There are two main types of scale, major and minor; in a major scale, the interval between the first and third notes is a major third (four semitones); in a minor scale, the interval between the first and third notes is a minor third (three semitones)

- There are several types of minor scale; in a harmonic minor scale the interval between the sixth and seventh notes is three semitones – an augmented second

Tip: Singers may ask why an interval of three semitones can be called either a minor third or an augmented second. Remind them that in any scale, each note name is only used once and that intervals are named after the number of steps between note names. The interval from F to A flat is a third because it has three note-name steps (F, G, A). The interval from F to G sharp is a second because it has only two note-name steps (F, G). Words like 'major,' 'minor' and 'diminished' describe the size of intervals.

This is a lot to absorb. The workbook explains everything methodically; revisit the ideas often until they are fully understood. Always reinforce the theory with singing and listening. Singers should encounter the sound of the minor scale before the theory: play and sing up and down the scale thoroughly, as specified in the workbook.

In the workbook

- *Page 20*   A minor staircase – check and discuss if necessary; ask singers to sing the scale, paying particular attention to the intervals

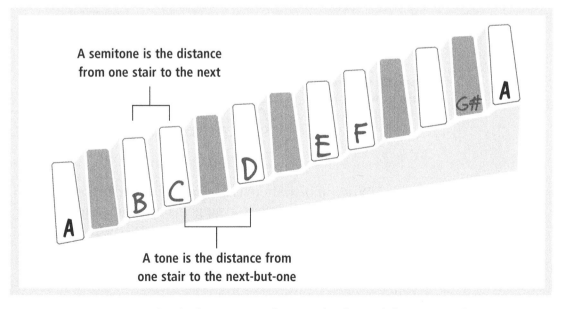

- *Page 20*   Check the write-in box at the foot of the page – there are three semitone steps from F to G sharp. Make sure singers have understood the concept of the augmented second – and can sing it.

Pages 21–24 of the workbook introduce the theory and notation of relative major and minor keys. (Before you begin this, you may wish to check briefly that singers have retained the material about scales, key signatures and accidentals learned at Light Blue.) Via singing activities, puzzles and explanations, the workbook demonstrates the following important points:

- Every major key has a related minor key (and vice versa)

- The sixth note of a major scale is the key note of its relative minor

- The key signature of a minor key is always exactly the same as its relative major

- In harmonic minor scales, you use an accidental to sharpen the seventh note, but this doesn't appear in the key signature

In the workbook

- *Page 21*   Write-in boxes: the relative minor of G major is E minor; the key signature needs one sharp, F sharp

- *Page 21*   E minor staircase – check and discuss if necessary; ask singers to sing the scale, paying particular attention to intervals

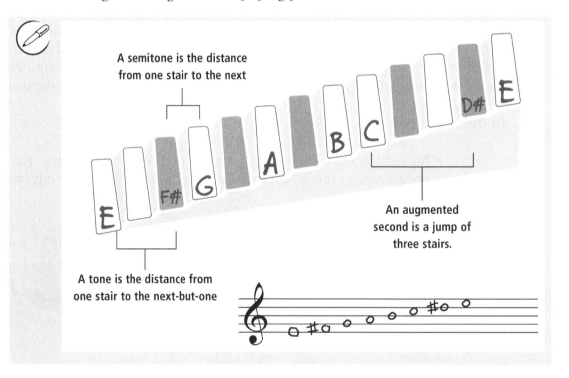

- *Page 21*   Write-in box: there is a semitone between the second and third notes of the scale (can singers name the notes?)

- *Page 22*   The relative minor of F major is D minor; the key signature needs one flat, B flat

- *Page 22*   D minor staircase – check and discuss if necessary (see opposite); ask singers to sing the scale

- *Page 22*   The seventh note of this scale is C sharp

- *Page 22*   Discuss (and sing) songs in major and minor keys

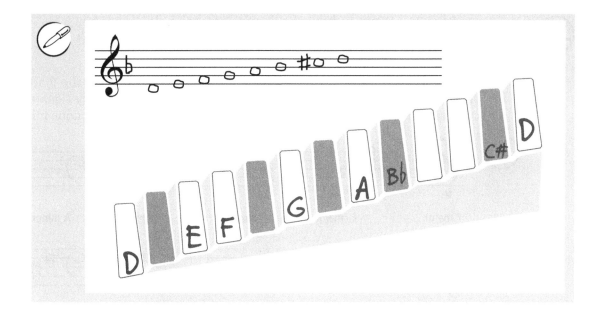

Pages 23–24 of the workbook introduce all the major and minor keys up to three sharps and flats (the limit of the requirement for Dark Blue). Encourage singers to identify and sing music they already know in these keys; sing and name the notes of each scale; and follow all the exercises and directions in the workbook.

Tip: Some choir trainers ask singers to identify different 'qualities' in keys. For example many musicians regard A major as a 'bright' key, E flat major as more mellow, C minor as quite sombre. This doesn't work for everyone but it can be a useful suggestion. Other musicians associate keys with colours or words. Anything that aids singers to identify and 'fix' keys and their signatures is valid.

In the workbook

- *Page 23*   Write-in boxes: the relative minor of D major is B minor; the relative major of G minor is B flat major

- *Page 23*   Key signatures: A major has F sharp, C sharp and G sharp; its relative minor is F sharp minor

Draw a clef on this staff and then write the key signature for A major and its relative minor. (See the next page or ask your choir trainer for help.)

- *Page 23*   Key signatures: the key signature of E flat major and C minor is B flat, E flat, A flat

Draw a clef on this staff, then write the key signature for E flat major and C minor. (See the next page or ask your choir trainer if you need help.)

- *Page 23* Write-in box: check answers (see below); are key signatures correctly written? Check position of sharps and flats

On the staves below, write the key signature of each key using only the sharps and flats in the circles above. Remember to draw a clef before each key signature. As you use each sharp or flat, cross it out in the circle. The first one is done for you.

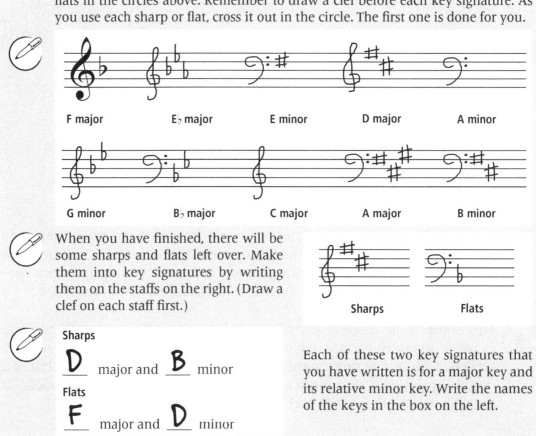

When you have finished, there will be some sharps and flats left over. Make them into key signatures by writing them on the staffs on the right. (Draw a clef on each staff first.)

Sharps

D major and **B** minor

Flats

F major and **D** minor

Each of these two key signatures that you have written is for a major key and its relative minor key. Write the names of the keys in the box on the left.

More help with keys and key signatures

There are many ways to teach key signatures and singers learn them in different ways. Some easily relate the graphic image at the start of the stave to a key; at first, others may need different strategies. For this level, the following hints may help:

- In sharp key signatures, the last sharp on the right is a semitone below the key note of the major scale for that key signature (count up one semitone to find the key note)

- In flat key signatures, the last flat on the right is a fourth above the key note of the major scale for that key signature (count down a fourth to find a key note)

- Once you have found the tonic of the major key, the key note of the relative minor is a minor third below the tonic.

- The order and position of sharps and flats in key signatures never changes. The first sharp is always F sharp; the second always C sharp; the third G sharp and so on; likewise with B, E and A flats.

Tip: It can help also to encourage singers to think of C major and A minor as a key signature of 'no sharps or flats' rather than 'having no key signature' – the absence of sharps and flats itself represents a key.

Pages 25–26 of the workbook introduce the idea of chords in general and triads in particular, making the following principal points:

- a chord is two or more notes sounded together

- when chords are written down, the notes are placed one above the other to show that they are sung or played at the same time

- notes with stems can share a stem when written as a chord

- chords can be written in different clefs and different staves

- in choral music, chords are often shown in closed score (singers have already encountered this in Module A of White level)

 Tip: Make sure you relate the theory in the workbook to real music (both as notation and sound). Can singers spot different types of chords in scores? Count the number of notes? Identify individual notes within chords?

The practical games, tests and exercises at this level in *The Voice for Life Guide to Musicianship* will help significantly with the theory here, and vice versa. Develop the two together as far as possible.

 In the workbook

- *Page 25*　Write-in boxes: check the answers as shown below

 This stave shows two notes. On the same stave, write them as a chord.

  The stave on the left shows four notes. On the same stave, write the four notes as a chord. Make the chord a quaver by adding a stem and a tail.

 If notes to be sounded together are in different clefs, they are still written one above the other. Below you will see two notes: one in the treble clef and one in the bass. Write these notes as a chord on the larger staves on the right.

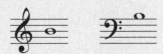

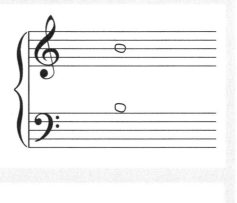

What is the interval between these two notes?

An octave

- *Page 26*　Write-in boxes: the tenors sing A; the altos F sharp

Triads

Pages 26 and 27 introduce and explore the idea of triads:

- A triad is a chord with three notes.

- There are several types of triads, classified according to the type of scale they are based on.

- A **major triad** is based on the first, third and fifth notes of a major scale; a **minor triad** on the same three notes of a minor scale

 Tip: It is important to ensure that singers can hear the difference between major and minor triads, as they are fundamental to the aural and sight-reading targets at Dark Blue. Can singers spot triads in printed music? Can they sing them or play them?

 In the workbook

- *Page 27* Write-in boxes: check responses – can singers sing the different intervals involved? And the triads (see opposite)?

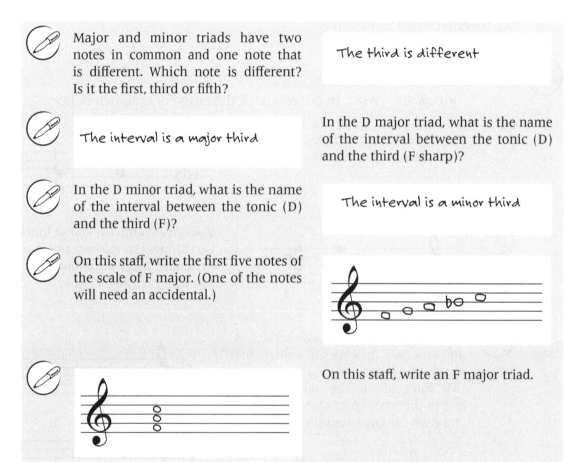

What singers say

'It can be hard to understand the difference between major and minor thirds at first, but if you sing them a lot, they feel different when you go from one note to the other. This helps you to hear the different sounds too.'

Liam, 11

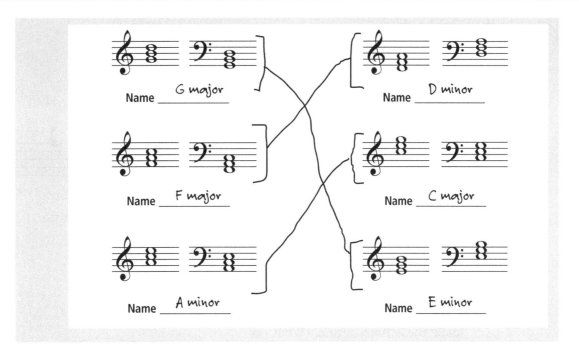

Performance instructions

At Dark Blue, singers need to remember all the signs and symbols they learned at earlier levels – chiefly dynamics and 'architectural' instructions like repeats. (For a summary of these, see pages 45–46 of the workbook.) In addition, an understanding of Italian tempo indications is required for the first time, together with some basic styles of articulation (staccato and legato). Pages 28 and 29 of the workbook contain the full list of terms and symbols.

Tip: Ensure that singers look at real music to spot these words. When they spot them, can they say what they mean? Your choir should perform and listen to music with a variety of speeds and moods so that singers become familiar with these. It can help to make explicit the link between these tempo indications and the speed of the pulse, perhaps by having singers beat time or conduct to music at various tempi.

The choir can physically embody tempo in other ways too – for example, by walking, tapping or gesturing to a pulse. Once singers are able to internalize a pulse, they will more easily understand changes to it when they are singing. Ask them to beat pulses at different speeds. One singer could conduct a group of others in these activities.

For the articulation symbols, once again, make sure singers experience these as part of real music, spotting notes in scores that are staccato, and those that are joined legato with slurs. Explore with them the physical sensations of these instructions so that these link to the graphic representation and the sound.

There is more advice about teaching performance instructions on pages 134–135.

What singers say

'It's a lot to remember at first. Lots of different things. You have to keep them all in your brain at once! It gets easier though, the more you do it.'

Pearl, 12

In the workbook

- *Page 29* Write-in boxes: check responses below

- *Page 29* Choosing tempo: check singers have done this activity at least once – ask them to clap their rhythm for you at the tempo they have chosen, with any additional changes as marked. If you change the tempo marking, can they clap at a different speed?

 More about teaching performance instructions
Dark Blue stretches singers in a variety of ways; they may start the level as relative beginners, but will complete it with a basic but nonetheless comprehensive grasp of what it means to be a musician. The targets require considerable skills in all five modules: central to this is an ability to read and understand music with a degree of independence. It is your job as a choir trainer to bring this about. The remarks below about teaching reading apply across all levels, but are particularly pertinent here.

 Pearl's comment on the previous page ('It's a lot to remember at first') may sound obvious, but it is heartfelt. As a skilled musician, you may forget what it feels like to be a beginner – how hard it can be to find your way around a score, remember what everything means, watch the conductor, produce a decent sound that blends with everyone else, stand or sit well and generally make a good impression on the audience or congregation. The following strategies may help:

Whenever you approach a new piece with your singers, make sure that everyone understands the markings in the music. You may want to do this separately from learning the actual notes (this is very helpful for 'pre-reading' singers who will want to follow the structure and spirit of the score even if they cannot read the actual notes). By Dark Blue, singers are expected to identify a wide range of notational features. Encourage them to examine the music for:

- 'structural' signs (repeats, codas, the *segno* and so on)
- signs and symbols relating to dynamics (letters, words, 'hairpins')
- signs and symbols relating to articulation (slurs, staccato dots, breath marks and so on)
- performance directions or signs relating to tempo or mood, and any changes to these as the piece progresses
- any other directions or advice

 Tip: It can be useful to allow singers unguided time to familiarize themselves with the music; but it also works well if you frame the task by asking them to comb the score for a few specific items such as:

- a particular dynamic symbol
- a short sequence of notes
- a few words from the text
- a repeat or *segno*
- a rest of a specific length

This sort of 'treasure hunt' activity encourages singers to engage with the printed copy in a really dynamic way, and to complete this they will be sifting visual information and identifying different elements of notation.

Once they have done this, ask them to read, sing or beat time to short extracts of the score. Guide them as they do this. This 'spotting' helps them to recognize landmarks visually, aurally and physically. It also accustoms them to moving quickly around the score and using the notation in different ways.

Elicit from them the meanings of any performance directions they find when reading music. If they have already heard or sung the piece, they may already have ideas or clues about the meaning of certain symbols. Your more experienced singers will understand more than the beginners, but try to give the latter a chance to contribute too.

 However in detailed rehearsals of a particular piece, where you require specific musical outcomes, it is sometimes preferable to tell singers what you want rather than referring them back to the score too often. Younger singers may be a little overwhelmed by constant exhortations to watch dynamics or obey tempo changes if they are already trying hard simply to sing the right notes at the right time. Have mercy: help your singers to process the information and don't berate them too much!

Red level

The fundamentals of music literacy and theory are assumed now. Red level introduces more notational details, compound time signatures, further intervals and keys, and more performance instructions. Once again, theory must go hand in hand with opportunities to sing more complex music. When choosing repertoire, try to provide singers with concrete examples of the theory they are learning.

Leger lines

Page 17 of the workbook introduces leger-line notes above and below the stave. In the treble clef, singers already know A above the stave and Middle C below; in the bass clef, Middle C above and E below. Now the following notes are added:

- above the treble clef: B (above the first leger line); C and D (on and above the second leger line) and E (on the third leger line)

- below the treble clef: B (below the first leger line); A and G (on and below the second leger line) and F (on the third leger line)

- above the bass clef: D (above the first leger line); E and F (on and above the second leger line) and G (on the third leger line)

- below the bass clef: D (below the first leger line); C and B (on and below the second leger line) and A (on the third leger line)

Tip: Make sure singers hear, read and write these notes. And of course they should sing leger-line notes within reach, though not everyone will manage high E or Low F!

In the workbook

- *Page 17*   Check the write-in boxes (see below)

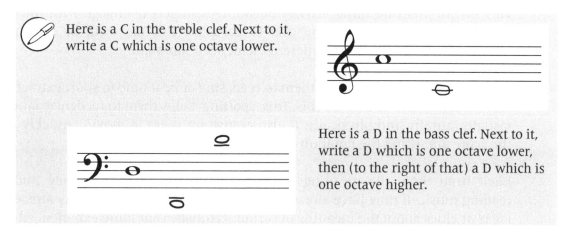

Here is a C in the treble clef. Next to it, write a C which is one octave lower.

Here is a D in the bass clef. Next to it, write a D which is one octave lower, then (to the right of that) a D which is one octave higher.

- *Page 18*   Check the write-in boxes (see below)

Here is a B in the treble clef. Next to it, write a B which is one octave higher.

- *Page 18*   Word game: FEED, AGE, FACE: Letter box: BRITTEN

Page 19 of the workbook explains that slurs (introduced at Dark Blue) join notes of different pitches, while ties (introduced here) always link notes of the same pitch. The following principal points need to be understood:

- A tie tells you to add the durations of the notes it links to make one long note

- Ties often run across barlines, linking a note in one bar to a note in the next

 Tip: Ask singers to find examples of tied notes and slurs in printed music. Encourage them to sing both and hear the difference in the sound. It's also important to stress that singers should keep the pulse in mind and count the beats of the bar carefully while singing tied notes. The continued regularity of the pulse helps the placing of all notes, whether tied or not.

 In the workbook

- *Page 19* Check the write-in boxes (see below). If possible, have singers tap, sing or play the passages to check.

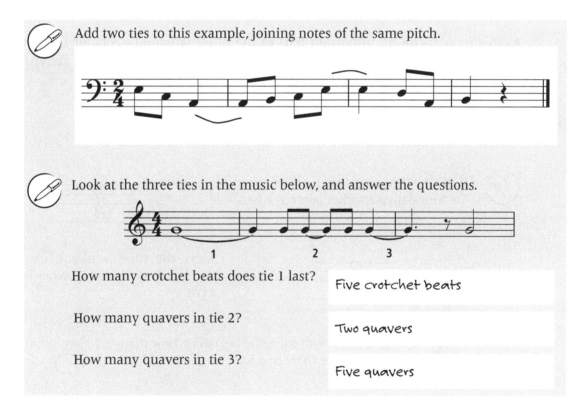

Add two ties to this example, joining notes of the same pitch.

Look at the three ties in the music below, and answer the questions.

How many crotchet beats does tie 1 last?   Five crotchet beats

How many quavers in tie 2?   Two quavers

How many quavers in tie 3?   Five quavers

What singers say

'Sometimes you need to work things out by reading the music, but sometimes it's easier to learn what it sounds like then just use the music to remind you. Eventually, when you know a piece well enough, you just use the music to help your memory. You don't need to read everything note by note once you know the music. I didn't realize that at first.'

Kate, 16

Singers already know 2/4, 3/4, 4/4 and 2/2, all of which are known as **simple** time signatures because the beat can be divided into two. Page 20 of the Red workbook introduces **compound** time signatures in which the beat is counted in dotted crotchets, each divided into three quavers:

- 3/8 (one dotted crotchet beat per bar)
- 6/8 (two dotted crotchet beats per bar)
- 9/8 (three dotted crotchet beats per bar)
- 12/8 (four dotted crotchet beats per bar)

 Tip: In practice these are unlikely to be new to Red-level singers. They will probably already have sung music in compound time signatures – but this is the first time in *Voice for Life* that they are expected to learn the theory of them.

There is no substitute for clapping, singing, gesturing and moving in these time signatures so that the physical 'feel' of the pulse is properly embodied. Don't underestimate the amount of time it may take for some singers to absorb the concept fully. Refer as often as possible to music singers already know. Can they beat time to it? Can they feel the way the beats are divided?

As this topic forms an important part of the musicianship targets for this level, *The Voice for Life Guide to Musicianship* contains plenty of help, advice and activities.

 In the workbook

- *Page 20* Check the write-in boxes (see below).

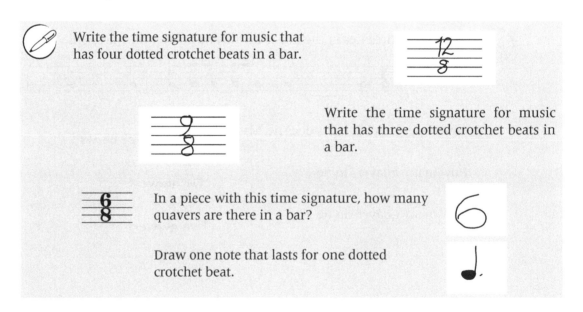

What singers say

'Our conductor asked us to move in time to the music. I was worried because I'm not really ... well, I don't like dancing. But she said the idea was to get what a 9/8 rhythm feels like and not to worry because no one was watching! I was a bit self-conscious at first, but she was right. It did help. The music felt different after that. More lively.'

Ben, 14

At Red level, singers are expected to know all the major, minor and perfect intervals within an octave. These are outlined on pages 21–23 of the workbook. This means that, in addition to those learned at previous levels, singers must be familiar with:

- the minor second (already encountered as a semitone)
- the major second (already encountered as a tone)
- the minor sixth
- the major sixth
- the minor seventh
- the major seventh

 Tip: Insist on singing and hearing, as well as 'measuring', reading and writing. Have singers spot different intervals in music they sing on a regular basis. Can they identify and sing an interval you play? Can they find that interval in the music?

The major version of an interval is *always* larger than the minor version. Some singers find it hard to distinguish between them. They need to hear the contrast frequently, and practice singing them to feel the physical sensation of each. (Remember too to practise descending intervals as well as ascending.)

 In the workbook

- *Page 21*   Check the write-in boxes (see below). Sing the intervals.

Major sixth

On the staff on the left, write a note that is a major sixth higher than the one shown.

On the staff on the right, write a note that is a minor sixth higher than the one shown.

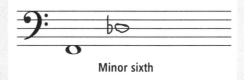

Minor sixth

Think of a tune that begins with a major sixth and one that begins with a minor sixth. Write their names here.

Major sixth

My Bonnie lies over the Ocean

Minor sixth

Close every door to me (from 'Joseph and the Amazing Technicolor Dreamcoat')

- *Page 21*   Write-in box: there are two minor seconds in a major second.

Pages 22 and 23 of the workbook explore major and minor seconds and major and minor sevenths. Again, insist that singers hear, sing and (if appropriate) play these intervals wherever possible.

 In the workbook

> • *Page 22*   Check the write-in boxes (see below). Sing the intervals.

 On the staff on the right, write a note that is a major second higher than the one shown. Sing these notes at an octave that is comfortable for you.

Major second

On the staff on the left, write a note that is a minor second higher than the one shown. Sing these notes at an octave that is comfortable for you.

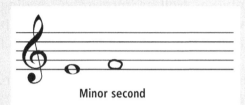

Minor second

 Think of a tune that begins with a major second and one that begins with a minor second. Write their names here.

 Major second

Frère Jacques

Minor second

The Londonderry Air ('Danny Boy')

 How many semitones are there in a major seventh?

Which note is a major seventh higher than C?

11

B

> • *Page 23*   Check the write-in boxes (see below). Sing the intervals.

 On the staff on the right, write a note that is a major seventh higher than the one shown. Sing this interval at a comfortable octave.

Major seventh

On the staff on the left, write a note that is a minor seventh higher than the one shown. Sing this interval at a comfortable octave.

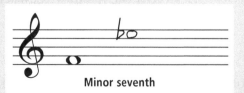

Minor seventh

• *Page 23*   Check the write-in boxes (see below).

Major seventh
The first and third notes of 'Somewhere over the rainbow' form a major seventh

Minor seventh
'There's a place for us' from 'West Side Story'

Link these intervals in order of size. Start with the smallest.

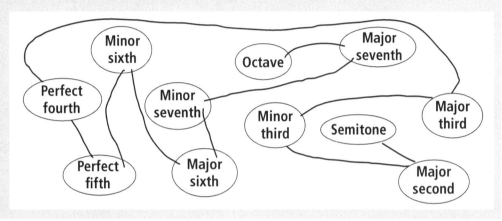

New keys and key signatures

Pages 23–26 of the workbook introduce all the major and minor keys up to five sharps and flats (the limit of the requirement for Red level). Encourage singers to identify and sing music they already know in these keys; sing and name the notes of each scale; and follow all the exercises and directions in the workbook.

Tip: At this stage, as singers move into some fairly advanced theory, it may be wise to check that the basics are secure. Check, for example, that singers remember the concept of relative minor keys. If they are unsure, refer them back to pages 21–23 of the Dark Blue workbook. You might also want to revisit:

- the key signatures up to three sharps and flats (major and minor)

- the order and position in which sharps and flats are written on the stave in key signatures (see page 130)

- the order of tones and semitones in a major scale (Light Blue workbook page 26)

- the structure of the harmonic minor scale (Dark Blue workbook page 20) and the augmented second in that context

What singers say

'Now I know a bit about how music works, choir practice is easier. Theory makes my singing more secure, so I think I make a better sound now. It's more than just singing with the others. It's kind-of like I own what I sing. That's important. I love that feeling.'

Mike, adult

In the workbook

- *Page 24*   Check the write-in boxes. The sharps are: F, C, G and D.

- *Page 24*   A flat major staircase – check and discuss if necessary; ask singers to sing the scale

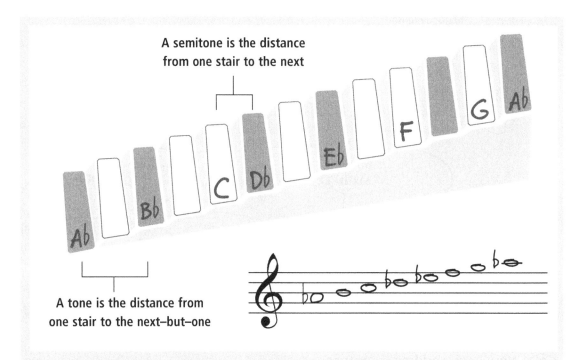

A semitone is the distance from one stair to the next

A tone is the distance from one stair to the next–but–one

How many sharps or flats are there in the key signature for A flat major and F minor?

_____ sharp(s)   4 flat(s)

Draw a treble or bass clef on this stave and then write the key signature for A flat major and F minor. (See page 26 or ask your choir trainer for help.)

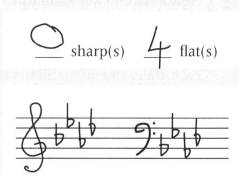

- *Page 25*   Write-in box: the relative minor key of B major is G sharp minor. Check answer, and sing both these scales.

- *Page 25*   Write-in boxes: check answers below and opposite, and sing all scales

 Name the five flats in the key signature above.

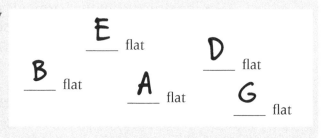

E _____ flat

B _____ flat

A _____ flat

D _____ flat

G _____ flat

Here is a key signature of three flats. What is the name of its major key?

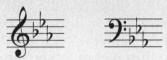

_____ **Eb** major

Write a clef on this staff and then write the key signature for B minor and D major.

Which two keys have a key signature of four sharps?

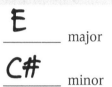

_____ **E** major

_____ **C#** minor

• *Page 26*   Check the write-in boxes. See below. Sing the scales.

On the staves below, write the key signature of each key using only the sharps and flats in the circles above. Remember to draw a clef before each key signature. As you use each sharp or flat, cross it out in the circle. The first one is done for you.

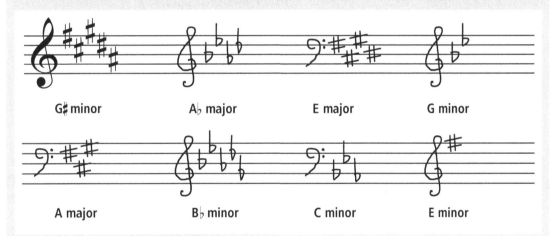

G♯ minor	A♭ major	E major	G minor
A major	B♭ minor	C minor	E minor

When you have finished, there will be some sharps and flats left over. Make them into key signatures by writing them on the staves on the right. (Draw a clef on each staff first.)

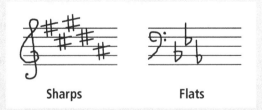

Sharps   Flats

Each of these two key signatures that you have written is for a major key and its relative minor key. Write the names of the keys in the box on the left.

Sharps

B major and **G#** minor

Flats

Eb major and **C** minor

On page 27 of the workbook, the material in the Dark Blue workbook about chords is developed to include arpeggios. This ties in with the requirement in the Red level targets that singers should sing a one-octave major or minor arpeggio. The following principal points are made about arpeggios:

- An arpeggio is formed when the notes of a chord are played one at a time

- A major arpeggio contains the first, third and fifth notes of a major scale (the same notes that form a major triad)

- A minor arpeggio contains the first, third and fifth notes of a minor scale (the same notes that form a minor triad)

- In an arpeggio, the notes are played one at a time, usually in order, either upwards or downwards (or both)

Tip: Make sure singers sing and hear a variety of arpeggios. Also ask them to identify them in printed music.

In the workbook

- *Page 27*   Check the write-in boxes (see below). Sing the arpeggios.

 Name the first, third and fifth notes in the scale of A major.

First: **A**

Third: **C#**

Fifth: **E**

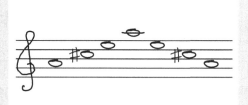

Put a clef on this staff, then write an arpeggio of A major, ascending. Start with the tonic, then write the third and fifth notes, then write the tonic an octave higher. One of the notes will need an accidental.

Put a clef on this staff, then write the key signature of A major. Then write the arpeggio, as you have done above. This time you will not need the accidental.

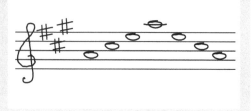

What singers say

'A while ago, when looking through a new score, I realized I knew in my head what the music would sound like before I actually sang it. I could imagine the sound it would make. I can't do that with everything yet, but of course the more I do it ...'

Phoebe, adult

At Red level singers need to remember all the signs and symbols they learned at earlier levels and also become familiar with the terms and instructions introduced on page 28 of the workbook. The growing list reflects the broadening range of repertoire that singers acquire as they progress through *Voice for Life*, and many of these terms appear in the sight-reading tests for the level. (The general points about teaching performance directions on pages 133–135 are equally pertinent here.)

 Tip: By now, these instructions extend beyond volume and tempo to sophisticated descriptors of mood and texture. Singers should not only know their literal meanings: they must also be able to make them part of their singing. For example, many singers (younger ones in particular) may be able to tell you the meaning of 'maestoso' but not be able to sing majestically. The following strategies can help:

- Talk around the term – for example discuss what 'majestic' means and what majestic singing might sound like (would it be loud? quiet? fast? slow? legato? staccato?)

- Play a recording of some music that uses the term in question: ask singers to identify which elements of the performance embody the term (what features of the singing or playing are 'maestoso'?)

- Can singers think of any other music which has the same mood?

- Ask singers to imagine what the mood feels like (can they walk it, gesture it, speak it?)

- Finally, go back to the piece in question and sing it again, bringing some of those details to the performance

 In the workbook

- *Page 29*   Check the write-in boxes. The correct answers are:
    - Getting faster – *accelerando* or *stringendo*
    - Go back to the original speed – *tempo primo*
    - Sing with expression – *espressivo*
    - Sweetly – *dolce*
    - Suddenly loud – *subito* (or *sub.*) *forte* or *subito* (or *sub.*) *f*
    - Very lively – *molto vivace*
    - Getting slower – *rit.* or *ritardando* or *allargando*
    - A little – *poco*
- *Page 29*   Check that singers can apply the terms in the panel at the foot of the page to scales, arpeggios or vocal exercises

What singers say
'It's simple. If the music is meant to be sad, you try to think sad. If it's meant to be happy, you try to think happy. Just thinking it seems to change the way you sing. I don't know how it works.'

Josh, 11

Yellow level

Singers will now engage easily with printed music and should have a firm grasp of the theoretical concepts covered so far. From this point, the theory in *Voice for Life* becomes more deductive and intuitive, introducing ideas that need both careful thought and practical experiment. Yellow level introduces a range of new concepts about keys, scales and modes; intervals and chords; cadences; pulse and rhythm; and notation. It also augments the list of performance instructions.

Tip: Once again, the learning of theory must be accompanied by the experience of more complex music. For example, singers should not just learn about modes: it is your responsibility to find examples of modal music for them to hear and sing if they have not already done so.

New keys and key signatures

Pages 19 and 20 of the workbook introduce the remaining major and minor keys (six sharps and flats). The circle of fifths – a way of visualizing the keys as they get sharper and flatter by degrees – is shown on page 52 of the workbook.

Tip: Before beginning this theory, it may be useful to check that singers can remember the names of the keys they learned at Red level.

In the workbook

- *Page 19*   Staircase puzzle – check the answer (see below) and sing the scale

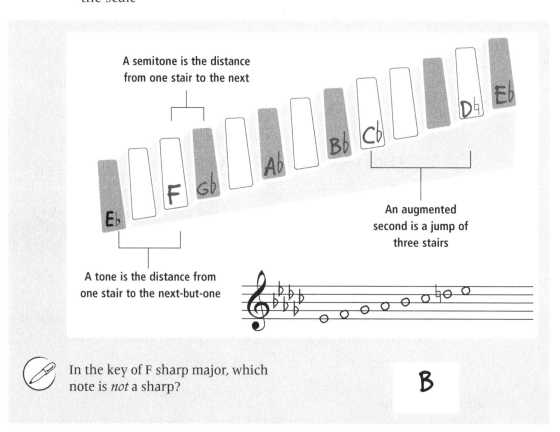

• *Page 20*   Check the write-in boxes (see below) and sing the scales

Name the six flats in the key signature of E flat minor.

What is the relative major of this key?

G flat major

B flat   **E** flat

A flat   **D** flat

G flat   **C** flat

What is the key signature of B minor?

2 sharp(s) **0** flat(s)

Can you link these keys in order according to how many sharps their key signatures have?

Circle the key with the most sharps. What is its relative minor?

C sharp minor

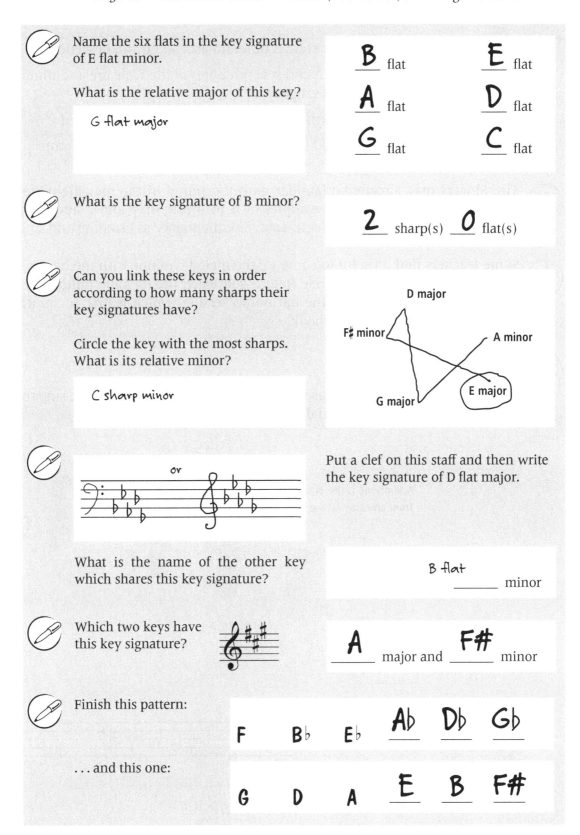

D major

F# minor   A minor

G major   E major

or

Put a clef on this staff and then write the key signature of D flat major.

What is the name of the other key which shares this key signature?

B flat

_____ minor

Which two keys have this key signature?

A _____ major and **F#** _____ minor

Finish this pattern:

F   Bb   Eb   **Ab Db Gb**

...and this one:

G   D   A   **E B F#**

Tip: The activities above require both a level of basic knowledge and an ability to use knowledge of the rules of theory to arrive at the correct answers. When assessing singers for the targets in this section, every so often it can be helpful to ask how they arrived at a particular answer.

Pages 21 and 22 of the workbook introduce the melodic minor scale, making the following principal points:

- The melodic minor scale is different ascending and descending
- Ascending, the sixth and seventh notes of the scale are a semitone sharper than the key signature
- Descending, the sixth and seventh notes are not sharpened
- Accidentals are used to modify notes outside the key signature

 Tip: Singers may already be familiar with the sound of the melodic minor scale. Encourage them to think of examples of it in music they know, and to spot the modified notes in scores. And, as always, link the theory to listening and singing.

 Some teachers find it useful to compare the melodic minor with the harmonic, but this can confuse students at first. Before you teach the melodic minor, check that your singers are secure with the harmonic version, which is first encountered on page 20 of the Dark Blue workbook.

 In the workbook

- *Page 21, 22*   Staircase puzzles – check the answers below; sing the scale ascending and descending

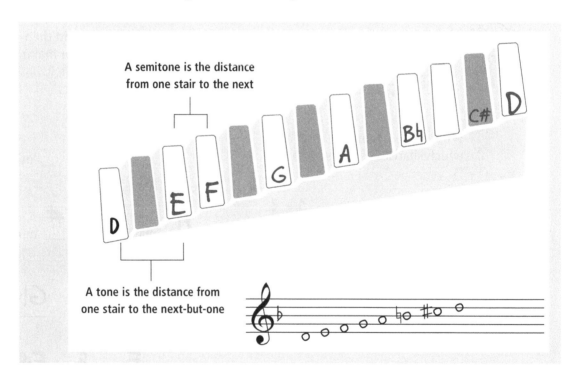

What singers say

'Some people think singing scales is boring when we do it in choir. But learning about different scales isn't boring because they're like the basis of all music. Knowing scales makes singing all music easier.'

Will, 15

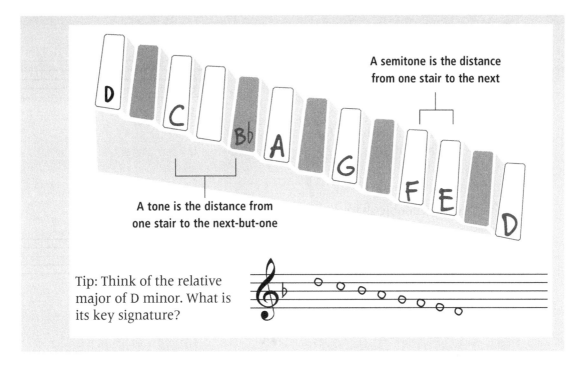

A semitone is the distance from one stair to the next

A tone is the distance from one stair to the next-but-one

Tip: Think of the relative major of D minor. What is its key signature?

- *Page 22* Check the write-in boxes and sing the scales: answers as follows:

  - In an ascending scale of E melodic minor, the seventh note is D sharp; the interval between this note and the one above is a semitone

  - The note below E in a descending scale of E melodic minor is D natural; the interval between this note and the one above is a tone

  - The note in A major but not A melodic minor is C sharp

  - This is the 3rd note of the scale

 ### Double sharps and flats

Pages 23 and 24 of the workbook introduce double sharps and double flats (accidentals that modify the basic note by two semitones), making the following points:

- Double sharps and flats are normally used in music that is already in very sharp or flat keys to further sharpen or flatten notes

- Though a double sharp is the same *pitch* as the note a tone above it, the double accidental is used because of the way scales and chords are 'spelled'

 Tip: You may wish to further explore this by revisiting the point that scales are normally spelled using the letters A to G in sequence – and that sometimes (particularly in the minor versions of very sharp or flat keys) the double accidentals are needed to maintain this sequence of letter names.

 ### In the workbook

- *Page 23, 24* Write-in boxes: check answers (shown overleaf)

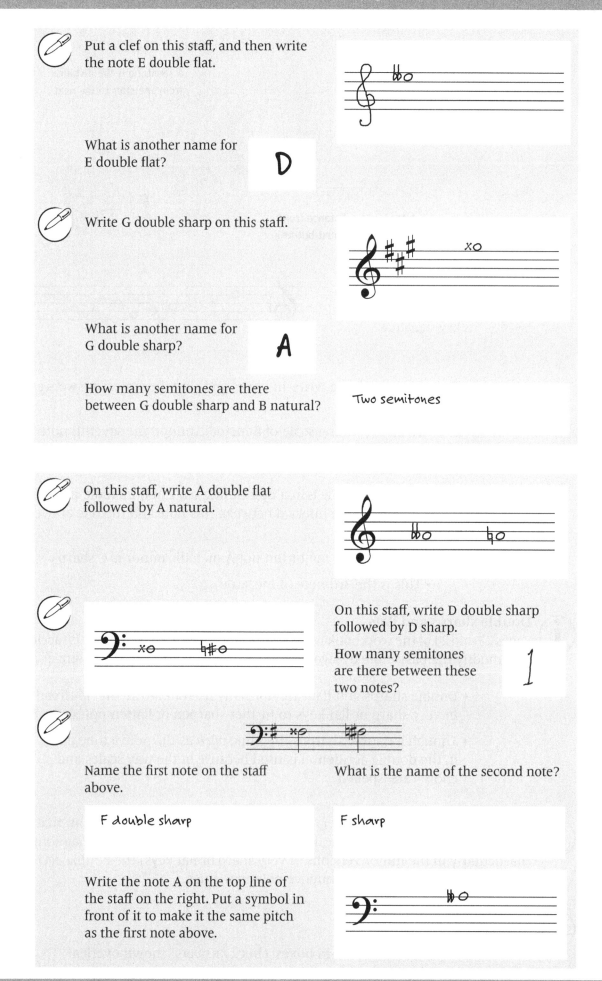

Put a clef on this staff, and then write the note E double flat.

What is another name for E double flat?

D

Write G double sharp on this staff.

What is another name for G double sharp?

A

How many semitones are there between G double sharp and B natural?

Two semitones

On this staff, write A double flat followed by A natural.

On this staff, write D double sharp followed by D sharp.

How many semitones are there between these two notes?

1

Name the first note on the staff above.

F double sharp

What is the name of the second note?

F sharp

Write the note A on the top line of the staff on the right. Put a symbol in front of it to make it the same pitch as the first note above.

Pages 25 and 26 of the workbook explore augmented and diminished intervals:

- Augmented means 'made bigger' – an augmented interval is one to which an extra semitone has been added (for example, if you add a semitone to a perfect fourth, you get an augmented fourth; singers encountered the augmented second at Dark Blue as part of the harmonic minor scale – see page 127)

- Diminished means 'made smaller' – a diminished interval is one from which a semitone has been taken away (for example, if you reduce a perfect fourth by a semitone, you get a diminished fourth)

- An augmented fourth sounds the same as a diminished fifth – its size is between a perfect fourth and perfect fifth. It is also known as a tritone.

- These intervals are written and described in different ways according to the harmonic 'spelling' of the music

 Tip: It is particularly necessary with these more complex intervals that singers learn how they feel in the voice. Sing them frequently, in contrast with perfect intervals. Can singers sing, from the same base note, a perfect fourth followed by an augmented fourth followed by a perfect fifth, and back again? Can they identify these intervals in music they hear and read?

 In the workbook

- *Page 25*   Write-in box – check the answers below and sing the intervals

 Link these intervals in order of size. Start with *either* the largest *or* the smallest.

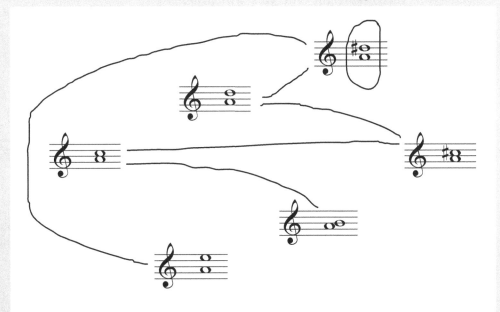

One of these intervals is an augmented fourth. Draw a circle around this interval.

Yellow level: New intervals

• *Page 26*   Write-in boxes – check the answers; sing the intervals

On this staff, write a note which is a minor second above the one shown.

How many semitones are there between these notes?   *1*

On this staff, write the note a diminished fifth above the one shown.

How many semitones are there between these notes?   *6*

Link the six intervals below in order of size. Start with the largest *or* the smallest.

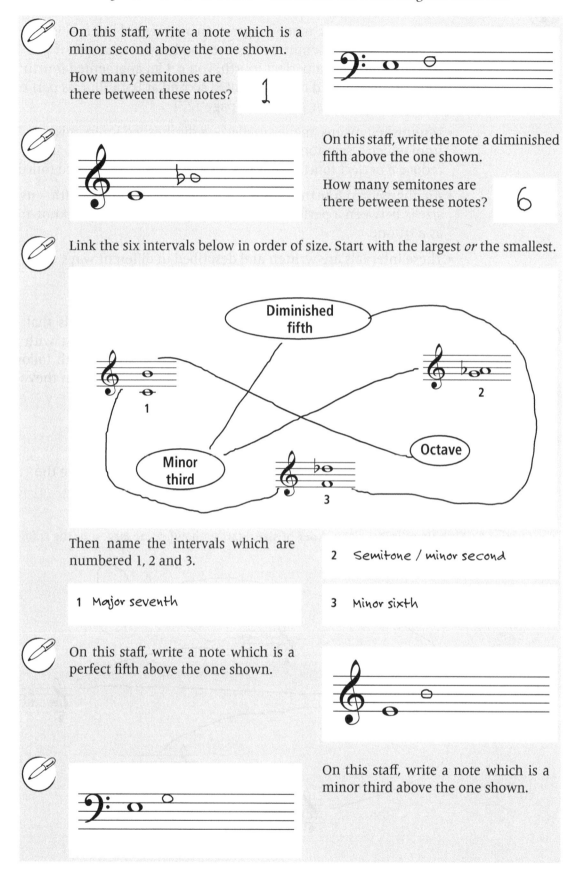

Then name the intervals which are numbered 1, 2 and 3.

1   *Major seventh*

2   *Semitone / minor second*

3   *Minor sixth*

On this staff, write a note which is a perfect fifth above the one shown.

On this staff, write a note which is a minor third above the one shown.

 Tip: Encourage singers to identify intervals you play to them and write them down. This ties in with the practical musicianship targets for this level.

Triads were introduced at Dark Blue, but now singers must understand the structural relationships between different triads. Pages 27 and 28 of the Yellow workbook look in more depth at types of chord and their construction and relationships:

- The note on which a triad is based is called its **root**

- The other two notes in a major triad are a major third and a perfect fifth above the root (the **third** and **fifth** of the triad)

- The other two notes in a minor triad are a minor third and a perfect fifth above the root (the **third** and **fifth** of the triad)

- A triad based on the tonic (key) note of a scale is a **tonic triad**

- The fifth note of a scale is called the **dominant**, and a triad based on this note is a **dominant triad**

- The fourth note of a scale is called the **subdominant**, and a triad based on this note is called a **subdominant triad**

- The name of a note or chord depends on the scale and key. In G major, D is the dominant. But in A major, it is the subdominant.

- The tonic, dominant and subdominant are the **primary chords** of a key. All the others are called **secondary chords** (these are named on page 52 of the workbook).

 Tip: Encourage singers to hear and identify primary chords in context. The exercise in the workbook to find them in a range of songs is very useful – don't neglect it. Many singers may already be familiar with the notion of primary chords by another name. The notion that you can accompany songs using only chords I, IV and V is so common among guitarists that it is known as the 'three chord trick'.

 There are so many songs using only the primary chords that it is difficult to know where to start listing them. A few examples are given below. The important thing to point out is that it is possible to harmonize all of them with only the tonic, dominant and subdominant, even though singers may know them in more sophisticated versions which use a wider range of chords. Wherever possible, demonstrate this to singers on the keyboard or guitar – or ask them to do so.

- Nursery rhymes: *Twinkle, twinkle, little star*; *Lavender's Blue*
- Christmas carols: *Silent Night*; *Good King Wenceslas*
- Religious songs: *Kum ba yah*; *Simple Gifts*; *Swing Low, Sweet Chariot*
- National anthems: *God save the Queen*; *The Marseillaise*
- Traditional songs: *Streets of Laredo*; *Auld lang syne*
- From classical music: *Lullaby* (Brahms); *Bridal Chorus* (Wagner)

Remember to identify primary-chord music in your choir's repertoire too.

 Tip: During this exercise, you may also like to point out to singers the gravitational pull from dominant to tonic. This will be necessary for the practical musicianship targets and also for an understanding of cadences (see page 156).

In the workbook

- *Page 27* Make sure singers have identified some well-known songs or tunes which use only primary chords in their harmony. If possible, check this with singers by adding – or better, asking them to add – the chords to the tunes they have chosen.

- *Page 28* Check the write-in boxes – in the key of E major, B is the dominant note, and A is the subdominant; see below for answers to the remaining questions

 On the staff on the right, write the tonic triad in the key of F major.

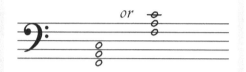

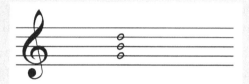

On the staff on the left, write the dominant triad in the key of C major.

 Look at the chord on the right, and answer the questions below to describe it in different keys:

In the key of A minor, what is the name of this chord?

The tonic

What is the name of this chord in C major? (Use a Roman numeral.)

Chord VI

What is the name of this chord in E minor? (Use both a Roman numeral and a chord name.)

Chord IV (subdominant)

 Page 29 looks at ways the different notes of a triad can be arranged or **voiced:**

- A chord with the root at the bottom is in **root position**
- A chord with the third at the bottom is in **first inversion**
- A chord with the fifth at the bottom is in **second inversion**
- The notes can be arranged in many different ways; this is called **voicing**. A chord where the notes are as close together as possible is in **close** or **closed position**; a chord where the notes are spaced out over more than one octave is in **open position**.

Tip: Make sure singers hear these types of chord in context, and can identify them in real music. In the practical musicianship tests, singers will need to be able to recognise them both by sound and by sight. Be patient – this can take some time. (For guidance about identifying the sounds of inverted chords, see *The Voice for Life Guide to Musicianship*.)

 In the workbook

> • *Page 29*   Write-in boxes – check the answers below and sing the individual notes of each chord

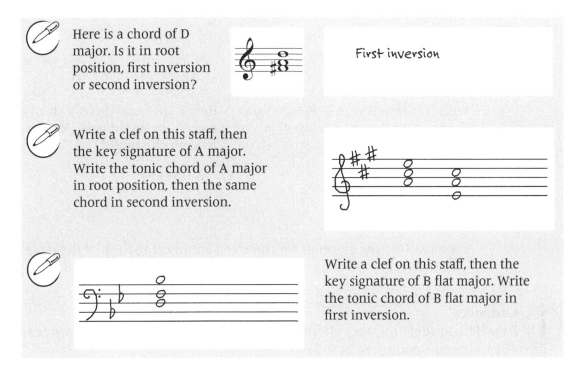

Here is a chord of D major. Is it in root position, first inversion or second inversion?

First inversion

Write a clef on this staff, then the key signature of A major. Write the tonic chord of A major in root position, then the same chord in second inversion.

Write a clef on this staff, then the key signature of B flat major. Write the tonic chord of B flat major in first inversion.

 Page 30 considers more complex chords in which extra notes are added to triads. Explore these with singers, pointing out that:

> • the added note is named after the interval it makes with the root of the chord
>
> • the chord is named after the triad and extra note
>
> • all types of chords can be shown by symbols in written music

 Tip: By this stage, singers should be familiar with the sound of more complex chords from the music they sing – but they may not be able to identify them by name when they hear or read them. From time to time, pick out a chord in a score and encourage singers to analyze it on the spot. Can they:

> • name it, and name and sing the notes it contains?
>
> • identify the inversion and voicing?
>
> • describe it in context of the key of the piece?

It may take time for singers to become accustomed to this, but it is worth persisting.

In the workbook

- *Page 30* Write-in boxes – check the answers below and sing the individual notes of each chord

This is the dominant chord in the key of D major. Add a seventh to the chord to make it a dominant seventh.

What is the name of this chord? (Name its root, and then decide whether the chord is major or minor.)

E minor

Here is the same chord with an added note. Is the added note a sixth, a seventh or a ninth?

A seventh

- *Page 30* The symbols for the three chords at the top of the page are: G7; C6; C9

Cadences

Page 31 considers the way chords are combined at phrase ends to form **cadences**. The important points are as follows:

- A cadence is a group of chords played one after another, like musical punctuation at the end of a phrase, section or piece

- There are four main types of cadence: **perfect** (V–I); **imperfect** (I–V or IV–V); **plagal** (IV–I) and **interrupted** (V–VI)

Tip: Singers need to hear cadences in the context of real music. If cadences are to be correctly identified (as they must for the musicianship targets), there is no substitute for regular hearing, reading, singing and playing of the various chord groups at cadential points. There is more about the aural identification of cadences on page 155 of *The Voice for Life Guide to Musicianship.*

It may be unwise to begin work on cadences before singers are comfortable with the material on pages 27 and 28 about chords and their relationships. Wait until they easily identify the tonic, subdominant, dominant and submediant.

In the workbook

- *Page 31* Write-in box – the cadences are: imperfect (IV–V in B flat major); plagal (IV–I in A major); and imperfect (IV–V in F major)

New time signatures

Page 32 looks at some new time signatures, specifically 5/4, 5/8, 7/4 and 7/8. Yellow-level singers should take these in their stride. The notational features are unchanged: the upper figure shows the number of beats in each bar; the lower figure, the type of beat. The difference here is that the beat groupings are uneven, but if singers are familiar with a range of contemporary music this is unlikely to cause problems

Tip: The challenge with time signatures like this is more aural than theoretical. As they are a feature of the aural tests at Yellow level, you will find help on page 160 of *The Voice for Life Guide to Musicianship*. In addition, follow the clapping and singing activities in the workbook. Singers need to hear real music in these time signatures and read, clap and identify the beat groupings.

In the workbook

- *Page 32*   In 7/4, groups of two and three beats can be combined in three ways: **2+2+3**; **2+3+2**; **3+2+2**; clap and count these groupings

Modes

Choral singers usually encounter modes in church music written before 1750, and also in jazz, rock and traditional music. While not specifically featured in the Yellow aural tests, modes may occur in the sight-reading and singers may need to understand them when discussing repertoire for Module C. Make sure singers' scale theory is secure before you begin modes. Page 33 of the workbook makes the following points:

- Some music is not in a major or minor key, but based on special scales called modes

- Like major and minor scales, modes form patterns of tones and semitones – but each mode has its own distinctive pattern

Tip: See page 33 of the workbook for examples of the five most common modes. Help singers to sing and play these, and also to recognize modality in the choir's repertoire or other music you play to them. (It will certainly be useful if they can spot modality when they hear it, even though they do not need to name the specific mode.)

In the workbook

- *Page 33*   Check the write-in box and sing the modes.

In the treble clef, write one octave of a Dorian mode, starting on C. You will need some accidentals.

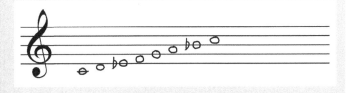

In the bass clef, write one octave of a Phrygian mode, starting on A. You will need some accidentals.

At Yellow level, singers need to remember all the signs and symbols they learned at earlier levels and also become familiar with the terms and instructions introduced on pages 34 and 35 of the workbook. At this level, singers will encounter a wide range of terms and should be able to react to them accurately when they see them in music. (The general points about teaching performance directions on pages 133–138 are equally pertinent here.)

 Tip: The performance directions at this level require a considerable grasp of stylistic and interpretative nuance. There are a few ways to help singers with this (and also to assess their abilities in this respect):

- Play recordings or perform music singers do not know, and ask them to suggest appropriate performance directions for it

- Ask singers to change the performance directions in pieces they already know and see if they can sing familiar music differently (this can have some memorable consequences, and also enhances interpretative and critical skills)

- Ask them to apply terms one by one to scales, arpeggios and vocal exercises. If one singer does this, can others guess what the chosen direction is?

Note that with these activities there is often no one correct answer – you may get many suitable responses, all of which are suitable for discussion. Doing this will help your singers to develop a sense of musical style.

 In the workbook

 Find the composer
Write the Italian words for the terms given below into the boxes. If you get them right, the letters in the shaded boxes will spell the name of a choral composer.

1) Silent, don't sing		T	A	C	E	T	
2) Slow and solemn	G	R	A	V	E		
3) Voice		V	O	C	E		
4) Heavily	P	E	S	A	N	T	E
5) Sadly		T	R	I	S	T	E
6) Nothing, no sound		N	I	E	N	T	E
7) Without		S	E	N	Z	A	
8) Furiously	F	U	R	I	O	S	O

- *Page 35* Check that singers can apply the terms in the panel at the foot of the page to scales, arpeggios or vocal exercises

What singers say

'Once, we were doing a hymn ... and ... it was supposed to be happy. But our conductor said it didn't sound happy enough. So he asked us to sing it sadly. It was really strange. It was hard to sing a happy song sadly, but when we went back to happy again, it ... sounded much happier. [Laughs.] No, it really did.'

James, 13

MODULE C

Repertoire

CONTENTS

Module C: Repertoire

This module aims to develop understanding of the musical and historical contexts of music performed by the choir or individual singers. It draws on the theoretical understanding gained in Module B, and develops singers' ability to gather information about pieces from various sources and to present this in an original form, acknowledging those sources where necessary.

How Module C is delivered

In the workbooks, this module is often referred to as 'Understanding the music we sing'. It is delivered via a number of worksheets and projects about the choir's repertoire. In order to complete a level in Module C, singers have to finish the worksheets and projects specified in the targets (shown opposite and at the back of the workbooks).

Sometimes singers are required to complete a section of the workbook just once; in other instances, tasks need to be repeated several times, each for a different piece of music. For this purpose, photocopiable worksheets are provided in the workbooks (and at the back of this book), though you may choose to request responses in a different format. Some projects have additional tasks for preparation and follow-up; you may want to vary these according to the culture and context of your choir, and the age and understanding of the singers.

To complete a project, singers must research it and present their responses either in the workbook itself, on a photocopied worksheet or on a separate sheet of paper; you should use these responses as the basis for assessment and further discussion before signing the relevant target box. If you have assigned extra tasks or requested follow-up, make sure you check these too.

Tip: Remember that it is not necessary to do all the tasks at once – they should form the basis of teaching, discussion and activities that unfold over time while singers are working on any given level. The more singers do of this work, the more they will acquire an overview of music history and the application of theory – which is a principal aim of this module. There is no time limit for these activities: allow participants as long as they need to develop the necessary skills and perspectives.

The more singers understand about the history and context of what they sing, the better able they are to make informed decisions about *how* to perform music of different periods and styles – these are key skills for any musician.

How to use this part of the book

After the targets, you will find some general thoughts about delivering Module C (pages 165–170), followed by some practical advice about assessing your singers' responses (page 170). Information about the individual tasks and projects, level by level, begins on page 171.

What singers say

'I thought I'd find Module C boring as I'm not really interested in history and all stuff like that. But it's funny how when you find out a bit about a piece, it kind-of affects the way you sing it. If you understand why it was written, and who wrote it, it's good.'

Jake, 16

White level

To complete Module C, singers are required to:

- fill in the sheet on page 31 of the workbook for at least *three* pieces of music

 Light Blue level

To complete Module C, singers are required to:

- complete the section on repertoire on pages 35–37 of the workbook
- show that they know how to take a piece of music and:
    - find out who composed the piece and when
    - read aloud the text of a piece (in English only)
    - make simple observations about the meaning of the text and mood of the piece

 Dark Blue level

To complete Module C, singers are required to:

- complete the section on repertoire on pages 30–32 of the workbook
- show that they know how to take a piece of music and:
    - find basic biographical information about the composer (e.g. date of birth, death, home country)
    - name any famous works by the same composers or name another composer active and living at the same time
    - briefly explain the meaning of the text (finding a translation of foreign texts where necessary)
    - undertake some simple music analysis (for example, major/ minor, the key/time signatures, the number of vocal parts)
    - describe the context in which the piece would normally be sung (for example, in a church service during a particular season, or in a concert)

Module C: Targets

Red level

To complete Module C, singers are required to:

- complete the section on repertoire on pages 30–32 of the workbook
- show that they know how to take a piece of music and:
  - find out who wrote the music and when (e.g. which period or century)
  - find the source of the text (e.g. the Bible, a poem, a prayer)
  - discuss in simple terms the relationship between the music, the text and the mood using some basic music analysis (learned from Module B)
  - find some simple information about the life of the composer (e.g. family, job)
  - find out whether the piece was originally composed for a particular event, or commissioned and/or written with a certain individual or group in mind
  - turn this information into programme notes

Yellow level

To complete Module C, singers are required to:

- complete the section on repertoire on pages 36–38 of the workbook
- show that they know how to take a piece of music and:
  - discuss the themes of the text and what it communicates
  - describe how the composer has set the words (for example, syllabic, melismatic, repetition, word-painting)
  - discuss the composer's use of different colours and textures and how this reflects the text and affects the mood of the music
  - look at the events of the composer's life, their historical/political background, and discuss any connections with his/her musical output
  - discuss the characteristics of the musical period in which the composer lived
  - name other pieces in the same genre and compare/contrast them
  - discuss any performing conventions that would have affected the piece and compare this with how it is performed today

Musical skills and understanding should grow together; as the voice develops, singers also need to understand what they are singing and why. Throughout *Voice for Life* singers are encouraged to expand their range of repertoire and gather the skills necessary to do the following for everything they sing:

- understand the text

- understand the music

- understand the purpose of a piece

- understand the historical background of a piece

- understand the style or genre of a piece

- understand how to research and present information about music

For each of these six points, you will find overleaf some key training ideas and useful sample questions to stimulate discussion and research. Note that the questions are for guidance only, as not all of them will be relevant for every item of repertoire. You may need to adapt them to the pieces that your singers are studying. The workbooks also contain further questions for your singers to think about.

 Tip: The sample questions overleaf are also very useful when preparing singers for the RSCM Bronze, Silver and Gold awards (see page 9).

 As a choir trainer, it is important to think about all the points above from the outset. In Module C, while the tasks and expectations of singers change from level to level, the issues about repertoire change very little. Hence many of the questions overleaf are relevant in some way to all singers; it is just that the more complex ones are more appropriate for more advanced students. (Within each point, the questions get progressively more difficult too, so the later ones are more suitable for higher levels.)

This means that you must frame the questions appropriately for singers at different levels. The tasks in the workbooks reflect the growing competence expected as the scheme progresses but you may find that you need to explain or adapt them to make them appropriate for your own singers or for a particular piece. Sometimes, to check the validity of singers' responses, you may want to rephrase questions or ask for answers in a different format.

 Remember too that:

- some young singers may lack the vocabulary to express their feelings about music (discussions will help this)

- some young singers may struggle with complicated research tasks (make sure everything is well explained in advance)

- some singers may question the relevance of these tasks to 'singing' (if you encounter this, try some of the arguments on page 162)

- some older singers at lower levels may feel they are too advanced for the lower-level tasks (encourage free expression and, if appropriate, make the tasks more complex)

Understanding the text

If singers are to communicate a text successfully to an audience, they need to be aware of its meaning and significance. They must understand:

- basic vocabulary (what the words mean: this includes an ability to source translations of foreign texts if necessary)

- literary, religious or social context and message (when the text was written, by whom, and for what purpose)

- the emotional weight and content (what it is trying to express)

Tip: Further details about the text may also be useful, such as: the biography of the author; whether it is part of a larger work; other works by the same author; whether the same text has also been set by other composers; and whether the original text has been edited or changed in any way to make it suitable for musical use.

Useful questions about the text

- Who wrote it?

- When and where was the author born? Where did he or she live? And when did he or she die?

- What is the source of the text? Is it part of a larger work?

- Why was the text written?

- If the text is in a foreign language, which? What does it mean in English?

- What are the themes and moods of the text? What is it trying to communicate?

Understanding the music

Text is set to music for a reason: otherwise performers could simply read the words to the audience. In order to work with repertoire, singers need to consider how music and text interact. It is important for them to understand:

- how setting a text to music can intensify its expressive power

- how different settings of the same text can express different things

- how music can highlight or add intricacies that the text did not appear to contain at first sight

- how music can change the meaning of a text altogether

To describe music and the way it fits the text, singers need the theoretical knowledge gained in Module B. The questions below encourage singers to look in detail at the score and talk about the notes. Again, you need to think about what it is appropriate to ask at each level, based on the contents of Module B.

Tip: Don't forget that listening to the music is fundamental here. Singers should react to what a piece sounds like (either from singing or recordings) as well as the score.

Useful questions about the music

- What is the key of the piece? Is it major or minor?
- What is the time signature of the piece, and the tempo?
- How many parts are there, and is there an accompaniment?
- How do the parts fit together? Are they all equally important?
- Where is the melody? Is it always sung by the same part?
- Are any melodic motifs repeated? Where and how?
- How do the music and text fit together? Do they work together to create one particular mood?
- How is the text set to music? Is the setting syllabic (one note per syllable) or melismatic (several notes per syllable)? Has the composer used word-painting (musical descriptions of the text)?
- What is the form of the piece?
- Can you think of any other settings of the same text? How do they compare or contrast with this one?

Understanding the purpose of a piece

Music is often created for specific occasions or seasons. It is useful to understand this when choosing repertoire, as not all music is appropriate in all contexts at all times. For example, although the Latin text 'Pie Jesu' is from the Requiem Mass and thus originally associated with services for the dead, many people choose musical settings of it for weddings. It can be interesting to compare the original function of the piece with its modern use. When selecting repertoire, singers need to know:

- the original religious or social purpose of a text or piece
- if it was written with a particular person, group or event in mind
- if changing its context and use is appropriate

Useful questions about the purpose of a piece

- Was the piece written for a particular event, occasion or season? What?
- What other music does your choir sing for the same event, occasion or season?
- Was the piece commissioned by a particular person? Who and why?
- Was it written for a particular performer (or group of performers)? Has this affected the music in any way (for example the style, level of difficulty, number of parts and so on)?
- In what context would the piece normally be performed now? Is this context the same as the composer's original purpose for the piece? Is this context the same as the way you will be performing the piece? If not, in what way is it different?

Understanding the historical background of a piece
The social, political and historical context of a composition often sheds more light on it for singers. While it is possible to perform a piece in isolation from its past, knowing its background can add extra dimensions, making for a more rounded interpretation. Singers should be aware of:

- biographical details of the composer and creator of the text

- specific events relevant to the creation of the music and text

- the historical, political and cultural contexts of a work's creation

For example, a composer's choice of a love poem as a text might reflect romantic events in his or her own life; Britten's *War Requiem* was a personal reaction to the horrors of World War II; and many composers, including Palestrina, Mozart and Shostakovich, altered their writing styles to suit religious and political circumstances.

Tip: An ability to draw parallels between composers' biographies and their music, and to understand why pieces exist in their present form, adds depth to performance. This sort of research can also capture your singers' imagination, leading to greater engagement with and enjoyment of the music.

Useful questions about the historical background of a piece

- Who wrote the music?

- When and where was the composer born? Where did he or she live? When did he or she die?

- How was the composer employed?

- What do we know about the composer's family life?

- Were there any major events that took place in the composer's life that may have affected their music (such as the death of someone close to them, an illness, political change, war)?

Understanding the style or genre of a piece
To perform a piece appropriately, singers need to know about stylistic conventions and interpretation. For instance, to be historically accurate a baroque piece may require the rhythmic notation or dynamics to be rendered in a certain way (which may not be evident in the score). An important part of musicianship is the ability to understand these stylistic customs and nuances as they change through history, and whether or not to adhere to them, and why.

Useful questions about style and genre

- What musical period was the composer writing in?

- What are the musical characteristics of this period?

- Are there any aspects of the composer's style that are typical? If so, can you name another piece that contains these characteristics?

- Can you name some other pieces written by the same composer?

- Can you name other composers writing around the same time?

- Can you name any of their works? Can you think of any that are similar in style or were written for the same occasion or purpose?

- What would the performing conventions of the day have been? Are these conventions still followed today?

- Will you be following the original performing conventions in your own performance? Can you explain your reasons?

 Developing research and presentation skills
The research and writing skills required in this module of *Voice for Life* have many benefits for singers. The ability to identify and consult reliable sources of information, and to turn found facts into relevant, original text is an invaluable skill. Music is not just about performing: it is about understanding and explaining too. Musicians should be able to write concise, interesting programme notes for their concerts.

Moreover any singer wishing to study music at school or in higher education will need to undertake research and presentation projects. Explain to your singers that these skills are fully transferable: the ability to process the opinions of others and then formulate one's own ideas is a vital part of study, employment and general life.

 Finding the information
There are many sources of information that that singers can use when researching their music. Encourage them to consult as many sources as possible, and point out that it is inadvisable to rely on one source alone. Explain that the wider the range of sources, the better the overview and more reliable the conclusions. (This also helps counter the temptation to copy large amounts of text from one source.)

Encourage your singers to use the self-completion sheets in the workbooks to help them collect information about their chosen piece. (These photocopiable sheets can also be found at the end of this book.) At the higher levels, once they have collected all the relevant information, they can then focus on putting this together into an interesting and informative programme note.

Useful sources of information

- Books – there is a list of useful reading at **www.rscm.com/vfl**

- Notes to recordings (CD booklets, or information accompanying downloads)

- Introductions to scores

- Programme notes written by other performers

- Magazines, newspapers and periodicals

- The Internet

- The choir trainer (you should always try to introduce basic facts about each new piece of repertoire)

- Other choir members (encourage singers to ask each other about the music they sing)

Expressing the information

Having collected their information using the worksheets, singers must present it in their own words. Answers may be hand-written or on computer. Some singers may choose to write in their workbooks, while others may prefer to present their answers on a separate sheet. Some may want to present their answers as a list of bullet points, while others may write more extended prose.

Tip: Information found in research projects can be expressed in many different forms. For example, some choir trainers ask singers to give informal presentations of their findings to the choir. Group discussions about repertoire can be a useful way to encourage singers to share their thoughts about what they sing. Bear these activities in mind as a way of varying singers' approach to their projects.

Assessing your singers' work for the targets

There are no standard 'right' answers for Module C. The essential requirement is that singers engage fully with the specified tasks, to the best of their ability, according to their age and level. Obviously you will expect different things of different singers, but certain principles are standard. When assessing research and presentation, consider:

- The accuracy of the information supplied
- The amount of information (the higher the level, the more detail you should expect)
- The variety of information
- Accuracy of presentation (key names, dates and words should be correct and consistently expressed)
- Logic of presentation: unless there are good reasons otherwise, the information should proceed from the most general (about the composer's life, for example) to the most specific (about the piece in general, then compositional details)
- Readability – can you understand everything?
- Physical presentation (neatness and clarity are not everything, but they do indicate whether singers have taken the task seriously)
- Evidence of original thought (and keep an eye open for material that looks familiar – discourage singers from 'borrowing')

Sample questions and answers

On the following pages you will find examples of questions set by choir trainers for these projects, based on the workbooks, together with responses quoted verbatim from answers given by singers of differing ages and abilities. The children and adults have approached this task in different ways, and each singer has their own individual writing style. Note that despite the differences in grammar, style, presentation and the occasional spelling mistake, they have all answered the questions given.

A note about other languages

In many choirs, repertoire requires even junior members to sing in other languages. For all such pieces you should know and demonstrate correct pronunciation, explain clearly the meaning of the text, and point out any important words or phrases.

White level

People who know about music take for granted a number of 'obvious' facts that may not be obvious to young singers. The most important of these is that pieces of music don't simply 'exist' or come into being unbidden. Nearly everything the choir sings was created by a composer or arranger and, if there is text, by an author too. (Explain terms like 'anonymous' or 'traditional' if your repertoire makes this necessary.)

At White level singers are required to work in English only, not other languages. They are encouraged to:

- Read aloud the words of each piece they sing

- Think about the mood of the words and music

- Make a note of any words they don't understand

- Learn some of the words from memory

Try to make this a habit with each new piece of repertoire, so that singers become accustomed to these basic methods of familiarization. Photocopy the worksheet on page 31 of the workbook (and page 223 of this book) as often as necessary.

In the White level workbook

To achieve the target, singers should complete the worksheet for at least *three* pieces. When assessing the work, look for evidence of some thought and research. You may well have provided much of the necessary information informally when introducing a new piece, but make sure it is accurately expressed on the worksheet. The handwritten notes below suggest things to look out for. Don't forget to talk to your singers about their responses, however briefly, before you sign the target box.

Write the name of the piece here ...

Make sure spelling and capitalization are copied accurately from the score. Look out for spelling mistakes.

... and the name of the composer or arranger here.

Make sure spelling and capitalization are copied accurately from the score. Look out for spelling mistakes.

Tick when you:
have read the words
from start to finish ☐

can say some of the
words from memory ☐

What is the mood of the piece?
Look for a variety of descriptive terms here. Discuss if necessary.

Is it for a particular event or festival?
Discuss if necessary. Young singers may need help with this.

Make a note of any words you don't understand.

Young singers in particular may struggle with vocabulary, and with old or unfamiliar versions of modern words. Make sure you are able to explain carefully anything that singers do not understand.

Light Blue level

The basic skills acquired at White level are developed quite substantially at Light Blue. Singers must be able to:

- identify the composer, arranger and author of a piece and provide details of when they lived

- understand and pronounce all the words (in English only)

- describe the mood of the text and music

- explain how they found the information

In the Light Blue level workbook

For the target, singers must complete pages 35 and 36 of the workbook and be able to fill in a copy the worksheet on page 37 (and page 224 of this book) for any piece you request. A good way to train singers for this research task is to have them do it for each new piece you begin with the choir, and for any other pieces you find appropriate.

- *Page 35, panel 1*
  Lavender's Blue
  Do we know who composed this piece? No, the piece is traditional.
  Has the piece been arranged by anyone? Yes, by Dave E. Burnsell.
  (Sharp-eyed singers will note that 'Dave E. Burnsell' is an anagram of 'Lavender's Blue'.)

- *Page 35, panel 2*
  Ave verum corpus
  Who is the composer of the music? W. A. Mozart
  Has the piece been arranged by anyone? Not as far as we can tell

- *Page 36*
  Who is the composer of the music? Robert Lowry
  Has the piece been arranged by anyone? Yes, Geoff Weaver
  Who wrote the words? Robert Lowry

- *Page 37*
  Singers should complete the worksheet for a few pieces of music, one of which should then be assessed and discussed for the target. (See the sample answers below.)

Sample answers for page 37

Singers were given a copy of the hymn 'Rejoice, the Lord is King' with music by Handel. They were asked the following questions, based on the worksheet:

- Who wrote the music?

- What musical period/century was the composer writing in?

- Explain in your own words what you think the words are about.

- What do you think is the mood of the piece?

The singers' answers are concise and, in the main, correct; some are more developed than others. Note the range of words used to describe the mood: 'springy' may not be standard music-criticism vocabulary, but it communicates Michelle's thoughts well. In a sense, her response is more informative than the others because it comments on *how* the music creates a joyful mood – 'fast notes and quavers'.

Chris's comments are brief, but they do answer the questions adequately. In Laurie's responses, one might be tempted to ask where in the text one would find evidence for some of the religious sentiments expressed; for all that these might be valid statements of belief, they are somewhat superfluous to the question.

You might also note the various ways singers have written Handel's name. While none of these is actually wrong, there are certain standard formats that might be pointed out in the interests of promoting consistency and historical accuracy.

Michelle, 10

Rejoice the Lord is King

Georg Friedrich Handel wrote the music. He was writing at the beginning of the 18th century.

I think the words are a hymn to praise God and tells people to rejoice that the Lord is king and that Jesus sits at the right hand of God.

It is a very joyful, springy piece as it has a lot of fast notes and quavers.

Chris, 12

Rejoice the Lord is King

The music was by G F Handel.

He wrote this in the Baroque period.

The words mean that they are rejoicing the Lord and whilst being so happy.

I think the piece is in a triumphant mood.

Laurie, adult

Rejoice the Lord is King

The music for 'Rejoice the Lord is King' was written by G. F. Händel during the musical period of Baroque.

The piece is like an invitation to celebrate and give thanks by means of meditation and song. It invites to celebrate the fact that Jesus is truth and love personified, that he died for our sins and defied death. It is because of this that ultimately all people will come to love Jesus. The mood of the piece is positive and celebratory.

Dark Blue level

Some research skills from Light Blue should now become second nature, like finding basic biographical details for the composer of a piece. Theory from Module B should start to inform research and presentation, and Dark Blue requires awareness of the context of a piece (when it might be sung, for example) and of individual works within a composer's output. Repertoire will not only be in English: where necessary, singers are required to find and understand translations of foreign texts.

In the Dark Blue level workbook

- *Page 30, Datequest*

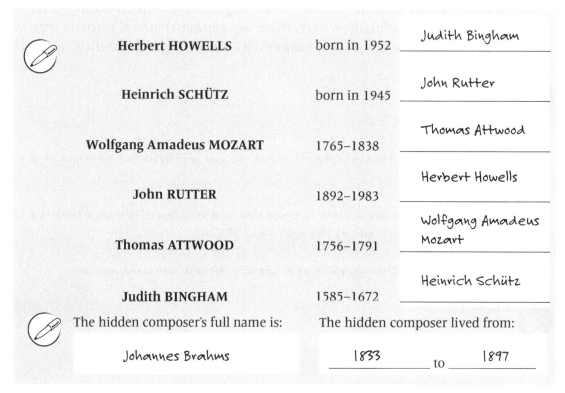

Herbert HOWELLS	born in 1952	Judith Bingham
Heinrich SCHÜTZ	born in 1945	John Rutter
Wolfgang Amadeus MOZART	1765–1838	Thomas Attwood
John RUTTER	1892–1983	Herbert Howells
Thomas ATTWOOD	1756–1791	Wolfgang Amadeus Mozart
Judith BINGHAM	1585–1672	Heinrich Schütz

The hidden composer's full name is:

Johannes Brahms

The hidden composer lived from:

1833 to 1897

- *Page 31, 'The Lord's my Shepherd'*

Who is the composer of the music?	James Leith MacBeth Bain
Has the piece been arranged by anyone? If so, who?	Yes – Malcolm Archer
Where are the words from?	Psalm 23 from the Scottish Psalter, 1650

- *Page 32*
  Singers should complete the worksheet for a few pieces of music, one of which should then be assessed and discussed for the target. See the sample answers below.

Sample answers for page 32
Singers were given a copy of the anthem 'A Gaelic Blessing' by John Rutter. They were asked the following questions, based on the worksheet:

- Who wrote the music? When was he or she born? What country does he or she live in?

- What century or musical period was the composer writing in?

- Can you name any other pieces by the same composer?

- Explain in your own words what you think the words are about.

- Describe the music in simple terms (for example the key signature, the number of vocal parts, any instruments involved and the general mood).

- When would this piece normally be sung? (In church or for a concert? At any particular time of the year or for a special event?)

The first thing to notice is that the Dark Blue questions have provoked longer and more detailed answers than those at Light Blue level. Below each answer you will find a few comments of the type that might be relevant for assessment purposes. In addition, there is an interesting postscript on page 177.

Grace, 12

A Gaelic Blessing was composed by John Rutter who was born in 1945 in England. John Rutter wrote this piece in the 20th century (1900s) in a modern-day style. Rutter also composed the 'Requiem', 'For the Beauty of the Earth', 'The Lord Bless You and Keep You' and 'All Things Bright and Beautiful' all of which are very well known.

The words are adapted from an old Gaelic tune talking about God as part of the nature of Earth with all the peaceful parts standing out. The piece is written for upper voices (soprano and sometimes alto) and either piano or organ. The piece is set with the key signature of D major (C sharp and F sharp) and the time signature at 3 crotchets per bar. The piece should be quite quiet and flowing.

'A Gaelic Blessing' is an 'all round' piece so it can be sung at any time of the year. It is sung in both normal and special church services and is sometimes sung during a wedding or Christening as this piece is a blessing.

All the questions have been answered, though some of the responses might be probed to check that everything has been fully understood:

- In the first paragraph, the phrase 'in a modern-day style' is fine as far as it goes – but an older singer with more listening experience and descriptive skill might articulate this more precisely.

- As an assessor, you might want to discuss what is meant by 'with all the peaceful parts standing out' in the second paragraph. It is unclear whether this refers to the text or the music. You might also want the singer to give you the evidence for the last sentence of this paragraph (performance directions, for example).

Andrew, adult

<u>A Gaelic Blessing</u> was composed by John Rutter (born, London 1945). Very much in demand as a composer and conductor, he divides his time between England and the USA. Although Rutter's music belongs to the twentieth and twenty-first centuries, his attractive and accessible idiom is light years from the more strident output of so many 'contemporary' or 'modern' composers (mentioning no names). His large scale works include a fine Requiem (1985), and a setting of the Magnificat (1990); he has written scores of shorter songs and anthems, including the delightful 'All things bright and beautiful'. Notable in his output is a large amount of Christmas music; with Sir David Willcocks, he co-edited four volumes in the Oxford 'Carols for Choirs' series.

The text to 'A Gaelic Blessing' is said to be 'adapted from an old Gaelic rune', perhaps carved on a Celtic cross, or a sarcophagus, or even a charm bracelet. There are several versions of the text, all of which call down a blessing on the one hearing it: 'Deep peace to you'.

Rutter's adaptation begins by invoking the four elements: water ('the running waves'), air ('the flowing air'), earth ('the quiet earth') and fire ('the shining stars'). All of these examples convey a picture of the deep peace of nature, and the hope of sharing in it. The last of these phrases opens out to include the 'healing light' of the moon and stars at night-time. And these thoughts about the peace of natural world lead on to the bringer of peace himself, and the closing lines: 'Deep peace of Christ the light of the world to you.'

Rutter's music exquisitely captures the peaceful mood of this text: a gentle 3/4 rhythm, marked 'flowing and tranquil', with rocking chords from the organ (or piano), support a liquid D major melody for solo or unison voices. For choral performances, the composer has provided a second part for just three bars, but this is a masterstroke, occurring at the climactic phrase of both text and music: Christ is described as the 'light of the world' and the melody reaches its highest note (F sharp).

Since the terms of this blessing are not specified, the piece may be used on any occasion where Christ's peace and light are invoked, either on individuals (weddings, funerals, baptisms) or whole bodies of people (in services of wholeness and healing, or penance and reconciliation, or in time or war or unrest).

Andrew's response is thorough and informative. The fourth paragraph is particularly well thought out: he has carefully considered, and described in detail, the way elements of the score create a particular mood. However certain aspects of these answers could be explored further in discussion:

- The questions did not ask for comment about the work of other (in this case 'nameless') contemporary composers: the remarks about this in the first paragraph are superfluous. (As a choir trainer, you might consider how singers might gain an understanding of – and even a liking for – music they currently find difficult.)

- Secondly, Andrew has not cited his sources. While the questions did not specifically request this, by Dark Blue singers should be aware of its importance. This is something that could usefully be addressed in the assessment discussion.

Clare, adult

John Rutter composed the music for this setting of 'A Gaelic Blessing'. The words have been taken from an ancient prayer – one of the many beautiful prayers found in the Gaelic / Celtic tradition.

John Rutter is a modern English composer and arranger who has rejuvenated many over-familiar hymns and carols into fresh and stimulating anthems, i.e. 'All things bright and beautiful'; 'For the beauty of the Earth'.

This setting of 'A Gaelic Blessing' is for solo or unison voices with a keyboard accompaniment, and an optional harmony in bars 32–34. I have sung this anthem using the SATB version but there is no lesser beauty in the simplicity of the single voice melody.

The words and style of the music make it a very suitable anthem for a bereavement, healing, meditative service; Perhaps after communion has been taken; perhaps around Remembrance Sunday or when the world is oppressed by thoughts of war. However it is by no means a miserable sounding piece. It has been written in a major key providing a positive sense of serenity. It is in 3/4 time and the piece, or should I say 'peace' flows throughout, emotively created by sustained notes across the barlines, disguising the obviousness of the beat, while the accompaniment runs with quavers underneath.

It would be particularly appropriate at the end of a service or concert to say 'God be with you' in song.

Clare's answers are concise and to the point, and they cover most of the points in the questions. Yet the style is informal and the information perhaps less carefully organized. In discussion, the following could usefully be explored:

- Rutter's birth date would be useful – it is not safe to assume that all readers will interpret the word 'modern' as 'living'.

- There is very little about the meaning of the text.

- Clare assumes that we know there is an SATB version of the piece: it might be sensible to state this explicitly (though it is good that she has made reference to it).

- In the fourth paragraph, the remarks about how the music creates the mood are very perceptive; the pun on the word 'peace' may be appropriate for some contexts but not for others.

Postscript

This task illustrates the importance of ensuring, when assessing singers' responses, that your information is as up-to-date as possible. When these answers were written, the information was accurate as presented by the singers. However John Rutter has since undertaken further research into the text and written the following:

> The text of A Gaelic Blessing, *long believed to be a translation of an ancient Gaelic original, is now known to be the work of the Scottish author and poet William Sharp who sometimes wrote under the pseudonym Fiona Macleod.*

Red level

Singers should by now be familiar with basic research techniques and sources, and be able to find and verify information about new repertoire and composers with little difficulty. Research and presentation will be firmly grounded in music theory and history; and singers will be able to scrutinize a wider range of pieces in a variety of languages and styles. A level of understanding of historical, stylistic and religious contexts is required.

In the Red level workbook

- *Page 30, Infoquest*

Infoquest

Do some research about the five choral composers below and match the names to the facts. The first letters of each name will spell the surname of another composer. Find the full name and dates of that composer.

LEIGHTON	TALLIS	STAINER	HAYDN	OUSELEY

Haydn _____ wrote 104 symphonies.

Ouseley _____ was born in 1825.

Leighton _____ died in 1988.

Stainer _____ wrote *The Crucifixion*.

Tallis _____ wrote a 40-part motet.

The hidden composer's name is: The hidden composer lived from:

Holst   1874 _____ to 1934 _____

- *Page 31*

  Singers should complete the worksheet for several pieces of music to prove that they are able to do this thoroughly. (This worksheet asks largely the same questions as the equivalent at Dark Blue level, but in more detail and requiring more intepretation.)

- *Page 32*

  Singers should take the information about one of the pieces researched for page 32 and turn it into a programme note. See the sample answers and comments below.

What singers say

'I joined a new choir last year. We were learning a carol and it was in French. Before we even started singing, the conductor asked us to work out together what the words meant. I was surprised. No-one had ever asked me that before. But of course it makes sense. If you don't understand the words, you can't sing it right, can you? And one of the choir members was French and she helped us to pronounce it all properly. It was fun.

Hannah, 15

Sample answers for page 32

Singers were given a copy of 'Locus iste' by Bruckner and asked to complete the worksheet on page 31 of the workbook. They were then asked to turn this material into a programme note.

This task is necessarily more complicated than previous levels because it requires singers to express a range of researched facts in a coherent and engaging fashion that an audience or congregation will want to read. All the responses below were successful, but they demonstrate how singers of different ages and at different stages of development will approach the task.

Hayley, 12

Locus Iste

Locus Iste is an anthem written by Anton Bruckner and edited by David Hill. Anton Bruckner was born in Austria in 1824 and died in 1896 (nineteenth century). He wrote ten symphonies during his life including: Te Deum which was written in 1881, Requiem started in 1848 and finished in 1849 and a string quintet starting in 1878 and finishing in 1879. He was an organist in two places: Sankt Florian Abbey (1856-68) and Imperial Chapel (1878-06). He then became a professor at Vienna conservatory in 1871 for four years. Other composers around this time were Franz Liszt and Frederic Chopin. The name of the musical period Locus Iste was written in was called the Romantic period.

Locus Iste is an anthem written in Latin for a four part choir (soprano, alto, tenor and bass) plus an organ or piano. Its time signature is four crotchet beats in a bar and is in the key of C major. It is marked 'Allegro moderato' which means moderately fast. The English translation for this piece is 'This place has been made by God a pure and holy one – this is indisputable'.

The words in this piece of music come from the Bible as it says that God is pure and holy and that he made everything and everyone. I think that this text is trying to get the point across that God is powerful and no one can argue with it weather they like it or not. This piece would generally be sung in a church at any time of the year.

Hayley has carefully collected most of the information required for the worksheet and written it up into an interesting programme note. The biographical facts about the composer are well organized and informative (though see below). However certain things would have improved the note:

- It would be useful to know when and why the piece was written as this would give historical background to the chosen text.

- There is little comment about the mood of the piece and how technical aspects of the score create this.

- Though the research appears to have been thorough, a number of the biographical details and dates are actually inaccurate.

- A little more information about the origin of the text would be useful – 'from the Bible' is perhaps too general a response to this question at this level. The last sentence, too, could be more specific.

Megan, adult

'Locus Iste' was written by Anton Bruckner in 1869. Bruckner was born in Ansfelden in Austria on 4th September 1824 and died in 1896. He wrote 9 symphonies, the last one unfinished when he died, 3 choral masses and about 30 motets.

He was writing in the Romantic period along with other composers such as Brahms, Puccini, Fauré, Chopin and Debussy. He was heavily influenced by Wagner and he in turn inspired Gustav Mahler.

Bruckner studied at the Vienna Conservatory and became Cathedral Organist in Linz.

Locus Iste is written for four parts, in simple time and in the key of C major and is sung unaccompanied. The music has long, Gregorian chant-like lines which create a very sustained sound and peaceful atmosphere. It alternates between very quiet and very loud passages through the three sections of the piece.

The piece was written to celebrate the dedication of the votive chapel of Linz Cathedral and is used in mass services for the dedication of a church.

The words mean 'This place was made by God, a priceless mystery, which is beyond dispute' and therefore focusses on the sense of the presence of God in his building, the Church.

 Megan's programme note is well-researched and concise. The material in the fourth paragraph is particularly well expressed, linking technical details with the mood of the music. But a few minor details would make the note more interesting:

- It might be sensible to make an explicit link between the fact that Bruckner was the organist at Linz Cathedral and the fact that 'Locus iste' was written for the dedication of a chapel there.

- Some extra information about when pieces with this text are sung might help to place the music in general context.

- Some indication of the origin of the text itself would be appropriate.

There are also a few aspects of the text that might usefully be explored in discussion:

- The second paragraph implies that Chopin, Bruckner and Debussy were contemporaries, which is only very loosely the case, even from a chronological perspective. (Bruckner outlived Chopin by nearly 50 years; Debussy was born nearly 40 years after Bruckner.)

- Debussy is rarely thought of as a Romantic-era composer and his music has very little in common with Bruckner's. (Has the singer properly understood the notion of 'Romanticism'?)

Jonathan, adult

This setting of <u>Locus Iste</u> was written by the Austrian composer Anton Bruckner (1824-96). Bruckner is mainly known as a symphonist (he composed nine, the final one being unfinished at the time of his death), and as a composer of large-scale choral works.

He was a controversial figure as his fame grew towards the end of his life. He was a close friend of Richard Wagner, with whom he was (in the common view of the time) allied through their progressive harmonic style against the more conservative classicism of Johannes Brahms.

Bruckner's upbringing was as a provincial choirmaster and schoolteacher. Through hard work and study, an abundance of talent and the generosity of benefactors, he was able to secure the post of cathedral organist in Linz (1855) and, later, the Professor of Harmony, Counterpoint and Organ of the Vienna Conservatory (1869).

Locus Iste was composed in 1869 for the dedication of a new votive chapel at Linz Cathedral. The text is that traditionally used for the dedication of a church. In the Catholic liturgy it is usually performed as a Gradual, the musical interlude between the Epistle and the Gospel.

The piece is typical of the influential 'Cecilian' movement that flourished during the nineteenth century, which strove for a 'purer' style of sacred music. This appealed to Bruckner's upbringing and temperament, as well as to his devout Catholicism.

Locus Iste is a motet based around a tonal centre of C major. Its homophonic style and tertiary form is underpinned by a strong bass line in the outer sections which could be seen to represent the 'cantus firmus' of an earlier style of sacred music.

This programme note is detailed, clearly written and highly informative. The facts researched for the worksheet have been coherently assembled into a text that manages to blend fact and considered opinion. Nevertheless even here there are a few details that could be discussed during assessment:

- While we are told about the use of the text, we are not told about its original meaning.

- It might be interesting for the reader to know just a little more about the Cecilian movement – where it began, who belonged to it, what its aims were. As this paragraph stands, the information seems to provoke more questions than it answers.

- The last paragraph assumes quite a lot of technical knowledge on the part of the reader. Will the audience understand words like 'homophonic' and 'tertiary' or do they need to be further explained?

- For all the details, there is little description of the mood of the music itself – this could usefully be added to the last paragraph.

Yellow level

Research skills, evaluation of sources, and ability to express information clearly and engagingly for a variety of readers are all requirements for Yellow level. Links between words and music must be carefully explored. Assertions in the programme notes will be based on a sound grasp of music theory and history; and singers will be able to scrutinize a wide range of pieces in a variety of languages and styles, displaying sophisticated understanding of historical, stylistic and religious contexts.

In the Yellow level workbook

- *Page 37*
  Singers should complete the worksheet for several pieces of music to prove that they are able to do this thoroughly. (This worksheet asks largely the same questions as the equivalent at Red level, but in more detail and requiring more interpretation.)

- *Page 38*
  Singers should take the information about one of the pieces researched for page 37 and turn it into a programme note. See the sample answers and comments below.

Sample programme notes

Singers were presented with copies of 'Wade in the water' arranged by Geoff Weaver. They were asked to create programme notes based on their answers to the questions below (which are based on page 37 and 38 of the workbook):

- Who wrote the music? What were the events of the composer's life and the historical and political background of the time? How might this have affected the music?

- What century or musical period was the composer writing in? What are the characteristics of this period?

- Can you name any other pieces in the same genre? Compare and contrast them with this piece.

- Who has arranged the music?

- Where do the words come from? Explain in your own words what the text is trying to communicate.

- How is the text set to the music? (For example, is the setting syllabic or melismatic? Are repetition or word-painting used?)

- How do the text and music fit together? Do they work together to create one particular mood?

- Describe the music (key and time signatures; number of vocal parts, any instruments involved; the general mood).

- Can you think of any other musical versions of the same text? Compare and contrast them.

- When would this piece normally be sung? (In church or for a concert? At any particular time of the year or for a particular event?)

Part of the complexity of this task is that the (relatively standard) questions asked about most music within the western classical tradition do not apply to 'Wade in the water'. So singers have to evaluate the piece from a different historical, theoretical and cultural perspective. In addition, there are many ways of interpreting the facts and the theory at this level. Both the responses below were successful – but they show various ways of approaching the assignment.

 Rachel, 19

'Wade in the Water' is an example of what was traditionally known as a spiritual. Therefore the actual composer is unknown. Spirituals are Christian songs that originated during the enslavement of Africans in America. Spirituals were inspired by the Gospel message of the Bible and the words of Jesus. The lyrics are tightly linked with the lives of their authors. They were an important source of encouragement and a way of expressing the desire for salvation.

The text of this piece refers specifically to the 'underground railroad'. This was an informal organisation existing at that time to help slaves escape and find their way to freedom. Other spirituals like 'Gospel train' and 'Swing low, sweet chariot' also refer to this escape route. Sometimes when walking through the night to escape, slaves would need to wade through water to ensure their tracks could not be followed, and it is to this that 'Wade in the water' refers.

The arranger of this particular version is Geoff Weaver. It has many characteristic traits of a spiritual, for example, syncopation, 'blue' notes (i.e. flattened thirds and sevenths), imitation and repetition in both the lyrics and the music itself. It is the syncopation in conjunction with effective use of dynamic range that makes for particular interest. It is set for soprano, alto and men with a piano accompaniment. There are two short verses, which come in between the main chorus sections. The first chorus section is in unison and then it splits into three parts for the rest of the piece.

 This answer is full of historical detail about the genre and the song itself. Rachel has paid a lot of attention to the historical context of the piece and the meaning of the words. Yet certain issues could be addressed during discussions:

- The first paragraph appears to imply that all spirituals are anonymous. Is this the case?

- Some dates and historical facts about slavery and its abolition might be useful for context here. Do we know where and when this song would have been sung first?

- Should the note include biographical details of Geoff Weaver? (Readers may not know who he is, and may think he is contemporary with the song.)

- Is it possible to explain how the song would have been in its original form and then look at what the arranger did to it to make his version special?

Module C: Yellow level

 Martin, adult

<u>Wade in the water</u> – Words and music: Spiritual, arr. Geoff Weaver

A spiritual is a religious song from the southern states of the USA. Used both in the church, and in the fields as a work song, the spiritual tended to be of the call-and-response type, with a leader and chorus singing antiphonally. This simple structure allows great freedom, as the solo part can be improvised, and the tag line or refrain repeated by the chorus ('God's a gonna trouble the water') is easy to pick up, which was important as these spirituals would originally have been learnt by ear.

The text of spirituals was biblical, often intensely moving and having a strong feeling of melancholy, which is perhaps not surprising considering that the Afro-American people in the deep south of USA had their roots embedded in slavery. 'Nobody knows the trouble I seen, Lord' or 'Sometimes I feel like a motherless child' identify the singer's troubles with the suffering of Jesus.

Spirituals were sometimes adapted from popular English hymns, such as those written by Isaac Watts (1674–1748), whose 1820 edition of hymns had wide circulation in southern USA and was very popular with the black community. Many other spirituals use the language of biblical passages that speak of liberation, particularly the Book of Revelation, as well as the books of Moses and Daniel. There is little doubt that these were effectively songs of protest in code, and that the words had meaning that was as much earthbound as spiritual.

 As ex-slave Frederick Douglass wrote, 'A keen observer might have detected in our repeated singing of "O Canaan, sweet Canaan, I am bound for the land of Canaan" something more than a hope of reaching heaven. We meant to reach the North, and the North was our Canaan'. (The northern states of USA had abolished slavery by that time, but many parts of the south had not.) Spirituals such as Didn't my Lord deliver Daniel? must also have been sung with the hope, if not belief, that escape from slavery would come for all.

In 'Wade in the water' the words are reminiscent of God 'troubling the water' in the book of Exodus, turning back the Red Sea so that Moses could lead the Israelites through on dry land, out of the slavery that they had known in Egypt and towards the Promised Land and freedom. However, there is probably a less fanciful idea behind the words. Escaping slaves were told to literally 'wade in the water', i.e. wade along rivers so that pursuing dogs could not smell their tracks, once again seemingly biblical words masking the true meaning of not just a hope of freedom, but almost a coded escape plan!

This piece is written for three voices, (Soprano, Alto and Men), accompanied by a keyboard. It is in a quick 4 beats in a bar, with strong syncopated rhythms that often feature in spirituals, and in the key of F minor.

In churches and schools where it is not always possible to have enough singers for a standard SATB choir, this type of composition is a useful resource. Not only is there one part only for the men, instead of splitting into tenors and basses, but the two other voices are actually equal soprano parts rather than soprano and alto, the top F and E flat in bars 19 and 23 being exceptionally high for most altos in amateur choirs. The keyboard part would perhaps be best played on a piano, as its percussive attack would help bring out the syncopated rhythms, or on an electric keyboard, rather than a traditional church pipe organ. Similarly, this piece would perhaps be more suitable for a concert, school assembly or youth service, rather than a traditional reflective service.

This note is well researched (with quotations to back up assertions in the text); carefully constructed and highly informative. But there are still issues one might discuss during assessment:

- As a programme note for a general readership, this assumes quite a lot of technical knowledge. Terms like 'call-and-response' and 'antiphonally' may be familiar to singers, but may be less so for ordinary listeners.

- It may be worth pointing out that the songs cited in the second paragraph are other examples of the spiritual genre.

- The historical information is excellent but there is little detail given about the musical aspects – the material in the sixth paragraph could be expanded here.

- There is no biographical detail about the arranger here – as with the previous note, it would be useful to the general reader to know who he is and what he has done to the song.

- The final paragraph is a useful additional piece of information that, while it may not be particularly useful to a concert audience, displays considerable awareness of the piece's suitability (or otherwise) for different types of performer.

What singers say
'If you'd told me when I joined the choir that I'd end up writing programme notes for our concerts, I would have laughed. But our choir director asked a few of us to try it. The research was interesting and I enjoyed putting everything down so that the audience could learn a bit about the pieces. Now I do most of the notes. It's sort of what I do in the choir now. I'm proud of the booklets I make. It's expanding my knowledge about music too.'

Adam, adult

MODULE D

Belonging to the choir

CONTENTS

Module D: Belonging to the choir

This module is concerned with what it means to be a choir member. It encourages singers to view the choir as a team of which they are an invaluable part. It requires choir members to be committed, responsible and polite. It also emphasizes the importance of reliability.

At the lower levels, Module D emphasizes regular attendance and attentiveness at rehearsals. Later on, singers are encouraged to take responsibility for other less experienced singers in the choir. They should set an example through their singing, attendance and behaviour. They are encouraged to develop their own initiative by looking for ways they can facilitate the smooth running of rehearsals and performances, responding to the needs of the individual choir.

Module D addresses the following issues that, unless you have the perfect choir, will at some time or other concern you as a choir trainer:

- Singers' attendance, punctuality and commitment

- Singers' effort, concentration and contribution

- The development of individual singers into responsible members of the choir

- How to provide an environment in which all singers can flourish

As with all the other modules, the aims of Module D are assessed by means of targets for each level. These are listed opposite, and at the back of each of the workbooks.

How Module D is organized

The attributes necessary to achieve the Module D targets cannot really be delivered by means of activities or exercises. They are motivational values that singers develop over time as a result of being active, committed members of the choir, and as a result of your persuasiveness as a choir trainer. They are in turn reinforced in the workbooks by advice to singers and by self-assessment sections (which you will check and discuss as part of the targets for each level).

How to use this part of the book

In the main, you will not need to train singers level by level for this module as the values are general ones that apply across the scheme. A general introduction outlining the principal concepts of Module D begins on page 191. This is followed by advice about encouraging reliability, commitment and responsible behaviour in your choir. After this you will find brief sections relating to what you should expect of singers at each level, and how to assess for the targets.

By reading the Module D material in the workbooks, you will familiarize yourself with what singers encounter at each level.

The Voice for Life Guide to Choir Training contains more detailed information about how to foster commitment, responsibility and leadership in your singers. In addition, the RSCM publishes a number of resources to help with these things, including the *Voice for Life* Weekly Standards Chart and General Progress Chart (see pages 10–11).

White level

To complete Module D, singers must:

- attend rehearsals regularly and punctually
- tell the choir trainer in advance when they are going to be absent
- make a positive contribution to the choir
- meet any other target(s) as specified by the choir trainer

 Light Blue level

To complete Module D, singers must:

- be a committed and punctual member of the choir, who informs the choir trainer before being absent from rehearsals, services or concerts
- be focused during rehearsals, services or concerts
- understand that they are singing as part of a group and that they need to contribute to the overall sound

 Dark Blue level

To complete Module D, singers must:

- be a committed and punctual member of the choir, who informs the choir trainer before being absent from rehearsals, services or concerts
- be focused during rehearsals, services or concerts
- understand that they are singing as part of a group and that they need to contribute to the overall sound
- be helpful to less experienced members of the choir

 Red level

To complete Module D, singers must:

- be committed, reliable and punctual, always informing the choir trainer before being absent
- lead other singers by example with attendance, singing, and behaviour in rehearsals, services and concerts
- understand the difference between solo and choral singing
- help less experienced members of the choir without causing fuss or distraction

Module D: Targets

To complete Module D, singers must:

- be committed, reliable and punctual, always informing the choir trainer before being absent

- be an outstanding member of the choir, setting an excellent example to other singers through attendance, behaviour, commitment, and musical standards

- understand the delicate balance in a choir between giving a strong musical lead and blending with other singers

- understand that the choir is a team, and the importance of participating in the practicalities of running that team – setting up rehearsal rooms, collecting music, for example

- take responsibility for less experienced singers

What singers say

'It's not just about singing. In fact, singing's the easy part! Making the commitment and finding the time for practice and rehearsals is harder. It's worth it though.'

Robert, adult

Put bluntly, singers should gain the following messages from Module D: turn up regularly and punctually; concentrate; help others; and take responsibility as an individual within the group. In theory this should be straightforward but, as any choir trainer knows, in practice it can be difficult to get these messages across to singers. Your role is to keep making these points in a number of different ways, and to foster and develop commitment and cooperation in your singers.

From Light Blue level on, the workbooks use and develop the metaphor of a sports team and the various roles of its members. In rehearsals, you can use this from the outset with singers of all levels. Share the following ideas:

In a sports team, every member must work hard. If some members don't make an effort, the others have to work harder, so the whole team gets tired quickly and plays badly. A choir is the same. If some members do not sing to the best of their ability, those who do must work harder. Everyone gets tired more quickly.

If a sports team contains members who do not cooperate and act too much as individuals, playing becomes difficult for everyone. A choir is the same. Unless everyone listens and takes part as a team member, the singing suffers.

And if the captain or manager of the team always has to organize everything with no help or contribution from team members, he or she will struggle. The team will be less efficient. A choir is no different. As well as singing to the best of their ability, singers need to help the choir trainer in all sorts of ways.

 ### Developing and motivating singers
As a choir trainer or teacher, you have the ability to 'grow' your singers, overseeing their transition from tentative first-timers through autonomous choir members to senior, responsible members of your training and management team. You can empower singers to gradually take more responsibility within the choir, developing their own initiative and improving their musical ability. The better you do this, the better the results will be from your choir.

There are a number of ways to do this. For example, you can facilitate each singer's personal development by involving them as much as possible in the general organisation of the choir. Delegating specific jobs to singers will make them feel that they are a valued and important part of the team. Overleaf you will find advice, level by level, about how to instil some of these values.

 Tip: It's very important to lead by example. Be punctual, well-organized, friendly, and co-operative. If you aren't, you can't expect your singers to be either.

 ### Parents: your ally
Young singers may be reliant upon their parents or other responsible adults to bring them to rehearsals and concerts. Make sure that these people understand the importance of punctuality and regular attendance. Children will have a better choral experience if their parents are committed to facilitating it. If attendance or punctuality become a problem, consider discussing the matter (gently) with the parent or responsible adult concerned.

Module D level by level

As this module unfolds, the workbooks and targets require different degrees of engagement from singers. Here are some details of what should be encouraged (and assessed) at each level.

White level

New singers may be rather anxious or disorientated at first, so your principal job is to put them at ease (with the help of more senior singers if possible). Above all, make the atmosphere welcoming. But it is also important that new singers know early on what you expect from them, and how to make the most of rehearsals. You may have informal terms and conditions of your own, but as a basis you can work with page 32 of the workbook, which suggests that singers:

- arrive on time

- know where to stand or sit

- concentrate and watch the conductor

- bring music to rehearsals, and a pencil to take notes

- inform the choir trainer if they have to miss a rehearsal or concert

- if skipping a rehearsal is unavoidable, find out from another choir member what they missed

- understand any special instructions for concerts or performances

- look after their voice and keep it in good condition

The White level workbook contains no specific activities for this module, but the targets will enable you to evaluate each singer's progress in this respect.

Tip: It can help to ask young singers frequently to remember the steps they need to take to prepare for rehearsals – what they need to bring with them; what they should do while they are in the rehearsal room; and what they should do in their own time between rehearsals. These things may seem obvious to you as a choir trainer, but good habits need reinforcing.

Light Blue level

By the end of this level, singers should be more aware of their responsibilities within the choir. The workbook stresses not only the necessity for regular attendance at rehearsals, but also for focus and concentration. The self-assessment boxes on page 38 of the Light Blue workbook encourage reflection – you should discuss the singer's answers in as much detail as necessary before you sign the targets. (With some young singers, it may be necessary to explain terms like 'focus' and 'commitment'.)

Tip: When commenting on singers' behaviour or performance – particularly younger ones – aim to praise more often than you criticize. Identifying positives is a powerful motivator, especially when you share these with the rest of the choir. But singers can get suspicious of constant unconditional praise, so don't be afraid to point out things that need improvement. When you do this, however, always identify the behaviour you want to change, and calmly criticize this rather than the singer as an individual.

Dark Blue level

This level reinforces good habits and practices learned at Light Blue, but makes new demands too. It asks singers to concentrate 'throughout rehearsals and performances' (quite a challenge for younger singers) and to help less experienced choir members. The self-assessment boxes on page 33 of the workbook explore these themes.

At this stage, while it is important to praise and reward good contributions, you should also be prepared to point out areas that need improvement, and maybe even wait for evidence of that improvement before you sign the target box. You may also feel it appropriate to ask a singer to demonstrate helpfulness to others in a specific way – looking after them during a break, perhaps – before signing the target.

Tip: When suggesting a specific task to a singer, make sure he or she understands what is involved and is comfortable with it. Never ask for a commitment that a singer cannot make, as failure is demotivating. Also, having asked a singer to perform a specific task, make sure you give feedback and show that it is appreciated.

Red level

At Red level, singers should be taking more responsibility within the choir. The workbook makes the analogy with a sports-team captain, reporting to the team manager (choir director). With this role comes the need to set an example to more junior members in terms of attendance record, behaviour and musical contribution. Red-level singers also need to understand the difference between solo and choral singing. The self-assessment boxes on page 33 explore these issues.

Tip: One Red-level target is to 'help less experienced members of the choir without causing fuss or distraction'. When asked to help junior members, some singers may be rather over-zealous, either to show off their new role to others or to impress you. Asking singers to help others is a great motivator, but make sure you monitor the situation. It can cause distraction or worse to less secure choir members. Keep your eyes and ears open and don't be afraid to intervene (gently) if need be.

Yellow level

At Yellow level, singers will be more or less autonomous musicians and reliability and punctuality should be second nature. They should now have some experience of helping and training less experienced singers effectively, so will be able to take on some of these responsibilities should you require them. A further requirement now is helping to run the choir – so you may want to assign specific administrative or practical tasks and monitor how these are performed.

Once again, there are self-assessment boxes (on page 39). At this level, you should be prepared to discuss each individual singer's responses in some detail. You could use this appraisal material as a way of establishing specific training or administrative roles within the choir for these advanced singers, and wait for evidence of competence before you sign the target boxes.

Tip: Yellow-level singers may enjoy directing part of a rehearsal or leading a section of the choir for a brief practice. But always ask them in advance and ensure they are comfortable: however confident they are, the responsibility may be daunting. Always help them to prepare thoroughly, and always give constructive feedback afterwards.

MODULE E

Choir in context

CONTENTS

Module E: Choir in context

This module is concerned with developing singers' understanding of:

- their role within the choir

- their choir's role in a wider context and the background and the motivation of its members

- how to gather information from various sources and present it in a coherent form, acknowledging sources where necessary

How Module E is organized

The module is delivered via a number of research projects on a variety of topics. With the exception of White, which has no formal targets in this module, there are three projects for each level; singers must complete the number of projects specified in the targets shown opposite. At each level, the first two projects listed are suitable for all choirs, while the third is specifically designed for church or worship choirs.

All the projects have a self-completion worksheet in the workbook. Some also have suggested tasks for preparation and follow-up; you may want to vary these according to the culture and context of your choir. To complete a project, singers must research it and present their responses on the worksheet; you should use this as the basis for assessment and further discussion before signing the relevant target box.

Within any level, you can work on the projects in any order. You may want singers to cover them all over time, or you may find some are more appropriate for some singers or choirs than others. (You could try asking singers to choose the projects that really interest them – they may find it motivating to be given the choice.) When a singer completes the number of projects required for the level, sign the module off in their workbook even if you still want them to look at the other projects later.

Tip: You may also find it useful to revisit or recycle projects from time to time. This can help to show singers how they have developed over time within the choir. If you do this, make it clear that this is the reason for your request – ask singers to identify the changes in their thoughts, findings and attitudes since the last time they worked on the topic. Many choir trainers use these projects in various ways over time to keep singers focused on the wider issues of choir membership.

As there are no formal skill tests for this module, the results may be less obvious and tangible than other modules. But as they work on projects, singers acquire skills and qualities that are vital for well-rounded musicians. Moreover, much of what is learned here is carefully examined in the RSCM Awards (see page 9). So don't be tempted to skip or rush Module E. Singers should give the project work the care and attention it deserves; and you should do the same before you sign the target boxes.

How to use this part of the book

Overleaf you will find some general thoughts about Module E, with practical advice about organizing projects and assessing singers' responses. Resources for all twelve projects listed opposite begin on page 201, level by level. For ease of reference, the project introductions as they appear in the workbooks are included in full. Blank photocopiable masters of all the worksheets can be found at the back of this book. These are useful if you need extra copies to give to singers.

Module E: Targets

 White level

There are no formal targets for Module E at White level. Nevertheless it can be useful to involve White-level singers in Module E – there is more about this on page 200.

 Light Blue level

Singers must complete at least *two* of the following:

- Project 1: The gift of music (page 201)
- Project 2: The power of music (page 202)
- Project 3: Places of worship (page 203)

 Dark Blue level

Singers must complete at least *two* of the following:

- Project 1: What is a community? (page 204)
- Project 2: The community of your choir (pages 206–207)
- Project 3: Festivals in the Christian year (for layout reasons, this appears on page 205, before Project 2)

 Red level

Singers must complete at least *one* of the following:

- Project 1: The wider community (page 208)
- Project 2: The roots of our choir (page 210)
- Project 3: Music in worship (page 212)

 Yellow level

Singers must complete at least *one* of the following:

- Project 1: The changing repertoire of our choir (page 214)
- Project 2: Serving the wider community (page 216)
- Project 3: Thinking about regular services (page 218)

A choir does not exist in isolation. It is a community in its own right, and it belongs to a wider community too: a church, a school, a village or town, or even a whole county or region. It is a mutually supportive and caring group, as well as a group that works at singing together. Module E encourages choir members to explore the context of their choir's existence by asking some of the following questions:

- Why does your choir exist?

- Why do people sing in that particular choir?

- For whom does the choir sing and in what ways does it affect people's lives?

- What is the choir's role? What are its responsibilities?

- How do I as an individual relate to those responsibilities?

 Before you ask your singers to answer these, do so yourself. You will quickly realize that the responses are by no means straightforward; the questions deal not just with music-making but also with wider issues of service, responsibility and motivation. To help singers answer them, you need to have some ideas of your own to start with.

 Some practicalities
Module E requires interaction with the choir and community beyond rehearsals and performances. For example, for certain projects singers are asked to work in pairs or groups, interview other members of the choir or the public, or find out about local history. You may need to provide practical help with this, suggesting suitable partners or drawing up lists of willing interviewees or research sources. And, in any situation where younger singers in your care encounter other adults, make sure you follow your organization's safeguarding procedures.

 Tip: When selecting projects for singers, ask yourself whether the goals involved are realistic for them. For all sorts of educational or emotional reasons, some choir members may struggle with certain tasks. For example a young, timid singer may feel anxious about interviewing other choir members; one with dyslexia may have difficulty filling in the more complex worksheets. Be aware of these things – it can be useful to talk discreetly to parents or other choir members about this.

 Tip: When you start singers on a project, ensure that everyone involved is comfortable and informed about what is going on. Remember that the module is flexible: with a little thought and care you will find projects that will engage, challenge and reward each singer. Be sensitive to the needs of individuals.

 Tip: Module E involves considerable planning, reading and checking. You as the choir trainer could do this yourself, but consider asking senior choir members to help, perhaps as part of their Module D targets. This will reduce your workload, give singers the chance to interact, and encourage senior members to mentor more junior ones. If you do this, you will still need to look at the workbooks and monitor singers' responses before you sign off the targets.

 Tip: For the church and liturgy projects, consider involving clergy or other ministers. This is a good way of building links between the choir and the rest of the church, and may provide new and valuable insights into repertoire and context.

Assessing Module E

In Module E there are no formal tests to provide evidence of achievement, and every singer's answers will be different. As there is no single correct response to any of the questions, you need to assess your singers' work with care.

For various reasons, it is difficult to provide model answers like those shown earlier in Module C. Firstly, no two singers, choirs or communities are alike – everyone's details are different. You may not always know whether a singer's responses are historically accurate; you may not be able to verify the comments they have recorded from people they interview in the course of their projects. And some of the questions are about opinions and feelings rather than facts.

Secondly, not all singers at any given level of *Voice for Life* will be the same age. They may have different levels of experience and different ways of expressing themselves; younger singers, for example, may well find it harder than older ones to articulate their opinions on some of these topics. You can help by considering which projects might be most suitable for a particular singer, but when assessing the responses you should – to an extent – take age and level into consideration.

When looking at the completed project worksheets, the key point is to assess the individual's effort and contribution just as much as the 'quality' of the answer. For example, it is reasonably easy to tell whether a singer has put thought and care into the answers and their presentation – even the simplest of responses can be delivered well and clearly. By the same token, singers who fill the boxes with a lot of words may not have paid much attention to what they mean.

Sometimes you will be able to tell quickly from the worksheet that the project has been done well. If you are unsure, or there are things you wish to confirm or verify, talk to the singer and discuss their responses. Try to hold these discussions one-to-one or in small groups, away from the entire choir: remember that you are looking for an individual's responses in order to assess his or her contribution to the module. A few well-directed questions will be enough to do this.

Remember too that you can ask a singer to provide more information or rewrite an answer before you sign the project off. This may help to stimulate further reflection and new perspectives after your discussions.

Tip: Your choir may not operate in a worship context, but that need not prevent singers from undertaking the worship projects in this module if they wish to. If you feel unable to assess their work yourself, consider asking someone with more experience in this area to look and comment.

Starting on page 201, you will find the worksheets for each of the projects as they appear in the workbooks. In the spaces left blank in the workbooks for singers' replies, you will find hints and tips about what sort of answers to expect, how to continue discussions, and ways of ensuring that singers get the maximum benefit from their project work. Blank copies of the worksheets can be found at the back of the book for you to photocopy and give to singers as necessary.

Module E at White level

There are no specific projects or targets for this module at White level, but this doesn't mean that singers should be excluded from Module E activities. Occasional mention of some of the topics will help young singers to address a few of the issues they will encounter later on in *Voice for Life*.

Some of the questions asked in this module at Light Blue level may be relevant to White-level singers, even if they have only been members of the choir for a few weeks. In informal contexts, try using the following questions as a basis for discussion:

- When and how did you first start singing?
- Is singing an important part of your life?
- What music do you like?
- What do you like most about being in a choir?
- What do you like least?
- Do you think the choir helps other people?

These discussions can start to form the basis of thinking about the wider context of the choir within the community. They may also be very useful to you as a choir trainer, as junior singers may come out with answers that are far less guarded and moderated than those given by people who have been in the choir for some time. Singers who are used to talking about these subjects from the start are likely to contribute more as they progress through the scheme.

Tip: In some of the projects, singers are asked to interview other choir members about aspects of their choral experiences. Even the most junior members of the choir could be included as interviewees as long as this is carefully monitored. It will give a sense of belonging and involvement, as well as some sense of what the scheme involves at higher levels. It will also make the point to more advanced singers that the views and thoughts of even the most junior singers are important.

What singers say

'When I was in hospital recently, at least half a dozen people from my choir visited me at various times. I was a bit surprised, but really pleased. It made me realize that the choir is more than just 'some people I sing with every week' ...

Camilla, adult

At Light Blue, singers may already be thinking about some of these topics as part of general discussions you may have about the choir and its purpose. They may already be involved in a range of music-making in a variety of contexts – but this will not always be the case, particularly with young singers.

 Topic 1: The gift of music
Think about the idea of a gift – something you give or receive. This could be something material (like a birthday or Christmas gift), or emotional (like friendship), or something living (like a pet or a plant). You may have other gifts too, such as a talent for sport or science or drawing.

Now think about music. It is a gift in two ways. It is a talent given to many people, enabling them to perform music well. And it is a gift given to listeners whenever performers make music.

When and how did you first become involved in music?

 Singers will probably tell you the age they started, how and where.

In discussion you could ask if they play an instrument, or if they have family or friends who play. (Ask singers to write these details down on the worksheet if they haven't already done so.)

How has music become important in your life?

 You may be surprised at some of the answers!

In discussion you could ask singers about their current music-making opportunities and which they like most. (Ask singers to write these details down on the worksheet if they haven't already done so.)

How do you plan to develop the gift of music in the future? What help do you think you might need for this?

 Look for evidence of reflection and thought here. Do not assume that all singers will know what music opportunities are open to them. (You could ask them to find out as part of the project.)

Discussions could include helping singers to plan future music-making.

What singers say
'There are lots of jobs you can do if you want to be a singer! You have to be good at it though, so you need to practise a lot and join lots of choirs.'

Harry, 8

This project is intended to focus singers on music's potential to alter or intensify our emotions. Singers also consider their own role in the transmission of music's power to other people. Responses to this topic will vary considerably according to the singer's age and experience.

Topic 2: The power of music

 Think of the many things music can make you feel. Some pieces make you feel joyful, others make you sad.

Think about the sort of feelings music can inspire. List them in this box.

> Responses will vary depending on the age and experience of the singer. All reactions are legitimate – the more the better!
>
> During discussions, you may wish to help younger singers find a wider vocabulary for feelings.

 Choose a piece of music that is special to you – a 'powerful' piece that causes strong feelings. In this box, write its name and describe why it's powerful.

> If you do not know the piece cited here, listen to it. Singers come to choirs from a range of musical backgrounds and you may have a few surprises. Everything counts here!
>
> In discussion, it might help to ask singers to expand on their feelings and reactions to their chosen piece.

 Music's power is used in many different ways in the wider world, such as advertising or sports. In the box below, write some examples of the ways the power of music is used.

> It is possible to follow this up by asking singers to match certain pieces of music to certain events or products.
>
> In discussion you could ask why some music works in some contexts but would be unsuitable in others.

 List some ways in which the power of your own singing and music making has affected other people.

> Younger singers may struggle with this because it demands a degree of empathy with audiences. If this is the case, a brief discussion about how audiences react to the choir during services or concerts might prompt some suitable responses.

This project is intended for worship choirs. As some of the tasks are quite complex, you may find that it takes time and that you need to ask singers to revisit some of their answers after they have shown you their worksheet.

Topic 3: Places of worship

 Think about a place that is familiar to you (for example your office, your bedroom, your classroom). Think about the people who use it, and how the layout and the furniture it contains reflects their needs and lives.

The aim here is to have singers think about an environment that is not a place of worship.

Younger singers may need a little help with some of this.

Look around the church where your choir sings. Think about important places inside and outside the building, and also about the church furniture (altar, font and so on). List some of these features in the box below.

Some singers may not have the necessary vocabulary for this – more senior members of the choir may be able to help them!

'The Voice for Life Chorister's Companion' contains a useful section (starting on page 136) about church layout and furniture. (For more information about Voice for Life publications, see pages 10–11.)

Now choose three of the church features from the box above. Write each of them in the box below. Say what it is used for, when it is used, and by whom.

Check this carefully – try to make sure that singers have understood the purpose of each of their chosen features. Discussion will help here.

Find out about the history of your church. When was it built? Can you list some of the people involved in its creation and upkeep?

You may need to point singers in the right direction to find this information if it is not readily available.

Vocabulary may be a challenge for younger singers – make sure everything has been properly understood.

At Dark Blue level, singers should start to be more aware of their role within the choir, and the choir's role within the community. The projects require more thorough exploration of these concepts. (For reasons of space, in this section the projects appear in a different order from the workbook; project 2 appears overleaf.)

 Topic 1: What is a community?
No one lives entirely alone. We all belong to different groups or communities of people. Some are large (like a school or university); others are smaller (like your close family). Some are formal, like the scouts or a sports team, but you may also belong to other looser groups, like a set of local friends or an online network. In the box, write the names of at least *five* groups or communities to which you belong.

Look for plenty of different ideas here.

Younger singers may find this a bit tricky, either because they find the concept hard to understand, or simply because they belong to a rather limited range of communities. If this is the case, discussions or group work may help.

 Different communities have different aims and activities. Again, these may be formal or informal, based on different things: friendship, faith, or a shared interest or activity. You may feel closely linked to some communities and less so to others.

Choose *three* of the communities you named above. In each of the boxes opposite, write the name of one community, describe it, and say how and why you are part of it. It may help if you answer the questions below.

- What are its activities and how do you contribute to them?
- How closely do you belong to this community?
- Is music part of this community's life? In what way?
- Is this community like your choir or not? Why?

 Community 1

In the workbook, there are three boxes, one for each community selected; singers should complete all three, though not necessarily all at once.

As above, bear in mind that some singers may benefit from working in pairs or groups to complete this project.

When you discuss this topic, try to ascertain that the singer has fully understood the concept of community before you sign it off.

This project is intended for worship choirs. As some of the tasks are quite complex, you may find that it takes time and that you need to ask singers to revisit some of their answers after they have shown you their worksheet. *The Voice for Life Chorister's Companion* will be very useful for this project.

 Topic 3: Festivals in the Christian year
Think of the main events and periods in the church's year. Think of how they form a cycle that continues year after year. Most festivals reflect events in the life of Christ or a biblical story, while some mark people or events in the history of the church.

 Think how we celebrate these festivals in different ways. Some of them are joyful, but others require us to be more reflective or solemn. The prayers and music we use at each festival mirror its mood and meaning. Often, prayers and music are written with a specific festival in mind.

Choose *three* major festivals of the Church's year (for example: Christmas, Epiphany, Candlemas, Palm Sunday, Easter Day, Ascension Day, Pentecost Sunday, Christ the King, Wesley Day). For each festival you choose, fill in one of the boxes below and opposite. (You don't need to do them all at once – talk to your choir trainer about this.) You will need to:

- write the name of the festival at the top of the box
- briefly explain the biblical story or church history behind it
- name a psalm or hymn which helps to explain the significance of the festival, and say why it is suitable
- name an anthem or song for the festival, give a little information about it (who wrote the music, the words, and when), and say why it is suitable for the festival

 Festival 1   In the workbook there are three boxes, one for each festival. Remind singers that they do not need to do all three at once.

Biblical story / church history:

The wider the variety of these stories or events, the better.

For helpful information, singers could consult 'The Church's Calendar' - a section of 'The Voice for Life Chorister's Companion'.

A suitable psalm or hymn:

'Sunday by Sunday' magazine and 'Sunday by Sunday: Music for the Second Service Lectionary' contain suggestions for suitable hymns, psalms and anthems for every Sunday, feast and festival of the Church year.

A suitable anthem or song:

Most decent hymn books are also arranged in Church Year order, and will have recommendations for the major feasts and festivals of the Church Year. Other hymn books may also have a thematic index.

This project follows logically from project 1, developing the notion of the choir as a community of people with common goals. If you have time, you could use some of the questions here as a basis for general discussion with the whole choir before singers embark on the worksheet.

 Topic 2: The community of your choir
Your choir is a group or community of people. Think about everyone who belongs to it – not just the singers, but the other people who work in different ways to keep it going. You may be surprised when you think about all the jobs that have to be done to get your choir ready for rehearsals and performances.

In the box below, write the names of five people in the community of your choir, and briefly describe how they help it. (If you like, one of these people can be you.)

 The obvious people here are other singers, committee members and people responsible for the choir's music-making – but try asking singers to think more widely too.

Does someone write, prepare and print programmes or service sheets? Who designs posters? Who provides refreshment at rehearsals? Does someone provide transport to concerts or rehearsals?

 A choir is a complex organization with its own aims, rules, customs and skills. As a choir member, you are probably familiar with these things and may take them for granted, but think about them carefully. Answer the questions in the box below.

 When and where do you meet?

Ideally, questions like this will bring home to singers the realities of their choir's routines, and the amount of organization required!

Can anyone join? Do you need any special skills?

Depending on your choir's policies, the answers to these questions may not be obvious! Encourage singers to think about them and – if they are unsure – work out who they could ask to find this information.

Who is in charge?

There may be several answers. The choir trainer may be in charge of rehearsals and performances, but other people – or a committee – may hold positions of management responsibility. Explore this with singers.

How do you learn to be a good member of the community of your choir?

Answers to this may be telling! Ideally singers learn by example from other members, though they may also bring to choir habits (good and bad!) that they have learned in other communities elsewhere.

Imagine your choir was visited by someone who knows nothing about singing or choirs. (It may help to think of a visitor from another planet!) You would have to explain many things to them – why your choir exists, why you sing, how the singers work together, why you wear what you do, and so on. Think of *three* questions this person might ask. Write the questions and answers in the box below.

This activity is harder than it may seem at first glance. It is intended to encourage singers to examine the 'culture' of singing and choirs from first principles.

Questions can range from the very basic to the sophisticated – often the most basic ones will elicit the most profound answers, though even young singers may need help to put themselves in the shoes of people who know nothing about the subject.

If the questions and answers appear to take too much knowledge for granted, suggest a few basic ones yourself:

Why doesn't everyone sing at the same time?

Who is that person standing at the front waving their arms about?

What is this sound for?

Individual members of a choir may belong to it for different reasons. In the box below, say what you gain from being a member of your choir community.

Expect standard replies like 'The opportunity to make music' or 'Companionship' - but look out for other less obvious replies. They may tell you a lot about your choir and how to motivate singers in future.

Young singers may have a bit of difficulty here – if so, give them the opportunity to discuss this question with you.

Ask another singer what he or she gains from being a member of your choir. Write their reasons here. Are they the same as yours?

For young singers, it may be sensible to nominate another more senior choir member for them to question.

Module E: Red level (project 1)

 At Red level, singers are encouraged to look outwards, beyond the confines of the choir and its own routines and habits, to think about what singing means to those around it. The projects also explore the choir's historical context, and the way in which its activities can contribute to worship.

 Topic 1: The wider community
Your choir isn't only important to the people who sing in it. It affects the people who listen to it too. Depending on the context of the choir, these may be: your church congregation, your school, your concert audiences and so on. The aim of this topic is to find out how your choir operates within your community.

To do this, interview at least three members of your choir's wider community – anyone who is affected by it but who doesn't sing in it. They could be members of your choir's audience or congregation, or people who help to run it. Talk to your choir trainer, who will help you to organize this. You can do your interviews on your own or, if you will feel more comfortable, ask another singer to help you.

In the worksheet opposite, there are five questions to ask in the upper box. If you like, add a sixth question of your own. Then take some copies to do your interviews. Find three people to interview and write their names in the box below.

 Ideally singers will use their initiative to choose interviewees; if so, before the actual interviews begin, it may be wise to check that the people named in this panel are happy to participate. Alternatively, you could recruit and suggest appropriate people in advance.

 When you do your interviews, write the responses in the spaces on your copies. Think about the replies, and answer the following questions:

- Did people reply in the way you expected?
- How did you feel about the replies?
- What benefits does the choir bring to the community?
- Do the replies suggest ways to change what the choir does to serve its community better?

Now write your conclusions in the lower box on the opposite page, and share them with your choir trainer. (Use extra paper if you need to.)

What singers say
'Choir can be quite intense and hard work. You get wrapped up in rehearsals and routines and services. At one point I realized choir had become so important to me that I had almost forgotten it's also very important to people who aren't singers, the people who are listening. Sometimes it helps to look outwards, to think about them and their needs.'

Jane, adult

1) What contact do you have with the choir?

The more specific the replies here, the better. (Encourage singers to ask for more detail if they feel it necessary.)

2) What do you expect from the choir?

Answers may be surprising!

3) Does the choir meet your expectations?

Encourage singers to report their answers fully – however favourable (or otherwise) the responses may be.

4) How are you affected by the choir's singing?

It may be appropriate to advise singers that interviewees may say negative things as well as positive ones!

5) How could the choir contribute more to the wider community?

This could be a useful discussion point in general, beyond the confines of this activity.

6)

You may wish to look at any extra questions before the interviews, and discuss them with interviewers if necessary.

Your conclusions

Look for evidence that singers have absorbed the responses to the questions above, and used those as the basis for their answers to the bullet point questions in the box opposite.

Ideally singers will write a set of conclusions for each person they interview. However, a more general set of conclusions gathered from responses to all three interviews is acceptable as long as it is well constructed and clear.

It is possible that singers will encounter criticism of their choir – you may want to alert them to this possibility. If this happens, be sure to emphasize the positive aspects of the comments too, to avoid singers becoming demoralized. And you could ask if the criticisms are justified; if so, what is to be done to address them?

By placing the choir in historical context, singers learn to feel part of a community that changes through time rather than being static. This can form the basis of useful discussions about change, tradition and continuity.

 Topic 2: The roots of our choir

The aim of this topic is to encourage you to explore the history of your choir – to find out about how it began, to think about how it has changed, and to look at your choir as an organization with a past, a present and a future. Knowing a bit about our history can help us to understand who we are. This is true for individual people and for organizations such as choirs and schools too.

Before you start this topic, think a bit about yourself, your family and its history. Does your family name reveal anything about your background or origins? If you wanted to know about the history of your family, who would you ask? Now think about your choir in the same way. Can you tell anything about it from its name? And where would you go to find out about its history? Who would you ask?

 To complete this topic, you need to collect information about the origins of your choir. (Don't worry if your choir is quite new – it still has a history.) To do this you will need to decide on your sources – where to find the information. Are there people to ask (other singers, or members of your audience or congregation), or documents or websites to look at? Does your choir have a diary or archive you could consult? Talk to your choir trainer about this, or other senior members of your choir.

In the box below, list *three* sources you can use for information about the history of your choir.

> Encourage singers to select a variety of sources of information. If possible one of these should be the reminiscences of at least one more senior choir member, as the act of sharing the experience is beneficial to everyone concerned.
>
> You may want to see the list of sources before the singer begins the research project. That way, if you are aware of important sources of information that the singer does not list here, you can suggest amendments if you see fit.

 Make copies of the worksheet on the opposite page, and consult each of your sources by asking the questions in the boxes. You may not get an answer to every question from every source, but when you have all the answers, put the information together by writing it into the boxes opposite. (Don't worry if you can't find the answers to all the questions. If you find any other interesting facts, include those too. For example, has the choir given any important performances? Won any competitions? Had any famous members? Travelled far?)

The answers you write opposite will form a short history of your choir. Your choir trainer will discuss the results of your research with you. He or she may ask you more questions about what you have written, or ask you to find some extra information. You may be asked to give a short presentation to other choir members, or write a brief article (to go into a concert programme for example).

Who founded the choir? When?

Some of the questions on this page may be hard to answer if the facts are unavailable. But if singers fail find the information, they should at least be able to tell you where they have looked for it.

Why was it set up?

Long-established choirs may have historical records or documents, written in ways which may be hard for young singers to interpret. Bear this in mind and find help if possible.

How many were in the choir at the beginning? And what voice parts?

Singers may find conflicts of information where one source says one thing while a second says another. Singers should weigh up the evidence and reach a conclusion, or at least record the contradictions.

What were its original activities, pattern and place of meeting?

If the choir is not in its original place of meeting now, do singers know where it is? Is the original place still in existence?

What was its name? How was this chosen?

Singers should understand the meaning of the name (if it is in a foreign language) and the reasons for its selection.

What do you know about the music sung by the choir at the beginning?

Singers may need some of the repertoire skills from Module C here.

How has the choir changed since it was founded?

An additional point for discussion here could be whether the changes have been for the better or not, and why.

Are there any other interesting facts about the choir?

It can add a slightly different perspective to ask singers what type of facts they might consider to be interesting.

What singers say

'My choir is nearly a hundred years old! All those people!'

Ruth, 13

Red-level singers should have a reasonably sophisticated grasp of how music is used as part of worship. This project explores some of the important issues involved in the structure of regular church services and how music is incorporated.

Topic 3: Music in worship
In this topic, you will explore the links between music and prayer, and how music helps individuals and congregations to worship. (This topic follows on from topic 3 in Module E of the Dark Blue workbook – 'Festivals in the Christian Year' – so it may be useful to review that before you start.)

Think about a regular church service with which you are familiar (such as Eucharist/ Communion or Morning Prayer). It could be one in which your choir takes part, or one at a church you attend. Think about the structure of this service, and answer the questions in the box below. (Refer to a service book or card if you like.)

Write the name of the service you have chosen.

Practice will vary from church to church. If you are unsure about aspects of liturgy yourself, consult the priest or minister responsible.

List the different parts of the service. In brackets after each part, say whether it is spoken or sung.

Look for a reasonably detailed list here for the elements of a particular service. For example:

For Communion services, the sung parts might include: Kyrie; Gloria; Sanctus and Benedictus; Agnus Dei; Anthem; Hymns

For Evensong, the sung parts might include: Preces and Responses; Magnificat and Nunc dimittis; Anthem; Hymns

What role does music play in this service?

For the whole of this section, singers will find it useful to look at 'A Guide to Church Services' - a section of 'The Voice for Life Chorister's Companion'. (For more information about Voice for Life publications, see pages 10–11.)

Are some parts sung by the choir alone?

Does the congregation join in with the music? How?

Now think about texts that are regularly sung in services that are familiar to you – for example *Kyrie eleison, Glory to God, Holy holy holy, Lamb of God, Magnificat* or any other sung text from the service you choose. For *two* of these texts, write their names in the box below and briefly describe their origins, in the Bible or elsewhere. This may require some research.

Text 1

Text 2

Now think about the music that you have heard or sung in services recently. Choose one of your favourites, write its name in the box below, then answer the questions about it.

The title and composer of the piece:

You should look for accuracy here – correct spelling, accurate punctuation, perhaps a translation if the original title is not English.

Give the context of the piece in the service. Is it for a particular festival or occasion?

How is the congregation affected by this piece? How does the music help prayer and reflection?

Repertoire skills learned in Module C will be particularly useful here.

Think of an appropriate prayer and Bible reading to go with this piece.

By this stage, singers should engage actively with repertoire. Instead of simply waiting for the choir trainer to supply each new piece, Yellow-level singers should be aware of the range of repertoire available to the choir and be able to evaluate music for its technical, aesthetic and spiritual suitability. This project encourages singers to look at repertoire critically from a number of perspectives.

 Topic 1: The changing repertoire of our choir
For this topic, you are required to do some research about the music your choir has sung over the years and consider what it tells you about its history. You will also think about how the choir's musical preferences and choices have changed over time and how these might influence its repertoire today and in the future.

If your choir has a long history and a lot of repertoire, you might want to concentrate on one aspect, festival, or period of time. For example you could examine what pieces have been chosen for Easter Day and how these have changed over the years, or think about the music the choir performed in its earliest days.

 How you will find out about your choir's past repertoire? Where will you look? Who will you ask? For example, you may want to look at old service sheets or music lists. Does your choir have a library? Could you talk to the librarian? Has your choir made recordings, or been reported in the local or national press? Is there an archive? In the box below, list some of the sources you plan to consult.

 Bear in mind that old service sheets or music lists may be precious and fragile. If appropriate, make sure this sort of archive research is properly supervised.

Singers should consult as wide a range of sources as possible. You may need to direct singers in this respect, or check what they intend.

In the upper box on the opposite page, you will find some questions to think about when examining your choir's repertoire. Make notes of your answers on a separate sheet. You may not be able to answer all of them, and you may find information not covered by the questions that will also be useful, so make a note of that too. You may want to discuss some of the questions with your choir trainer.

Then, in the lower box, use your notes to write a repertoire report. Discuss what the repertoire history tells you about your choir, and say what new repertoire you would suggest and why. Continue on a separate sheet if necessary.

What singers say
'It used to irritate me a bit if we had to sing pieces I didn't like. But then I realized that you can find something enjoyable in nearly anything you sing, even if it's just the pleasure of singing well. Of course I still have my favourite pieces but I try to keep an open mind. Everything has a purpose and it's good that we all have different tastes.'

Jennifer, adult

Who chose your choir's repertoire in the past? Who chooses it today? Do you help to make the choices?

How has the choir's repertoire changed over the years? What do these changes say about the choir and its audience?

Is any repertoire more popular now than in the past? Why?

Is any repertoire less popular now than in the past? Why? Should any of it be revived?

What influences your choir's repertoire selection? (Think about: the ability and tastes of the singers; the choir's role in the community; the expectations of the audience or congregation.)

If you had to suggest new repertoire for your choir, where would you look?

Suggest some new pieces for your choir. Think about why they are suitable, how the audience will react to them, and what the new pieces will say about your choir's image or status.

Repertoire report

Many of these questions do not have straightforward answers. Look for depth of research and a willingness to consider the information from a number of different angles. Bear in mind that some of the responses rely on personal taste: your ideas may differ from those of your singers.

For example, you may think certain repertoire has fallen out of favour for very good reason, but a singer may think it suitable for revival. In cases like this, look at the quality and inventiveness of the singer's arguments rather than at the music itself. You might want to discuss the quality of the music as part of the assessment, but make sure you respect others' taste in the same way as they should respect yours.

From a practical perspective, make sure that singers are equipped with a range of sources of new music. These could include specialist music magazines; publishers' catalogues and websites; conferences and choral symposia; and so on.

At this level, singers should have a grasp of the various criteria that need consideration when evaluating repertoire:

- technical and musical suitability for the choir

- musical (and, if appropriate, religious) suitability for the audience or congregation

- what the selection says about the choir

This project asks singers to look beyond the choir into the community it serves, and to devise a practical scheme to forge links between the two. While this is a theoretical exercise, you may well find that you want to put some of the ideas into practice – and of course using singers' own project plans can be a powerful motivator for the choir.

 Topic 2: Serving the wider community
For this topic, you are required to conceive and plan a practical event or activity to build relationships between your choir and your community. This involves thinking about how your choir already relates to the people and places around it, and what could be done to improve this. First, answer the following questions. (You may have already thought about some of these in the Module E topics at earlier levels.)

 How does our choir already contribute to the community? (Consider performances, fundraising, non-musical, social, religious or pastoral activities and so on.)

 You may need to think about this question and the next quite carefully before assessing singers' replies.

Are there other ways in which the choir could contribute to the community?

This question in particular links back to the information gathered in Red level project 1.

Are there any special events or occasions coming up in the next year that could be a focus for the choir's contributions?

If there are no events or occasions scheduled, can singers think of any anniversaries or relevant events that ought to be marked?

 Now develop an idea for an event that your choir can organize for its community. If you want, discuss your idea with other choir or community members. It may not be possible for the event to take place, but plan it as if it were going to happen. Be practical and realistic. Think about the questions below to help you plan. Make some notes on a separate sheet, then fill in the worksheet opposite.

- What do you hope to achieve for the community?
- What do you hope to achieve for the choir?
- What tasks need to be done to make the event happen?
- What funds will you need?
- Who will take part?
- What help will you need?
- Whose permission will you need?
- How will you tell people about the project?
- How will you decide whether it has been a success?
- How will you keep a record of the event?

The worksheet will help you to draw up a detailed plan. You can take extra copies in case you would like to plan several different events or projects.

Briefly describe the project, saying who will benefit from it and in what ways.

Singers should look at this from all angles – benefits to the community, to the choir, to individuals and any wider implications.

When and where will it happen?

Think about practical considerations here – would the plan work for the time and place? Would there be enough performers / audience available? (Consider, for example, what happens during school holidays.)

List the key people involved and their roles.

Again, think practically. Does the list include everyone necessary to the project? Make sure there are no serious omissions. And would the people in question be willing and available?

Do you need special permission? Do you need equipment or resources?

Think about licensing, copyright or safety issues. (Is the venue big enough? Do you have permission to use the music you want?) If you choose to put the plan into action, you may need further advice.

How will you notify the community about the event?

Even if the project itself remains theoretical, this question can form the basis for interesting practical activities about marketing, publicity, poster and web design, and so on.

If you need to raise money to fund the event, how will you do this?

Encourage singers to think about drawing up a budget for the project and various means of fundraising for it. Is the event intended to raise money? If so, will it raise more money than it costs to produce it?

How will you decide if the project has been a success?

There may be many criteria for this (financial, spiritual, aesthetic, promotional, recruitment), with varying levels of importance. Singers need to identify these and work out how to assess them at the end of the project.

List any extra information you need, or add extra information about the project.

Are singers asking enough questions? Telling the prospective clientele enough about the project? Make sure the information is properly ordered and expressed. Can singers give a presentation about their project?

What singers say

'There's such an awful lot to organize! And so little time!'

Victor, adult

This project, directed at singers in worship choirs, requires considerable familiarity with services and liturgy. Once again, practice here will vary from church to church. If you feel unsure about liturgical matters, it would be sensible to consult the priest or minister responsible for this. By this stage, individual singers should feel able to do this without supervision from you.

 Topic 3: Thinking about regular services
Human life is full of patterns, regular habits and routines. This can sometimes be oppressive, but routines also help us build and run our lives. Think about some of the routines in your own life and how they bring structure to it.

Worship employs time-honoured structures and patterns which become familiar over time. Every act of Christian worship contains some basic elements: welcome (Greeting); the reading of scripture (Ministry of the Word); prayers (Intercession); and sending out (Dismissal). There are often other elements too, such as hymns, anthems, communion and a sermon. For this topic, you are required to look at the structure of individual services (and how music forms a part of them) and use your findings to develop a service plan (Order of Service) of your own.

 First, think about some regular services – either ones you attend for worship or ones in which your choir takes part, or both. You could look at several different types of service (for example, Morning prayer, Evening prayer or Eucharist/Communion/ Mass) or choose one particular type and study a few examples of it. Look at the prayer book for the services you are describing.

 Often the books only contain a few words and instructions, but in actual worship a lot more happens beyond this. Think about the various elements of worship: readings, prayers, blessings, acclamations, actions, music and so on. What gives each individual service its character? Describe each one on a separate piece of paper, referring to the points below.

- List the parts of the service in order, one after the other.

- For each part, say: *what* is happening; *whereabouts* in the church; *who* is involved; and *which* text or music is used (if any).

 When you have described at least *four* services in this way, think about the general questions below and write your answers on a separate sheet.

- What elements were common to all the services?

- What patterns or structures were common to all?

- Were there any big differences between the services?

- Were there any distinctive or unusual elements?

- What was the particular role of the music in each service?

 Now devise a short regular service of your own for one of these occasions: Advent; the Baptism of Christ; a Sunday in Lent; the day of Pentecost; or (if applicable) the Patronal Festival of your own church. Use a service book to help you with the basic structure, and add in the other elements yourself. For these you will need to look in the Bible, hymn books and other music resources, prayer or service books, collections of poetry and so on.

As you collect your ideas, you may also find it useful to talk to your choir trainer or other members of the choir or church. Use the worksheet opposite. If you like, take copies so that you can try this activity more than once.

1) Name the service and the season or festival.

For this section, singers will find it useful to look at 'The Church's Calendar' and 'A Guide to Church Services' - sections of 'The Voice for Life Chorister's Companion'. (See pages 10–11.)

2) Choose a passage of scripture (in your choice of translation) that is appropriate for this service, and say why it is suitable.

3) Write a suitable prayer, poem or piece of prose, and explain what you have written. It should be something you have created yourself. Include it on a separate piece of paper.

4) Select at least one suitable hymn or song for the congregation to sing, and explain your choice(s).

5) Select at least two suitable musical items which are not congregational hymns (for example a solo, a choral anthem or instrumental piece). Explain your choices.

Now list these items in the order they will appear in your service.

If you do not feel competent to judge the appropriateness of the choices and writings here from a liturgical perspective, consider asking a member of the church's clergy to comment.

Remember that the answers here may well be very personal and refer to deeply-felt convictions. If you feel the need to criticize them, or to request changes in order for the target to be achieved, do so sensitively and make your reasons clear.

Photocopiable masters

CONTENTS

The following pages contain photocopiable masters of all the *Voice for Life* worksheets, reproduced exactly as they appear in the workbooks.

Looking at scores

 The more you look at music, the easier it will be to understand and navigate. At first it may seem as though there is a lot to remember, but with practice you will quickly get used to it. The activities on this page will help you to feel more comfortable.

 Score study

In this activity, you need to look at some pieces of choir music. Ask your conductor or choir trainer to show you some suitable scores. For each piece you look at, answer the questions and fill in the boxes below. (Take photocopies of this page so that you have a sheet to fill in for each piece.)

 Write the name of the piece here

How many voice parts are there?

How many instrument parts are there?

Is the piece in open score or closed score (hymn notation)?

What is the time signature of the piece?

 Tick when you have:

followed the part you sing all the way through the piece ☐

read the words all the way through the piece ☐

followed another part all the way through the piece ☐

 Tick when you have spotted:

some one-beat notes	☐	some one-beat rests	☐	notes joined by beams	☐
some two-beat notes	☐	some two-beat rests	☐	a time signature	☐
some barlines	☐	a treble clef	☐	a bass clef	☐

As a choral singer, you sing for an audience or congregation. To do this well, you must understand the meaning of the words and the mood or background of each piece you learn. Your conductor will help, but you can do a few important things for yourself between rehearsals:

- Read the words of the piece aloud all the way through. Follow the line you sing in the music. Imagine you are telling a story.

- Think about the mood and meaning of the words. (Are they happy or sad? Do they tell a story? Are they connected with a particular event or festival?)

- Make a note of any words you don't understand, or don't know how to pronounce. At your next rehearsal, ask your conductor or another choir member.

- Learn some of the words from memory. This makes rehearsals more enjoyable.

 Like a story or a poem, music has to be written or created. Someone who writes music is called a **composer** or **arranger**. For each piece you sing, find out this person's name. (Ask another choir member if you aren't sure.)

Score study
For each new piece you start, copy this page and fill in the boxes below.

Write the name of the piece here …

… and the name of the composer or arranger here.

Tick when you:
have read the words
from start to finish

can say some of the
words from memory

What is the mood of the piece?

Is it for a particular event or festival?

Make a note of any words you don't understand.

What is the title of the piece?

Who wrote the music?

When did the composer live? (Give dates, musical period or century.)

Read the text aloud. Do you find any of the words difficult to pronounce? If so, write them here.

Are you unsure of the meaning of any of the words? If so, find out what they mean and write the definition next to each word here.

Word	Definition

Explain simply in your own words what you think the whole text means.

What is the mood of the music?

How did you find this information? Where did you look?

Understanding the music we sing

Make copies of this page so that you can repeat it with several pieces of music.

What is the title of the piece?

Give the name and dates of the composer.

What country did the composer live in?

Name another piece by this composer, or another composer who lived at this time.

Do you find any of the words hard to understand or pronounce? If so, write them here with their meaning or pronunciation.

Word	Meaning / pronunciation

What language is the text written in?

In the box on the right, explain in your own words what the whole text means, or what it is saying.

What key is the piece written in?

What is its time signature?

How many vocal parts is it written for?

What is the mood of the music?

When would it be performed?

How did you find this information? Where did you look?

Name the piece of music.

Name the composer.

Where do the words come from?

Give the composer's dates of birth and death.

What country did he or she live in?

When is the piece normally sung? At a particular time of year or for a particular event?

What century or musical period was the composer writing in?

Name some other pieces by this composer.

What key is the piece in?

Give the time signature of the piece.

Name some other composers who wrote in the same period.

What is the mood of the music?

Give any interesting information about the composer (for example, job, family, and so on) or the piece (for example, where it was first performed)

Writing programme notes

Concert programme booklets often contain **programme notes** – information to tell listeners about the music. For Red level, you have to write some programme notes using the information you collected for the worksheet on the previous page. Make copies of this page so that you can repeat it with several pieces of music.

Make your notes clear, easy to read, and interesting. Think about what your listeners would want to know. If you went to a concert and bought a programme, what kind of information would you like to have about the music? The following additional information might be useful:

- What is the text about? Explain it in your own words. (Is it in English? If not, your readers need to know what language it is in and what it means.)

- Describe the music. How many vocal parts are there? What instruments are used? What is the feeling or mood of the music? Why does it feel like this?

Name the piece of music.

Programme note:

You may want to continue writing on a separate piece of paper.

You may photocopy this page

1) What contact do you have with the choir?

2) What do you expect from the choir?

3) Does the choir meet your expectations?

4) How are you affected by the choir's singing?

5) How could the choir contribute more to the wider community?

6)

Your conclusions

You may photocopy this page

Who founded the choir? When?

Why was it set up?

How many were in the choir at the beginning? And what voice parts?

What were its original activities, pattern and place of meeting?

What was its name? How was this chosen?

What do you know about the music sung by the choir at the beginning?

How has the choir changed since it was founded?

Are there any other interesting facts about the choir?

You may photocopy this page

Name the piece of music and the composer.

Give some biographical details of the composer (dates of birth and death, where he or she lived, nationality and so on).

What century or period was the composer writing in? Name some other composers working around the same time.

Give the key and time signature of the piece.

Where do the words come from? What language are they in? Explain briefly what they are about.

Name some other pieces by this composer.

When is the piece normally sung? At a particular time of year or for a particular event?

Give any interesting information about the composer or the piece (for example, where it was first performed).

Describe briefly how the music is put together – the number of vocal parts, the instruments involved.

What is the mood of the music?

Briefly describe the project, saying who will benefit from it and in what ways.

When and where will it happen?

List the key people involved and their roles.

Do you need special permission? Do you need equipment or resources?

How will you notify the community about the event?

If you need to raise money to fund the event, how will you do this?

How will you decide if the project has been a success?

List any extra information you need, or add extra information about the project.

You may photocopy this page

1) Name the service and the season or festival.

2) Choose a passage of scripture (in your choice of translation) that is appropriate for this service, and say why it is suitable.

3) Write a suitable prayer, poem or piece of prose, and explain what you have written. It should be something you have created yourself. Include it on a separate piece of paper.

4) Select at least one suitable hymn or song for the congregation to sing, and explain your choice(s).

5) Select at least two suitable musical items which are not congregational hymns (for example a solo, a choral anthem or instrumental piece). Explain your choices.

Now list these items in the order they will appear in your service.

Lightning Source UK Ltd.
Milton Keynes UK
UKOW07f1946040216

267669UK00004B/37/P